Reaching
Audiences

Reaching Audiences

A Guide to Media Writing

Second Edition

Jan Johnson Yopp

University of North Carolina, Chapel Hill

Katherine C. McAdams

University of Maryland

Allyn and Bacon

Boston   London   Toronto   Sydney   Tokyo   Singapore

Senior Editor: Karon Bowers
Series Editorial Assistant: Leila Scott
Marketing Manager: Susan E. Ogar
Editorial Production Service: Ruttle, Shaw & Wetherill, Inc.
Composition Buyer: Linda Cox
Manufacturing Buyer: Dave Repetto
Cover Administrator: Jenny Hart
Electronic Composition: Omegatype Typography, Inc.

Library of Congress Cataloging-in-Publication Data

McAdams, Katherine C.
    Reaching audiences : a guide to media writing / Katherine C.
    McAdams, Jan Johnson Yopp. – 2nd ed.
        p.   cm.
    Includes bibliographical references and index.
    ISBN 0-205-28622-4
    1. Mass media–Authorship.   2. Mass media–Audiences.   3. Report
    writing.   I. Yopp, Jan Johnson.   II. Title.
P96.A86M38   1998
808'.066302–dc21   98-34457
                                                                CIP

Printed in the United States of America

10   9   8   7   6   5   4   04   03   02   01   00

CONTENTS

Chapter 4   **Beyond the Lead: Organization**   **73**

PART TWO
Improving Writing

Chapter 5   **Saying It Straight**   **117**

PART THREE
Gathering Information

PART FOUR
Other Media Writing Styles

PREFACE

Cable television. Video news releases. Databases. E-mail. Facsimile machines. Satellites. Web sites. Cellular telephones. Information superhighway.

Technology has created a multitude of new ways to send and get information and entertainment. We are truly in an information age. Although many audiences still rely on newspapers and television, they are attracted to a dazzling array of faster, electronic sources of information and entertainment. Wave after wave of invention invites attention, analysis, and adoption. Eager individuals spend hours deciphering the language to access the links that offer faster and often exotic ways to send messages. Developments seem to appear faster than they can be mastered.

Communicators are among the dazzled users. Most writers long ago abandoned typewriters for computers. Reporters and columnists transmit stories to and from anywhere in the world. Writers use computer databases to research stories and to access government storerooms of information. They even use e-mail to interview sources. Communicators send messages via fax machines or as video or sound files. They put notices on computer bulletin boards or list messages retrieved by special telephone numbers. Technology has enabled communicators to produce work more efficiently and quickly, just as it has allowed users to access information faster and in greater quantities.

Technology also has broadened the field for communicators. New writing markets have been created in publications and advertising for specialized audiences, electronic newspapers, online services, video news releases, graphic design, and literally hundreds of other jobs. Students in journalism and mass communication programs have many career possibilities beyond jobs on newspapers or magazines, in public relations or advertising, and in radio and television.

The key ingredient to success in any communications job is good writing. In today's world, good writing has suffered. Part of the decline can be attributed to technology. The proliferation of technology has diverted many communicators from their main task: good writing. In the rush to produce and send information, people often overlook the critical need for accuracy and proper spelling and grammar. Too many communicators believe that the first draft is good enough and do not spend time editing and rewriting. Such a philosophy has eroded informative, entertaining, well-crafted writing. Technology has enabled anyone with information, no matter how the content is structured, to put it out for public view. As a result, much information is poorly written and irrelevant to audiences.

Students, who need to learn the skills to become good communicators, seem to be less committed to the craft of writing. They rely on spell-checkers and grammar-checkers housed in computers, rather than on their own knowledge. They believe they have little need to know the basics of proper sentence construction. With video a major component of new technology, students want to focus on the visual, not on the text. As children of the television age, many have little patience for writing and rewriting.

Despite student sentiment, professors in journalism and mass communication teach—or, in many cases, struggle to teach—specific styles of writing. Students interested in print journalism first learn the inverted pyramid style of writing. Broadcast students follow a shorter and more casual electronic communication format. Advertising students learn copywriting. Public relations students practice writing news releases and brochures. Photojournalism students write cutlines. Graphic designers write legends. Each format has its prescribed guidelines.

Within each format, today's students must learn to make their writing clearer, more accurate, more relevant, and more appealing. They must think constantly about their audiences. They must know their audiences and their specific language uses and interests. Students need to understand the importance of good writing and be willing to take on the task. Professors must push students harder to pay attention to their writing and editing skills. Today's students are the communicators of tomorrow—regardless of what technology has developed and what medium they ultimately use.

The following chapters stress the basic writing skills essential to any student in any mass communications sequence: news-editorial, advertising, public relations, electronic communication, or visual communication. The essentials of good writing apply, regardless of format.

Part One presents the basic components of the writing process and the critical role of audiences. Students will learn the fundamentals of print journalism, how to write text for different formats including the Web, and the value of the inverted pyramid style of writing. Any informative writing must be grounded in the tenets of basic newswriting.

Part Two looks at refining writing. Specific tips are given to improve writing, from word selection to sentence length to grammar and usage. Students also will learn the steps of editing, a crucial part of the writing process, and how to avoid bias in writing. A grammar chapter includes proficiency tests on specific grammar problems.

Part Three reviews how to gather information through three principal methods: research, observation, and interviewing. Students also are introduced to online searches and resources.

Part Four discusses other media writing: electronic communication, public relations, and advertising. Each has its particular formats and communications tools for reaching audiences.

The first three appendices focus on narrower topics: libel and privacy, a list of abused words, and spelling hurdles. The last appendix contains the answer key for the grammar chapter exercises.

Mass communication at all levels needs writing that is accurate, complete, and concise. Writers constantly must consider their audiences. Writers today can no longer write solely for their own enjoyment. They must create messages that are well written and will reach the intended audiences.

The authors clearly embrace technology. Without it, they would not have been able to produce their writing efficiently and easily. They recognize that technology will not disappear, and no one would wish it away. But technology changes and fades. The importance of good writing does not.

Acknowledgments

Writing a book is never the work of just the individuals whose names are under the title. So it is with this book and its second edition. A number of colleagues and friends have provided invaluable contributions.

The core of the book would not have been done without Kevin Davis of Macmillan, who saw the potential in our initial concept and encouraged us to write, and our editor Karon Bowers at Allyn & Bacon and her editorial assistant, Leila Scott, who drove us across the finish line.

The second edition was written with the advice, counsel, and support of our colleagues at the School of Journalism and Mass Communication at the University of North Carolina at Chapel Hill, especially Dean Richard Cole, Associate Professor Harry Amana, Associate Professor Cathy Packer, Associate Professor Dulcie Straughan, Associate Professor John Sweeney, Assistant Professor Carol Pardun, Librarian Barbara Semonche, and student assistants Andy Johns and Mary Hill; and at the College of Journalism at the University of Maryland, especially Professor James Plumb, Professor Maureen Beasley, Professor Carl Sessions Stepp, and students Erik Bucy, Andrea Hoffman, and Encarnita Pyle.

We also thank Beth Haller at Towson University of the University of Maryland, Thom Lieb at Towson University, Eugenia Zerbinos at Michigan State University, Candace Perkins at Kent State University, Robert D. West at Kent State University, and Daniel T. Davis at Michigan State University. We also thank the people whose spirited support helped create the Grammar Slammer: Richard Cole, Jim Shumaker, Reese Cleghorn, Bill Cloud, Phil Meyer, Greig Stewart, and Chet Rhodes.

Beyond the university, we also acknowledge the contributions of Evelyn Hsu, John Greene, and our families, for their moral support and ability to manage without moms for a while.

Reaching Audiences

1

The Writing Process

Most mornings Evelyn Hsu's alarm rings at 6:30 A.M. Eyes still shut, she gropes for the remote control on the nightstand and turns on the TV to catch a local morning news show. She listens for the latest weather and traffic updates and ignores the rehash of yesterday's news.

She gets up, showers, dresses, and heads downstairs where her husband, Larry, has already set *The Washington Post* and *The New York Times* on the dining table. She scans the section fronts of both papers, looking for interesting stories to read when she gets home that night. She says good-bye to her husband and seven-year-old daughter.

Then it's through the kitchen, where a wall calendar holds scribbled notes about Brownie meetings, orthodontist appointments, and school performances, past the living room, where school fliers, bills, and magazines are piled on a chest, and out the door to drive a car pool to her twelve-year-old daughter's middle school.

Her half-hour commute to an office near Dulles Airport in suburban Virginia is quiet. No radio. At work, the red message light on Hsu's phone is lit. Three messages. A "Things To Do Today" ad sits on her desk, full of lists, scribbles, and notes on Post-its® from the day before. She checks her e-mail, the interoffice one first, then two Internet services. Twelve messages total. Two press releases and a computer training brochure are in her in box, along with a facsimile from someone who will be speaking at a seminar Hsu is organizing.

Hsu goes down the hall to check her mailbox. She develops training programs for newspaper managers. Her office subscribes to more than fifty magazines and specialty publications that reflect the interests and concerns of their subscribers: *American Demographics, Columbia Journalism Review, Harvard Business Review, Sales and Marketing Management, Wired*. Every day, three or four magazines are routed into her box. Hsu skims them, makes notes to file on the ideas and authors that catch her attention, then squeezes the stuff into the next person's box. Copies of *USA Today* and *The Wall Street Journal* are on a file cabinet. Hsu skims them as well.

It is 9 A.M., and Hsu has already mentally sorted hundreds of messages, alert for information that is new or makes a difference to her work or her family. Everything else is mentally discarded.

Like Evelyn Hsu, most people are bombarded by messages that come to them in a multitude of ways every day through radio, television, newspapers, brochures, e-mail, voice mail, U.S. Postal Service mail, telephone, fliers, and on and on.

Some messages are saved and others are discarded. The average person, such as Hsu, will quickly toss out messages that are unclear or unintelligible—that is, messages that are unfriendly. How the message is structured, its relevance, and its appeal will determine its success in reaching its audience. Thus the fate of any message lies in good writing.

This chapter discusses

- Why writing remains a critical task in communication,
- Stages in the writing process, and
- Why the writing process is important for all forms of mass communication.

Writing Is the Basic Task

No matter what the vehicle, most messages have a common basis: Each was written. Before they are printed, broadcast, aired, or distributed, messages are written. Communicators have to write first, regardless of what medium or technology they use.

For example, a school principal writes the monthly calendar of activities before announcing it at a Parent–Teacher Association meeting or printing it in the school's monthly newsletter.

A radio reporter types stories before she reads them on the 6 A.M. news show.

A working mother who wants her teenage son to start dinner leaves instructions on the kitchen counter.

An advertising copywriter creates an insert about credit card interest rates for a bank to put into customers' statements.

Three television journalists write their scripts before the weekly Sunday morning news program.

The editor of the campus newspaper writes two editorials for each edition, then updates the paper's Web site.

All communicators—whether they are journalism or mass communication students, newspaper reporters, or school principals—must write a message before it is sent to its intended audience. Once writers let go of the message—that is, once the message is aired or distributed—they have little control over whether the audience absorbs the message. Although the message may have arrived, it may be crowded out and ignored.

Getting through the Clutter

As we know from the Hsu example, writers today have competition from other media and from busy lifestyles. Children and adults today—including you—have developed the skills to sort constantly what will and will not be read, watched, or heard in the limited time available.

The good news is that audiences have an insatiable desire to be informed and entertained. They are looking for information. They are seeking leisure activities. They are investigating new media such as Internet publications and electronic bulletin boards. They want and need information that will help them cope with or escape from everyday life.

How do writers get through the clutter of media and lifestyles to reach waiting audiences? They do it with good writing. They write messages that are simple, clear, and accurate. Audiences will not stick with messages that are confusing, incoherent, or unbelievable. Writers must craft messages that attract and hold audiences with their content and structure and that are relevant and emotionally compelling.

Few communicators today can write messages for pleasure or for the sake of the task. Writers today have a purpose in writing. They want to tell of a family's trauma during an earthquake. They want to inform voters about candidates. They want to entertain viewers of a late-night talk show. They want to highlight a product's usefulness. They want to sell a client's services.

These writers want their messages to reach a destination, and they want audiences to pay attention.

For audiences to pay attention, writers must create messages that are accurate, appealing, organized, readable, relevant, compelling, clear, complete, and simple. Audiences today require good writing. An audience will gain no new information or entertainment if the message fails to be read or heard because it was poorly written.

The Good Writing Bonus: Jobs

The hungry audience and the new technology are a boon for good writers. Good writers are needed in hundreds of media outlets. Complete and readable writing is needed in manuals that teach people how to use new computer software. Accurate and relevant writing is needed to tell citizens how an expanded city park system will improve their lives. Compelling and appealing writing is needed to make elementary students read school bus safety rules. Clear, well-reasoned, and organized writing is needed in a letter asking for donations to the city's homeless shelter. Information must be updated continually on Web sites. The list goes on and on.

Technology itself demands more good writers. Many employees must become expert communicators as soon as they are given a terminal, a keyboard, word-processing software, e-mail, and access to the Internet. Good writers are needed in an information world in which much published material is produced by those who, professionally, are nonwriters and noneditors.

Students who can master basic writing and editing skills and who can craft appealing and compelling messages will find many ways to use their abilities. Within one career they may have half a dozen different, satisfying, and successful writing jobs. The changing environment for communication offers rewards to good writers.

Is Good Writing Inborn?

Many people believe that good, skillful writing springs not from teaching and learning but from inborn talent that eludes most ordinary people.

Nonsense.

Writing a straightforward message requires no more inherent talent than following a road map. Author Joel Saltzman compares learning to write with learning to make salad dressing:

This is the only way I know to make a terrific salad dressing: Mix up a batch. Taste it. Mix again.

The secret ingredient is the patience to keep trying—to keep working at it till you get it just right.

Do most people have the talent to make a terrific salad dressing? Absolutely. Are they willing to make the effort to develop that skill? That's a different question.

Good writing, like good salad dressing, can make even dry material palatable and can make good subject matter great. Like ingredients in a recipe, each word, sentence, and paragraph is selected carefully with one goal in mind: pleasing the consumer. The first bite will determine whether the diner eats more; good writing will sell a piece beyond the first paragraph. Like cooking, not every writing session will produce a masterpiece, but the end product must be palatable.

The Writing Process Explained

Writers today work in the same way as writers have worked throughout time—by following a regimen we call the writing process. Seven stages of the writing process are presented here: information gathering, thinking and planning, listing, drafting, rewriting, sharing, and polishing. But before a writer begins any part of this process, he or she must have an idea or topic.

What's in a Topic?

Research shows that no matter how readable a story is, a reader will be turned off immediately if the topic is unappealing. Studies show that readers prefer interesting topics, regardless of how well the pieces are written. These studies show that audiences may be willing to plow through difficult text if it promises important information.

To be viable, a topic must pass a five-question test. The writer must be able to answer yes to each of these questions before writing begins:

1. "Is my topic of interest to my audience?" Identify several specific individuals or groups that would want to know about the topic.

2. "Is my topic of interest to me?" The topic must be interesting to the writer to stimulate energy and the motivation needed to write appealing copy.

3. "Is my topic too narrow or too broad?" Readers resist biting off more than they can digest, such as a multipage article on the general topic of antiques. However, tiny topics, such as the story of one Chippendale chair, may be equally unsatisfying.

4. "Are high-quality sources of information on my topic both plentiful and available?" Writers owe their readers top-quality information. If a story topic, such as the landmark abortion case *Roe* v. *Wade,* requires an interview with a Supreme Court Justice who does not grant interviews, a writer might consider changing the focus of the topic rather than substituting second-rate or secondhand information.

5. "Is my topic of value?" No writer wants the audience to glance at a message and respond, "So what?" Janet Jackson wears sweatpants shopping— so what? Avoid topics that are trivial or inconsequential. Writing about a rock star's entire wardrobe would attract more readers.

If your topic does not pass the test—that is, if you answer "no" to any of these questions—try shifting your focus. If the topic *gymnastics* is too general, try focusing your writing on one gymnast or one gymnastics program. If getting authoritative interviews for a *Roe* v. *Wade* story is out of the question, write about local sentiments toward abortion rights.

Once your topic has passed the test, the writing process begins. It is important to note that three of the writing stages occur before the writer sits down to draft the actual message. In the information age, research and planning are essential to good communication. No amount of skillful writing can save a message that has been written without thorough, accurate information.

Stages in the Process

The same sequence of activities outlined here occurs in good writing of all kinds. All communicators must gather information, think about and plan the message, list key information, draft a message, rewrite the draft, share the message, and polish by checking and editing. Together these separate stages of activity form what we call the writing process: a set of behaviors common to all writers. The order of stages may vary, and some stages may be repeated, but each stage is essential to producing a good message.

Each stage in the writing process is briefly explained in the following sections; later chapters in this book will explain writing tasks in greater detail. You will be referred to relevant chapters as each stage is discussed here.

Keep in mind that following these stages will produce successful writing in business, education, advertising, public relations, the news media, and daily life. Throughout this text, you will learn what professional writers know: Writing is a skill that can be learned like other skills, one stage at a time. And the first stage is to go beyond yourself to gather information. Good writers are seekers.

Stage One: Information Gathering

Gathering information on your topic is the first stage of the writing process. To begin the search for information, you must answer questions that all people are prone to ask: Who? What? When? Where? Why? How? How much? Then what?

People of all ages ask these questions when they are curious, and new technologies put many answers at our fingertips. Basic facts and figures are easy to obtain online, but every writer needs to go beyond superficial statistics.

Never begin to write without talking to other people or reading their work. Good writing requires good external information. Once you know the questions, go outside yourself to find the answers. Even if you are an expert on your own topic, you must find other reliable authorities on it.

In writing an announcement of an art exhibit at a local high school, for example, a writer might begin the questioning by talking with obvious experts—perhaps the principal and art teacher—who can provide answers and can lead the writer to additional sources.

After answering basic questions, information could still be gathered to complete the announcement or add interest to it. For the exhibit announcement, we still need to know the following: What types of artwork will be shown? Will prizes be awarded? Will any special guests appear at a reception?

The new questions will guide your next steps in your information search. Generally, steps in research lead to one of three sources:

1. *Interviews.* Talk, in person or by phone, to authorities or to people your initial sources suggest. Interviewing is discussed in Chapter 10.

2. *Library and online research.* Any kind of writing can require research in libraries, Web sites, or databases. For example, if the art on display at Edwards High School celebrates Impressionism, the writer needs to find out about the Impressionists and their art. Basic research skills are included in Chapter 9.

3. *Other sources.* Brochures, publications, or archives can provide helpful information in old and new sources. For example, an article or brochure about last year's art exhibit could be located through a newspaper index or online archive. Chapter 9 explains how to use traditional and innovative reference sources.

It is important to gather information from a variety of sources. Ideally, a writer compiles more information than is actually needed so that he or she can be selective about which information to use.

Take notes on every source used in the information-gathering stage. A writer never knows when an important fact or statistic will emerge or when a quotable statement will be uttered. It is best to have the notepad always ready. In addition, careful notes enable writers to attribute interesting or unusual information to sources and to be accurate in what they have written.

Some writers refer to the information-gathering stage as "immersion" in the topic. Whatever it is called, this first stage of writing turns the writer into an informal expert on his or her subject matter.

Stage Two: Thinking and Planning

Once information is gathered, the writer studies the notes taken in Stage One and ponders them. The writer scans material to see what information seems most important and most interesting.

A good writer always makes decisions about priorities, keeping in mind the audience that will receive the message. Successful writers actually picture the probable audience, hold that image in mind, and plan the message for that imaginary group. Some writers say they write for a specific person such as the truck driver in Toledo or Aunt Mary in Hartford; a newsroom favorite is Joe Six-Pack, the average guy. More about audiences and their needs is provided in Chapter 2.

Sometimes the thinking stage will allow the writer to see possibilities for creative approaches to writing. More often, however, this stage of the writing process helps the writer to realize that more information needs to be gathered before listing and writing can begin.

Once the writer has gathered enough information, he or she will begin to evaluate and set priorities, asking, "What does my audience need to know? What does it need to know first? What next?" and so on. If no further gaps in information become apparent at this stage, the writer takes pen and notepad in hand and moves on to Stage Three.

Stage Three: Listing

Before committing words to paper, writers note the facts and ideas that must be included in the message. Some writers jot key words; others write detailed outlines. Whatever form this activity takes, it yields one or more lists.

What goes in these lists? In one list the writer should rank elements of the message that the audience must know. In a second list, the writer might note audiences for the message; in a third, the writer could list the values and goals of each important audience. Initial lists should be made by brainstorming, jotting down each important message element, and perhaps scratching out, adding, or combining items in the lists.

Once lists are committed to paper, the writer reviews them and attempts to rank the information in each list. Imagine, for example, that the top priority item on the message list is "student art shown." One of the top audiences is "parents," and one of the top audience goals is "nurturing our young people." Isolating the items guides the writer to structure a message that will feature student art, appeal to parents, and frame the event as a constructive, positive effort for young people.

In this stage, the writer imposes order and organization on the information. Chapters 3 and 4 deal with specific ways to organize messages.

Stage Four: Drafting the Message—As You Would Tell It

For most people, even experienced writers, writing seems somewhat unnatural. In contrast, conversational speech always seems to flow. So the efficient writer drafts a message by writing it as it might be told to a friend.

Checking the lists made in Stage Three, the writer would begin by "talking" about the first and most important element in the message—perhaps like this:

```
A student art show that displays the talents of twenty-
seven of the city's young artists will open at 7 P.M.
Wednesday at Edwards High School.
```

Once this telling process has begun, it continues easily. The writer will move smoothly through interesting aspects of the message to a stopping point after the listed priorities have been included.

By the end of this stage, the writer has created what is called a draft, rather than a message. The term *draft* distinguishes this version from a finished product. It is different from a polished message, and purposely so. Think of the draft as a raw lump of clay, in which substance is what counts. The stages that follow will shape the clay, giving form to the finished message. Drafting messages is discussed in Chapters 3 and 4.

Stage Five: Rewriting

In this stage, the conventions of the written language are imposed on the draft. Sentences are checked for completeness and coherence; paragraphs are formed and organized; transitions and stylistic flourishes are added.

A good portion of this book is devoted to the skills involved in rewriting. Only through rewriting—sometimes repeated rewriting—can a message be streamlined to reach its intended audience. All good writers rewrite; great writers pride themselves on painstaking reworking of their original phrases. Author E. B. White labored for three years over his slim classic *Charlotte's Web,* and he willingly revised much of his other work as many as fourteen times.

Of course, writers on deadline cannot afford the luxury of spending years, or even hours, rewriting a draft. Writers develop shortcuts to rewriting as they become familiar with print formats, as described in Chapter 4. But no good writer ever skips rewriting.

The rewriting stage is separate from polishing, in which fine points of style, such as capitalization, are debated. If a writer stops in mid-draft to debate a style point, the train of thought is interrupted, and the writing process stops. Small decisions are left for the last stage—a stage that may be conducted by someone other than the writer. Rewriting involves rearranging, adding, and subtracting information so that the clay of the draft takes a recognizable form.

Rewriting a draft is the bulk of the writing process. It is hard, time-consuming work; factors to consider in the process are discussed in Chapters

5 and 6. A rewritten draft is far from a finished work, however. Two stages remain in the writing process: sharing and polishing.

Stage Six: Sharing

The revised draft now must go to another reader—almost any other reader. By this stage, most writers have lost perspective on the message. They have become knowledgeable about the topic, and they may no longer be able to tell how the message would be received by an average member of the audience.

Sharing your work at this stage gives you a much better idea how an audience member may react. Outside readers will quickly let you know whether information is confusing or unclear, or whether any important details are missing.

It is a good idea to share your work with a naive reader—someone who knows far less about your topic than you do. Sometimes a colleague at work or a family member is an excellent choice for sharing because of that person's distance from your topic.

In large offices, outside review of your revised draft may be built in. Communication pieces in big companies usually are reviewed by one or more editors and often by top management. Such an editing process is helpful in many ways, and certainly it saves the time and trouble of finding someone with whom to share your writing.

Regardless of who is sharing and commenting on your work, you as a writer must never forget that you did the initial research. You have expertise on your topic that your colleagues, family members, or even top managers may not have. Be sure to get feedback from your outside readers in a setting where you both can talk. You may need to explain why certain parts of your message are written as they are. Good editing is negotiation; no editor is an absolute dictator. You as a writer need to work with, not for, editors and outside reviewers. Together you can produce clear, correct writing.

Stage Seven: Polishing

The final stage in the writing process is one that many people ignore or abhor. But editing or polishing is an essential and critical part of the writing process, and it is appropriately the last stage. Many young writers feel that all capitalization, punctuation, grammar, usage, and spelling must be perfect, even in an initial draft. Concentrating on perfection in all those areas is unimportant in the early stages of writing. You might spend ten minutes looking in the dictionary for a word that you eventually decide not to use!

Working on word-by-word perfection at the early stages of writing is wasteful and even paralyzing. Writers who worry about every comma will find it difficult to get through the stages of drafting and revising. Writing becomes a much more comfortable and speedy task when polishing is put off until its proper place at the end of the process. After the important substance and form of the message have been established, then spend time with style books, dictionaries, and thesauruses.

All writers should polish their work. But in truth, this final stage of editing may well be performed by another person. An editor or editorial assistant may make the final checks for correctness and consistency and put a message in final form. The polishing process comes last also because it may come after the writer passes the message along. Confident writers welcome assistance with this final, cosmetic touch, knowing that letter-perfect writing will add to the credibility and clarity of their message.

Chapters 5, 7, and 8 discuss the work of polishing your own or another person's writing. Chapter 6 outlines the editing process.

Consider the Audience

E. B. White in the introduction to *The Elements of Style* explains that good writing is a writer's responsibility to the audience. He tells how his professor and coauthor, William "Will" Strunk, taught rules to writers out of sympathy for readers.

> *All through* The Elements of Style *one finds evidences of the author's deep sympathy for the reader. Will felt that the reader was in serious trouble most of the time, a man floundering in a swamp, and that it was the duty of anyone attempting to write English to drain this swamp quickly and get his man up on dry ground or at least throw him a rope. . . . I have tried to hold steadily in mind this belief of his, this concern for the bewildered reader.*

Today it is time to return to Strunk's wisdom. As a teacher in the early twentieth century, Strunk knew that audiences were hindered by poor type quality and low levels of literacy. Today writers contend with new distractions Strunk could never have imagined. But the remedy in either era is the same: clear messages that show consideration for audiences.

The principles of effective communication are more important now than ever, regardless of the medium, as we discuss in Chapters 11 through 13. Even essential messages are in danger of being crowded out in an increasingly competitive media marketplace. This is the age of instant, constant communication. Challenges for writers have never been greater; at the same time, communication opportunities have never been so great. The potential power of media messages is unlimited in our society, where people are confounded by change and unlikely to have traditional networks of family, church, and community. Chapter 2 discusses the complexity of today's media audiences.

Today's complex communication environment calls for simple, direct messages. The chapters that follow provide a guide to writing messages that audiences will search for and understand in the information age.

EXERCISES

1. Try to remember the times during the day today, so far, when you have been exposed to media messages. List the exposures you can remember. For each exposure, record where it occurred and how—by what medium—each message came to you.

2. Look at your list of incoming media messages. Circle those that you would have missed if we were to substitute the technology of 1895 for the technology of today.

3. List three topics that you think pass the test for viable topics.

4. Select one of your topics from above and explain how you would gather information on this topic. Be sure to include research in each of the following: interviews, libraries, online resources, and other publications.

5. Write a few paragraphs describing the characteristics of the audience for your student newspaper. Then explain how you could follow Strunk and White's advice to help the audience use and understand the student paper better.

REFERENCES

Joel Saltzman, *If You Can Talk, You Can Write.* New York: Ballantine Books, 1993.
William Strunk, Jr., and E. B. White, *The Elements of Style.* New York: Macmillan Publishing Co., 1979.

2

Audience, Audience, Audience

When writers complete the writing process described in Chapter 1, they have a message to send: a news item, a television script, a magazine advertisement, a brochure, a feature story, or a novel. But all the steps in the process are wasted if the intended audience ignores the message.

You learned from the Evelyn Hsu example in Chapter 1 that audiences do not accept or assimilate every message that comes their way. They sift through messages and choose which ones they will hear and read. Successful writers know that about their audiences. Writers must understand an audience's lifestyles, media preferences, interests, and language. That knowledge will aid them in selecting topics, writing a draft, and polishing the message so that it fits an audience's needs and interests.

Writers must find out who makes up their audiences. Audiences change just as society changes. During the last four decades, audiences—and writers—have been affected by changing lifestyles, an increasingly diverse population, and new technologies. Good writers take into account the impact of these forces on their audiences.

In this chapter, you will learn

- How audiences and the world they live in today have changed,
- How writers can analyze audiences,
- How to be successful with audiences, and
- Roadblocks to messages reaching audiences.

How Audiences Have Changed

The 1990 census showed that most people in the United States live in households but that less than half of those household groups are what was once considered a stereotypical family: an American-born mother, father, and several children. Single-parent families and blended families are more common than the so-called typical family. Neighborhoods and communities, increasingly diverse, are home to many racial and ethnic groups.

The information revolution has directly affected audiences. New technology has given audiences greater access to information and entertainment. Consumers have welcomed new technology and its gadgets. The dramatic drop in the price of personal computers in the last decade has brought them within the price range of more and more people. Now millions of people have quick access to hundreds of Web sites and information databases that contain sound, film, and videotape, as well as text.

Media forms continue to evolve, stretching old definitions of newspapers and news broadcasting and taking audiences on a roller-coaster ride into an unimagined future of interactive and virtual reality. More specialized media, more ethnic media, more electronic media—in fact, more media of all kinds—are on the market. The media system grows and changes daily and is indexed by hundreds of cataloguing services. And all these media, old and new, compete fiercely for audience share and attention.

Today's media audiences are filled with people who have become accustomed to fast food, fast travel, and fast information. In 1994 a Times-Mirror study revealed "an American public that uses more media outlets more frequently than at any time in recent history." That has not changed. More and more people today are accessing the information superhighway. By the year 2000 about 200 million people worldwide will have Internet access. Increasingly sophisticated audiences are using the Internet and expect accurate, high-quality information.

Even though some audience members search for information and use new media, other audiences may be more resistant. Caught in the demands of daily living, they may be less ready, willing, and able to listen, and they may still rely on more traditional media for information. Or they may not have the financial means to buy computers and software to go online. Writers must be aware, therefore, of how to communicate in both old and new media.

Changing Lifestyles

The family that fifteen years ago may have started the day together at the breakfast table may now find itself scattered at sunrise. Adults and kids depart early and separately for demanding days in jobs and classes—sometimes both.

Lifestyles have become hectic. Lives are filled with distractions: children, media, sports, work, overtime, fatigue, more media, too much information at work, too much junk mail, housework, commuting, and family commitments, to name just a few.

Many U.S. women are in the workforce, and families increasingly lead busy lives like that of Evelyn Hsu in Chapter 1. Even after women have babies, more than half return to work. About three of five working women have children under age six. Women have less time as they work outside the home and still take on responsibility for most household and child-related chores.

Men, too, have found their lives to be changing from traditional patterns. Many men have less time because of increased work hours or because they have taken on additional home duties. What used to be leisure time may now be spent with laundry or children.

The trend toward less leisure time and more work is well under way as Americans approach the end of the twentieth century. The average white-collar workweek is almost forty-four hours, compared with forty-one in 1973. For manufacturing, the average workweek is forty-one hours, the highest since World War II. Executives average between forty-six and forty-seven hours a week.

An Increasingly Diverse Society

At the same time people's lifestyles are changing in the United States, the country is witnessing another trend that affects media use: diversity.

What used to be a primarily white, male-dominated society has changed significantly in the last twenty years. Women account for 55 percent of the United States population. Racial and ethnic groups are increasing. The latest United States census data show that minorities make up more than 25 percent of the population. The traditional categories—African Americans, Asian Americans, Hispanics, and Native Americans—lose meaning as new groups, such as Caribbean and Pacific Islanders, immigrate and as intercultural families become commonplace. Some young people of mixed heritage will no longer classify themselves a single ethnic category.

Demographic experts predict increasing shifts. By the year 2000, 30 per-cent of the country's residents will belong to groups once considered to be racial or ethnic minorities. By 2025, Hispanics will constitute the largest sin-gle ethnic group in the United States. And by 2056, whites not of Hispanic descent may constitute less than half of the United States population.

Although ethnic- and gender-specific media have long had a role in this country, the changing complexion of the United States has meant an in-crease in media that addresses specific groups and individuals. The changes have meant new topics, new discussions, and new themes. Media, particular-ly general-interest newspapers, cover issues that for many years were carried only in specialized media, such as the black or Hispanic press. Consider the growing numbers of some targeted publications: almost 200 black newspa-pers, almost 250 newspapers that serve forty ethnic groups from Hungarian to Japanese, and about two dozen gay and lesbian publications.

Changing diversity has meant that media are also working to hire employ-ees who represent differing groups so that newsrooms will more accurately reflect the makeup of the population in general. That has not been easy. Black, Asian American, and Hispanic American reporters, for example, are still few in number compared with whites. Experiences of white and minority profes-sionals in the newsrooms vary, and, in some cases, the differences cause minor-ity journalists to leave the profession.

The Associated Press Managing Editors Diversity Committee is just one group monitoring job satisfaction among minorities. Its 1996 diversity report set a baseline for tracking women and minorities in newsrooms and their feelings about work environment and promotion opportunities. The Poynter Institute and Ford Foundation have joined in forming Media Diver-sity Beyond 2000, a group whose goal is to help make newsrooms and news coverage more diverse. It has planned projects to help organizations connect with their communities and a database that would allow editors across the country to share techniques in recruitment and news coverage.

Information and Media Glut

Writers must remember that today's increasingly diverse society offers more to read, watch, and listen to than anyone could possibly consume, even with unlimited leisure time. Marshall McLuhan, more than twenty-five years ago, predicted today's trends, suggesting that new media would alter our society in dramatic, unanticipated ways.

> . . . *electronic technology is reshaping and restructuring social patterns of interde-pendence and every aspect of our personal life. It is forcing us to reconsider and re-evaluate practically every thought, every action and every institution formerly taken for granted. Everything is changing—you, your family, your neighborhood, your education, your government, your relation to "the others."*

He was right. Society has changed. McLuhan could hardly have envisioned the information explosion today. In the United States, the three commercial networks and scores of publications of thirty years ago have grown into a multimedia system that numbers 1,520 daily newspapers, 7,915 weekly newspapers, 8,843 magazines, 1,004 commercial television stations, 406 cable systems, and 10,238 radio stations. By 1998, more than 500 newspapers had online editions. News companies have joined to create online networks that contain features and national news stories.

No one person can possibly read or see the tiniest fraction of what is available today. Media pervade daily life. To the traditional media have been added new forms of communication, such as direct mail and telephone marketing, that can reach anyone who has a zip code and a telephone number. Technology has so overcome such barriers as geography and cost that almost anyone can buy the equipment to be in touch with anyone anywhere in the world. People in remote areas can tune into events via satellite dishes; a sailboat captain in the Caribbean can receive a fax on board or view an online copy of the latest *Wall Street Journal.*

Audience Impact on Traditional Media

The changes in lifestyle, emerging ethnic groups, and competing media have had a major impact on traditional media. Historically, American consumers spend about 4 to 5 percent of the country's gross national product on media. Even during good and bad economic times, the percentage has remained constant. That means that in times of prosperity, more dollars are spent on media, and media flourish.

Many of today's consumers spend on new media and invest in computers, digital color monitors, CD ROMs, and accompanying software. Consumers buy the equipment that gives them access to information. Such spending is not factored into the dollars spent on media but rather is hidden in the cost of electric bills, the amortization of equipment, online access, and telephone service.

The need for information and entertainment is constant, therefore, but the preferred sources change—perhaps for the good. But the change has not been so good for traditional media, such as newspapers. Research has shown that fickle audiences may not return to a medium once they have abandoned it for another means of getting information and entertainment.

Newspapers have been hard hit by change as audiences have moved to other technology to get information and entertainment faster. Since 1980, more than 200 daily newspapers have closed, whereas weekly newspapers have declined only slightly in number. The circulation of daily newspapers has dropped, although that of weeklies has grown. Professor Robert Stevenson, in describing the "vanishing newspaper reader," noted that 73 percent of people in a national sample in 1967 said they read a newspaper every day. That number had dropped to 59 percent by 1998, although slightly more said they read the Sunday newspaper.

Critics of the newspaper industry have said that newspapers have not kept up with the technology and changed enough to attract readers. Some newspapers have taken steps to reach out to readers, such as putting reporters' e-mail addresses at the end of stories and inviting readers to sit in on daily news meetings. Others have launched special reporting projects targeted to community interests. Newspapers such as *The Washington Post, The Wall Street Journal,* and *The New York Times* have established elaborate Web sites that may be accessed easily at home or at work.

Newspapers are not alone in experiencing a decline in audiences. Well-established magazines have faced competition for readers' time from a flood of specialized publications. One study found that 18 percent of respondents said they read a news magazine such as *Time* or *Newsweek,* and only 5 percent regularly read financial magazines such as *Forbes* or *Business Week.*

Watching television news, however, is still a daily activity for most Americans. Eight of ten respondents in a Times-Mirror study said they watched television news regularly. Although television appears to be the main source of news, it, too, has dealt with declining ratings and increased competition.

To attract and retain attention, media executives have had to stop and consider audiences more carefully so they can reach them successfully with advertising and editorial content. And to retain and attract audiences, they have had to consider content in relation to convenience, habit, interest, and other factors.

Media leaders are aware of the constraints that keep audiences away, such as money, lifestyles, increasing demands on time, and the lure of other media. The smart ones have realized that they must adjust and be flexible to reach specific audiences. They have recognized that often they need to create a profile of their audience, by research and other means, to find out exactly who they are and what they need. Armed with knowledge about audiences, media leaders—and writers—can do more to aim messages more specifically to their targeted destinations.

Analyzing Audiences

People who write tend to read more than the average person does. They are likely to be more educated, have a larger vocabulary, and exhibit a greater interest in various topics. They may write to please themselves or to satisfy what they think audiences want to know. As lifestyles have changed, they may be out of touch with their audiences and not know truly who their audiences are.

Such ignorance is dangerous. Writers are at risk if they do not know who their audiences are or if they assume that audiences are masses of uneducated folks. They also cannot assume that audiences can grasp complicated, technical messages. Successful writers take several pre-writing steps in an effort to know and to get in touch with their audience.

Steps to Audience Success

First, writers must accept that they have to work hard to win readers; second, they must consider and analyze their audience and its needs; and third, they have to invest time and energy in caring about their audience. Good writing requires that writers understand and practice these steps.

Step One: Acceptance

First, and perhaps most important, writers need to accept what has been laid out earlier in this chapter: Writers compete for audiences. They cannot change the ways in which audience lifestyle or diversity constantly changes, nor can they reduce the proliferation of media and new technologies that compete for audiences and distract them.

Before writing, writers must accept that they will have to work hard to craft a message that will catch and hold an audience. They must stretch to reach less cooperative audiences. They must also accept that audiences have a desire for information and entertainment and search both traditional and new media to satisfy that desire. To be successful, writers must know their audience and know what they want.

Step Two: Audience Defined

For many writers, defining specific audiences is a new experience. Throughout our school years, most of us think of "the teacher" as our audience, unless perhaps the teacher instructs us to "write a children's story" or "write a letter to grandmother." In such cases, few writers stop to describe and analyze that audience. Hardly anyone who is told to write a children's story ever stops to think, "Now which children do I want to reach? All children? Preschoolers?"

Asking such questions, however, is the most basic kind of audience analysis—whereby writers put their wants and needs aside and think about those of the audience. Such analysis is essential for today's writer and is obvious in the work of master writers.

Children's author Roald Dahl, an older writer at the peak of his career, thought constantly about children and what their lives were like. Dahl described his audience in *Meet the Authors and Illustrators*:

> They [children] love being spooked. They love suspense. They love action. They love ghosts. They love the finding of treasure. They love chocolates and toys and money. They love magic. They love being made to giggle.

In Dahl's *Charlie and the Great Glass Elevator,* the characters travel through time and space in a large glass elevator, along with Mr. Willy Wonka, a character made famous in Dahl's well-known book, *Charlie and the Chocolate Factory.* Dahl made the most of children's past experiences with elevators, with glass, with silly adults, and with his previous book. Rather than featuring a starship with alien creatures, Dahl used familiar thrills to build a great adventure for everyday kids—and it sold more than a million copies.

Here are a few questions that may guide a writer in defining audiences:

Who will read this?
Who needs to read it?
Whom would I choose as an ideal listener or reader?

Step Three: Audience Care and Feeding

The term *audience care and feeding* truly sums up priorities for writers in the information age. Good writers care about audiences and take time to learn about them, to think about them, and to please them rather than themselves. Good writers also feed audiences by giving them information in a palatable form—one that they can use and understand.

Dahl cared about his audience: children. "Unless you hold them from the first page, they're going to wander away and watch the telly or do something else," he noted. Dahl took the time to discover what elements appeal to children. Then he constructed his storybook in a format that children could use and understand. He created a fanciful world that captured children's imaginations and was related to their interests. He cared so much about his audience that he precisely crafted an appealing writing style and story. And his writing proved successful.

Writers must think long and hard about the audiences for their messages, just as Dahl did. Writers must care so much that if readers reject their work, the writers have also lost. They need to undertake careful thinking before a first draft is attempted.

Identifying Audiences

Few writers have a single audience, although many mistakenly write for what they call a "mass audience." In today's world, *mass audience* is only a rough term used to describe a conglomeration of many smaller, specific audiences. The members of the small audiences have much in common. Some typical smaller audiences are veterans, working mothers, union members, and power company customers. Your audience may be tiny (members of St. John's Parish), or it may be huge (Americans interested in better health care).

Regardless of size, every audience may be subdivided into smaller component audiences. For example, members of a church parish will include smaller audiences of children, teens, young adults, singles, marrieds, new parents, empty nesters, choir members, grounds workers, and so on. Even a smaller audience, such as veterans, could be further divided into veterans of specific wars, such as World War II or the Vietnam War.

Breaking an audience into its composite groups is an important activity for people who need to communicate essential messages. Each subgroup may have specific needs for information and a specific way of getting it. A university, for example, has many audiences, including students, faculty, staff, alumni, potential students, governing bodies, the press, and potential donors. No one message will effectively reach all of these publics. Most universities spend a great deal of time and money developing specific messages that are targeted to their many audiences, such as the alumni newsletter for alumni, direct mail for potential donors, and news conferences for the media.

Writers need to identify their audiences. A shortcut is to state the topic, then to ask the question, "Who cares?" The answer will be a list of groups or audiences that are potential consumers of the message.

Let's try the "who cares?" method for listing audiences for a message. You are writing an article for your company newsletter on a new policy that provides preventive health care benefits to employees who have children. "Who cares?" yields this list:

- Married employees with children,
- Single employees with children,
- Employees thinking about having or adopting children, and
- Employees who have no children but who wish they had preventive health care benefits.

Why is listing audiences important? Because even if writers go no further in getting to know their audiences, once they have at least listed them, they may change their writing approach. For the employee newsletter, your initial attempt at an introduction might have read

```
A new company policy will provide health care benefits for
preventive medicine.
```

But after you list audiences, your introduction becomes more personal:

```
As a single parent, staff geologist John Payne has worried
about the extra expense of annual medical exams for his
three children and a doctor's visit if children were only
mildly ill.
    But Mega Oil's new health benefits program will ease
those worries. The plan will reimburse employees with
```

children for preventive health expenses, such as office
visits and well-child checkups.

As audiences are subdivided and defined, so are writing tasks. When writers take time to identify specific audiences, such as single parents, messages can be targeted for those audiences. The approach, structure, and language can be chosen to suit the audience, and communication becomes possible—and even likely.

Researching Audiences

To be more successful at reaching audiences, writers should go beyond just listing them. Once writers have listed their audiences, they often need to do research, both formal and informal, to become familiar with audiences. Research gives writers information such as audiences' likes and dislikes, the media they use, and audiences' values and goals.

Audiences will not turn away from a message that is consistent with their values, needs, and goals. An audience interested in women's health will be attracted to a message that begins with "Free mammograms..." rather than with the name of the sponsoring agency or the name of the government official who announces the program.

Real estate agents frequently cite the three most important words in their business: location, location, location. They must know where house hunters want to live. Any good agent knows what matchups to avoid: Don't show the townhouse on a busy avenue to the couple with four young children or the retiree's garden apartment to the aggressive young professionals.

Much as real estate agents select a location or a sample of homes to show to potential buyers, writers can tailor messages once they know their audiences. Just as real estate agents need to find out immediately where clients want and need to live, so must writers find out what the intended audience wants and needs to know. A writer can't begin to write an effective message until the characteristics of the audience have been assessed.

To gather information about audiences, four techniques are commonly used by researchers. No single technique can provide complete information about any audience; most writers should use some combination of these methods.

COGITATION. Yes, that's right. Writers can just think about their audience. For example, when writing a letter to Grandma, gifted grandchild-writers stop to think, "What in my life is of greatest interest to Grandma? What kinds of things make her laugh? What will she want to know more about?" Asking these questions about Grandma is a form of audience research. Such analysis is also essential for today's writers, who must ask, "What do I think my audience is interested in?"

LIBRARY RESEARCH. Sometimes a writer needs to go to the library or to an online reference service. For example, when developing family management tips for working mothers, a writer may need to know how many working mothers are in the United States and in the potential audience. What kinds of jobs do they have? How old are they? How old are their children? What is their average income? Answers to these questions are available in census data and in articles about the census. The answers can tell a writer what kinds of information will appeal most readily to the working mother audience. For example, money-saving management tips may be well received.

INFORMAL AND FORMAL SURVEYS. Surveying is a scientific way of asking questions, usually from a wide variety of people. Informal surveys are part of a writer's daily life. Interviewing various people is a staple of daily journalism that works well for all writers as a way of learning more about audiences.

Spending time observing the way people live or conduct business can add to a writer's knowledge. The novelist who writes about life in Appalachia may spend months gathering oral histories, which will serve as the basis for a new book. Novice reporters learn the value of "hanging out" at the police station or at city hall, where they can talk to many people who are interested in their news beats.

More formal survey techniques are sometimes used for understanding audiences. Suppose that the circulation of a community sports newspaper has been dropping steadily. Before abandoning or changing the paper, the editor conducts a readership survey, asking people what they would change about the publication. Students who are thinking of starting a new on-campus publication may distribute surveys to determine audience interests and needs.

No formal survey is worthwhile unless careful methods are followed. Before attempting to conduct a formal survey, a writer should consult a professional or professor in public opinion research, or consult a book about survey research.

Both formal and informal surveys protect writers from making dangerous assumptions about their audiences. Perhaps the most common assumption is that everybody in the audience is alike—and is even like the writer! Audiences are diverse and ever-changing, and surveys can help today's writer monitor their varying needs.

FOCUS GROUPS. Focus groups are gatherings, usually of seven to ten audience members or potential audience members, to discuss audience needs and preferences. In selecting focus group members, researchers strive to represent all components of the audience or audiences. One of a series of focus groups for a statewide religious publication, for example, included nine people: two mothers of school-age children, a young father, a newlywed, an older woman, two retired men, and two active church women. The group was considered to be nearly an ideal representation of the church membership statewide. The nine-member group talked for seventy minutes and produced a variety of suggestions for improving the publication and many ideas about topics that should be covered. The church implemented their suggestions for change.

All types of media use focus groups to determine what their audiences do and do not like. Focus groups can be helpful for a public relations practitioner in evaluating a new service, such as a telephone call-waiting feature. Advertisers use focus groups to test packaging and assess the perceived quality of a product.

Some publications bring together focus groups solely for the purpose of generating new story and service ideas. Readers have a unique and private perspective on what they read, and the focus group is one of very few methods that allow writers and editors to share their responses and ideas. Many focus groups were held prior to the design of *USA Today Weekend,* the weekend magazine of *USA Today.* Discussion in the early focus groups led to a design of the new magazine based on what readers said they liked and did not like.

Professional users of focus group research advise caution in generalizing too broadly from the results. Researchers hear from only a select few people who are willing to take time from their lives to come and talk about a topic— perhaps an obscure topic. Writers or marketers should never base a decision on a single focus group and its conclusions.

All kinds of research on readers should proceed carefully and with the understanding that no study is perfect—and that audiences may not always know what they like. We must consider the audience in all that we do, but we also must remember that professional judgment is also needed to put audience comments in perspective.

Success with Audiences

Some general rules apply that may give a message an immediate winning edge. These rules will be reiterated in subsequent chapters in the book, but it is worthwhile to set them out here.

• *Give accurate information; check and recheck facts.* An announcement of freshman orientation must send new students to the right building at the right time on the right day. An error can result in a big mixup for hundreds of students and their families. Writing that misinforms or misleads an audience discredits the message, the writer, and the medium. Research has shown that accurate writing preserves a writer's reputation and the goodwill audiences have for the media.

• *Give complete information.* Every bit as frustrating as inaccurate information is incomplete information. And incomplete messages may inadvertently be inaccurate. Coverage of the death of Congressman Sonny Bono would have been incomplete—and wrong—if it had failed to include his earlier years as an entertainer and as part of the twosome, Sonny and Cher.

• *Don't make assumptions about your audience.* Writers often assume a certain background and lifestyle among their readers and listeners. If you write a lead that says

```
Remember the good old days when you were sick and your
mother fed you baby aspirin and chicken soup,
```

the lead assumes that the audience is a uniform age and old enough to have had a childhood in the days before acetaminophen. It also assumes that all audience members had a mother and that they grew up in a society where mothers stayed home with sick children.

• *Deal caringly and ethically with people you are writing about.* Avoid libel or information that may damage a subject's reputation or put that person in an unfair light. Appendix A explains the danger of libel that can occur in any writing. Make sure any descriptive words accurately define the person or people in your message.

• *Avoid offensive words or topics, except when they are crucial to the message.* Daily newspapers traditionally have cautioned writers to observe a breakfast-table standard: Don't publish information, language, or pictures that will make readers lose their appetite for breakfast. In reality, many media have moved quite far away from that advice. Television brings horror into living rooms and kitchens every day, and media have been roundly criticized for insensitivity. Writers need to be circumspect about the value of offensive, crude, or gory material and weigh it against audience needs and interests. The choice is often difficult. Look at the following example, which appeared in a newspaper. The writer might argue that the description shows good reporting, but audiences have little need to know all the details.

NEW YORK—A runaway elevator decapitated welfare clerk James Chenault, 54, as he straddled the doorway in an attempt to help his frightened fellow passengers to safety.

One made it out before the elevator, with the doors still open, shot up to the next floor, cutting off Chenault's head, police said.

The head, with stereo headphones still on, landed in the elevator with the three remaining passengers, police said. The body fell down the shaft.

Reaching Audiences

So where are we? In this chapter we have tried to show that writing is critical to communication, despite increased use of electronic media and other transmission devices such as facsimile machines. Most communication is written first.

We have considered the changes in audiences, both in lifestyle and in diversity. We recognize that every day people are bombarded with dozens of messages from television, newspapers, mail, flyers, magazines, billboards, other people, and on and on and on. In today's information age, many messages cruise from writer to audiences. Many reach their destination—audiences—but are immediately discarded before they have a chance to be assimilated.

Why? Because many factors must be considered as roadblocks between writers and audiences. Even when writers know their audiences, they have to overcome roadblocks.

To summarize and review, here are the major kinds of obstacles that exist between writers and their audiences:

•   *Taxing lifestyles.* Audiences today, despite labor-saving devices, are busier than ever with multiple commitments to work and family. People are spending more of their leisure time on family activities and household chores and less on media consumption.

•   *Diversity of audiences.* Audiences no longer resemble most writers. An increasingly diverse society has changed audience needs and interests from those of even ten years ago.

•   *Media and information glut.* More kinds of media become available almost daily. Each memo, letter, article, or news brief has infinitely more competition for an individual's attention than could have been imagined a decade ago. An overwhelming smorgasbord of media offers information. People use online services, direct mail, and an array of cable and satellite channels in addition to the traditional media. They are hungry for information, and they are able to choose media that are most relevant to their lifestyle.

•   *Unfriendly messages.* Poor writing interferes with messages getting through, just as do commuting, working, children, and too many media choices. A message that bores or taxes an audience or that takes too long to understand can be the greatest roadblock to complete communication.

Different Approaches
for Different Audiences

When the North Carolina Appeals Court returned an opinion, two media covered the case differently. The Associated Press wrote a straightforward account, relying on judges' opinions in the case as its sources. AP distributes its stories to a variety of newspapers throughout North Carolina. A reporter for *The News & Observer,* based in Raleigh, decided to take a lighter touch on the story. Compare the differences in approach, language, and style.

RALEIGH—Baring one's bottom in public may be offensive and indecent, but it doesn't meet the legal standard to be prosecuted for indecent exposure, the state Court of Appeals ruled in a divided decision.

The court ruled 2–1 Tuesday in a 1995 Mecklenburg County case. Judge William H. Helms refused to dismiss the indecent exposure charge against Mark Edward Fly. He was convicted of a misdemeanor after a jury decided Fly dropped his shorts and flashed a woman walking up a staircase to her condominium.

The Appeals Court ruled that state law prohibits the baring of "private parts" but that doesn't include a person's buttocks.

"We recognize that the conduct engaged in by the defendant in this case is indecent as that term is generally defined," Judge K. Edward Greene wrote for the majority in a divided three-judge court panel. "It is not within the province of this court, however, to vary from the natural and ordinary meaning of words used by our legislature to define the criminal offense.

"In this case there is no evidence that the defendant exposed his genital organs and the trial court therefore erred in denying the defendant's motion to dismiss."

In a dissenting opinion, Judge Ralph A. Walker said the court should include mooning as a violation of the indecent exposure law.

"The buttocks are a part of the human body which morality and decency require to be covered in the presence of others. Thus, our statute should be reasonably interpreted to include buttocks within the meaning of 'private parts' and to protect citizens from the exposure experienced by the witness on this occasion," Walker wrote.

(Reprinted with permission from the Associated Press.)

The News & Observer printed this account on its front page:

—Moonstruck? Well, there's no redress. Not right now in North Carolina, anyway.

In language not the least bit cheeky, the state Court of Appeals ruled Tuesday that baring one's behind in public may be bad manners, but it's not indecent exposure because state law doesn't consider the buttocks among a person's "private parts."

The buttocks in question belong to Mark Edward Fly, who revealed them to Barbara Glover on the steps to Glover's Mecklenburg County condominium in 1995 before riding off on a bicycle. Fly was convicted of a misdemeanor and appealed.

The appeals court ruled 2–1 that "private parts" means the reproductive organs only, and that because there was no evidence that Fly showed his, the case should have been dismissed.

Judge Ralph Walker, dissenting, had a more expansive definition of "private parts."

"I really don't know what message the decision sends," said Karen Eady, Fly's public defender. "It says on the one hand we have a free-for-all and we can go around mooning anyone in North Carolina that we want to. On the other hand, I don't think the average Joe Blow would base his actions on the decision like that."

Even if he did, Judge K. Edward Greene points out in a dictum to the decision, the conduct still may be considered a disturbance of the peace.

And even with this case, the end may not be in sight. With a split decision, the state attorney general can appeal the ruling to the state Supreme Court.

William Hart, an assistant attorney general, said his office is considering whether it will do just that.

(Reprinted with permission from *The News & Observer.*)

The Writing Challenge

Writers and communicators must accept that getting messages to people in today's society is an unparalleled challenge. Writers have to accept that they cannot do much to change individual consumer's lifestyles. They cannot reduce the number of media. They cannot modify society's diversity. They cannot alter the fact that only a few messages get through the daily clutter.

But they can control one aspect: the structure of the message. Trained writers know techniques for ensuring that messages reach their destination and are consumed. For some audiences, the succinct three-paragraph news story will suffice. Others will seek the longer, more detailed, narrative account. Good writers know which techniques and which structures best fit their audiences.

Today's technology dramatically increases the need for good writing. Although information may be packaged differently in the technological revolution, audiences still seek information that is accurate and relevant. They will abandon sources that fail to provide information clearly and concisely.

EXERCISES

1. Keep a media log for a twenty-four-hour period between today and the next class. Make a chart showing which media you used, how long you viewed or read, a summary of messages, and what else you were doing while using each medium. Indicate whether you had interference or distractions that prevented you from understanding the message. Be prepared to compare your media-use patterns with those of others in the class.

2. Get a written example of one of the messages recorded in your media log. Study it for clarity. Did you understand the message? How did the writer make it clear? What kept the message from being clear? If the message was not clear, rewrite it to make it clearer. List any missing information that would help the message be better understood.

3. Interview a relative about his or her media use, formulating questions based on your log. Explore how his or her media use has changed during the last five years, ten years. Where does the person get most news? Entertainment? Information that is dependable? In-depth information?

4. Get together with a friend or classmate. Identify his or her roles. For example, your friend may be a cheerleader, daughter, church member, sister, or Girl Scout, or have several other identities. Select one. Through an informal interview, find out what interests your friend when she is in one of those roles, such as church member. How does she get information pertinent to that role? Then switch to another role, say cheerleader. Compare the media she uses to get information in that role.

5. Pick a major national event that occurred within the past two weeks. Go to the library and select several sources that reported the event. Examples would be community newspaper, national newspaper, local daily newspaper, national news magazine, or online publication. Compare the way

each introduced and developed the story. Look at writing style, language, length of story, anecdotes, and quotations. Does the format for presenting the news fit the medium's audiences? How?

REFERENCES

Associated Press Managing Editors Home Page. Available: http:///www.apme.org.

Ian E. Anderson, ed., *Editor and Publisher Yearbook*, New York, Editor & Publisher Co., 1997.

Irwin Kirsch, Ann Jungeblut, and Donald Rock, "Reading Newspapers: The Practices of America's Young Adults." Paper delivered to the Education Writers Association, April 1988.

Deborah Kovacs and James Preller, *Meet the Authors and Illustrators.* New York: Scholastic Inc., 1991.

Marshall McLuhan and Q. Fiore, *The Medium is the Message: An Inventory of Effects.* New York: Bantam Books, 1967.

"News and Newspaper Reading Habits." New York: Newspaper Advertising Bureau, May 1988.

Newspaper Association of America Home Page. Available: http://www.naa.org.

Clarice N. Olien, Phillip J. Tichenor, and George A. Donohue, "A Changing Media Environment in the U.S." Paper presented at the annual meeting of the Association for Education in Journalism and Mass Communication, Boston, MA, August 1991.

Donald L. Shaw, *The Rise and Fall of American Mass Media: Roles of Technology and Leadership,* The Roy W. Howard Project. Bloomington, IN: School of Journalism, Indiana University, 1991.

The Poynter Institute Media Diversity Beyond 2000 Home Page. Available: http://www.poynter.org/dsurvey.

Times-Mirror Center for People and the Press, *The American Media: Who Reads, Who Watches, Who Listens, Who Cares?* Washington, DC, 1990.

Times-Mirror Center for People and the Press, *The People, the Press and Politics: The New Political Landscape.* Washington, DC, 1994.

U.S. Census Bureau Home Page. Available: http://www.census.gov/population/www/socdemo/fertility.html.

"Women's Lifestyles: A Special Report." *Scripps-Howard Editors Newsletter.* Cincinnati, OH: Scripps–Howard Newspapers, Spring 1989.

1990 Census of Population. U.S. Department of Commerce, Economics and Statistics Administration, Bureau of the Census, Washington, DC, November 1993.

3

Getting to the Point

When the president of a university spoke at her installation ceremony, she discussed the broad issue of improving undergraduate education and specific points to achieve that goal. Media wrote the story from different angles. The student newspaper focused on greater rigor in classroom teaching. A television station with a broad viewing audience began its report with her call for accountability to state legislators. A business publication examined her challenge for a more aggressive investment policy to increase the school's endowment. The university's alumni publication looked at the outcome: the continued strength of the university's reputation and the value of its degree. A donor newsletter picked up her request for additional funds for scholarships and teaching-excellence awards.

Writers who are familiar with their audiences know what information will be relevant and appealing. Writers must alert audiences to messages that are important. They know what will attract the attention of the individual who juggles time for job, home, spouse, children, hobbies, and friends.

Messages must therefore hook the audience. The hook must be set in the first few sentences or paragraphs, called the *lead* of the message. That is when writers must show the relevance of the message and attract, entertain, and inform. That is when readers or listeners will decide whether the message is compelling, entertaining, or informative enough to warrant attention. Why toil over constructing messages that do not hook or reach audiences?

This chapter will discuss lead writing, specifically

- The role of audiences,
- Elements in lead writing,

- News values, and
- Types of leads.

What's the Point?

To hook a particular audience, writers must know why they are writing. It sounds simple enough. But many people regard writing as an artistic endeavor, not as a craft. They avoid thinking about the substance of what they are going to say. These writers sit down to write with a broad purpose or goal in mind, such as informing an audience about government waste. They haven't figured out the main point of the specific message, an essential element in hooking the audience.

Determining the point requires critical thinking. Writers must look at the components of the message and weigh each as it pertains to audiences. They must lay out the facts and evaluate their importance and relevance.

What does a rural community need to know about issues in a state legislature? How about a professional association of school board members? These two audiences will need different hooks for the same information. As writers consider information and audiences, they get closer to the point of the message, establishing where they want to start.

Getting to the point is like eating an artichoke: As you peel off the outer leaves and examine them, you get closer to the real heart of your search. You may toss out heavy, less interesting leaves. Closer to the center, you will find more succulent, flavorful leaves worthy of attention. And finally, you unveil the heart.

Finding the heart, or kernel of your story, is essential to writing. Along the way, writers will discover facts and pieces that relate to the main point, surrounding and supporting it like the artichoke's tasty leaves. But the examining process must be completed first.

Consider the advertising copywriter who says, "I want to write an ad that will get more business for my client." He or she is still handling the whole artichoke—a big and unworkable problem. Thinking and planning— a stage of writing—will help in moving from the broad idea of producing an ad to the more specific task of communicating the client's specific benefit. The writer will get to the point.

If the client makes hand lotion, the advertiser's point may be beautiful hands or healthier skin or convenient packaging. If the client owns a tax service, the point may be customer peace of mind and the accountant's knowledge of tax laws. Once that benefit—the point—has been identified, the writer's job is to select precise words that will emphasize that point and grab a consumer's attention. And once writers have established where to start, they will know the direction to go.

In the Beginning Comes the Lead

In journalism the first sentences or paragraphs of a story are called a lead. The lead has a heavy responsibility. It is the bait to hook the reader. By educating, entertaining, or enlightening, it stimulates the reader to pay attention. The lead shows relevance and is relevant to the audience. It also entraps. A publisher once wrote that a lead must be provocative, vigorous, and even at times startling to the reader.

Every piece of writing has a beginning or opening statement; every piece of writing has a lead. Long-time syndicated columnist James J. Kilpatrick once wrote

> *The lead is vital to any writing, whether one is writing a novel, a short story, a book review, a term paper, a newspaper editorial, or a homily to be read in church on Sunday morning.*

Consider this lead from the *Pittsburgh Post-Gazette*:

> Meticulous to the end, Dianna Green organized her suicide with corporate precision.

The most important message was sketched out: A woman, probably in corporate America, planned her death in a precise, organized way. Instead of being bored by what could have been a routine lead, readers are hooked to find out why and how she arranged her death so meticulously.

The lead, therefore, sets out the message's relevance. The lead whets the reader's appetite to stay with the message. A church newsletter used this short lead to establish relevance for parishioners:

> —Hymnals continue to disappear from the church. They need to be brought back so they are here for use at Sunday services.

The lead contains the stimulus for reading, sets out the message's relevance, and gives the reader the most important information first. As the stimulus, the lead entertains, enlightens, and educates; as it sets out the relevance, it whets the reader's appetite to stay with the message; and in giving the most important information first, the lead ensures that the reader gets the point quickly.

By digesting the most important information first, audiences know the essential details after the first few paragraphs. They are informed. They have the information they need because the writer hooked them and got to the point right away. They can stick with the story or even move to other messages.

The lead must also set up the story. After reading or hearing the lead, audiences should know the main points of the message that follows. If not, the lead has misled them, and the writer's credibility is damaged. How does a writer know whether the lead sets up the story? When the story is complete, a writer must consider the main points in the body of the message and ensure that they are noted in the lead. The lead sets up the story; the story backs up the lead. For example, a story reports a robbery at the campus dining hall and includes details about the robber locking the dining hall manager in a closet. That fact should be noted in the lead, along with the information that the robbery occurred and how much money was taken.

Journalists, primarily print journalists, have recognized for decades that getting to the point is essential to attract and retain readers. Media writers have found that they immediately must set out the critical aspects of the message for their readers, listeners, consumers, or other audience members. Writing a lead has become a crucial assignment for any information-age writer.

How to Get Started

To construct a lead, writers must know their information thoroughly. They must evaluate the information, using their judgment and experience to determine what is most relevant to their audience.

As a pre-writing activity, some writers go through their notes and add priority numbers next to information. Before writing the lead that asks for hymnals to be returned, the newsletter writer listed information to be included: The budget for hymnals is $300 this year; forty-two books are missing and we need them back; 10 percent of hymnals have been taken since January 1 and we don't have money to replace them; if you want a home copy, we can order one for you for $15; replacement cost is $15 per book.

Next to each fact, the writer put a number corresponding to its importance to the audience.

In writing the lead, the writer determined that the audience did not need to know about book counts or budget information. Priority number 1 is that hymnals are missing and the church needs them to be returned. The writer sets out the main purpose of the story—to tell the audience that hymnals are missing—and the relevance—without hymnals parishioners can't sing during services.

Writers can avoid the actual numbering of facts through another approach. They can simply ask, "What must my audience know?" and then list three to five things in order of importance. In the case of the hymnals, the list would be something like this:

1. Hymnals are missing and must be returned.
2. If people want home copies, we can order them.
3. Cost is $15.

The main point would become the lead. Other main points would be fashioned into the rest of the copy. Writers have created in essence the format many journalists use—the inverted pyramid—that ranks information in descending order of importance. That format is discussed in Chapter 4.

Writers who struggle with ranking information and its relevance should remember that most people want to know the personal angle first. It all comes down to the audience's automatic question, "How does this message affect me?" The audience immediately looks for the explanation. In the hymnal story, the lead states simply how parishioners will be affected: no hymnals.

Sometimes stories or messages don't have that simple, personal component. Then writers must look beyond the "what about me?" question or relevance rule to other factors that make some pieces of information more important than others. Such factors are also guides to the selection of information for the lead. Those elements are called *news elements* and *news values* and are discussed next in this chapter.

News Elements

Certain elements are of interest in all writing. Journalists over the years have spelled out the elements that must appear in news stories every day: *who, what, when, where, how,* and *why.* That list is a basic starting point for any writer in determining what will go first.

These news components can form a question: "Who did what to whom, how, when, where, and why?" Every letter, news article, news release, or advertisement will answer this question.

Why are these elements important? Because people are most interested in other people, who they are, what they say and do, where they live and work, what happens to them, why they make certain choices, and how they deal with those choices. They are interested in conflict, competition, and achievements. People want to know about other people who overcome adversity, who are defeated, and who do the unusual.

—A Hollywood, Fla., man and woman exchanged wedding vows at 1,300 feet as they plummeted to earth hand-in-hand under silver parachutes five miles west of here Wednesday afternoon.

Grace Mason and John Kempner met while skydiving at a local club and decided it would be the most significant way to start their married life together.

The elements are there:

Who: Grace and John.

What: Got married.

When: Wednesday.

Where: Near Hollywood, Fla.

How: By parachutes.

Why: Because they wanted to start married life in a manner meaningful to their courtship and to them.

The two-paragraph lead summarizes what happened. Readers can decide whether they want to read further to learn more about Grace and John. The author has also set it up so that after reading two paragraphs, the reader knows the most important information and can turn to another message.

Where to Put Who and What

Putting all the elements in the first sentence can result in long, convoluted sentences. Consider the following lead and its clearer rewrite.

—Sam Atwood, an associate professor of political science at the University, told students in a speech Thursday in MacPherson Hall as part of the University's Bicentennial observance that they should be more concerned about world events that more and more directly affect their lives and their future.

Rewritten:

—Students should be concerned about world events that more and more directly affect their lives and their future, an associate professor of political science at the University said Thursday.

Rather than the professor's complete name, a descriptive phrase or identifying label can be used to describe him in the first sentence. The location of the speech and why he was giving it can be included in a subsequent paragraph.

Writers must decide which elements deserve emphasis and are most relevant before they write a lead. All elements will be included somewhere in the story. As a general rule, *who* and *what* will be in the first sentence. So will *where* and *when* because they take up little space. This formula also follows the natural order of the English language: subject, verb, object. *Who, what, when,* and *where* set-up an active structure: A masked man robbed the University dining hall of $3,000 Wednesday night and locked the dining hall manager in a closet. *How* and *why* can be included in the first sentence if they are unusual. A full explanation usually will require several sentences or paragraphs.

Consider this lead, which focuses on *who, what, when,* and *where.*

HO CHI MINH CITY, Vietnam—Fifty-five U.S. cyclists arrived here Wednesday after a grueling 22-day tour through the country's mountains and plains.

Who: 55 U.S. cyclists.
What: Arrived after 22 days of cycling through Vietnam.
When: Wednesday.
Where: Ho Chi Minh City is where the tour ended.

A Closer Look at the Elements

Let's define the lead elements and what role they play in the copy.

Who defines the person carrying out the action or affected by the story. *Who* may not be a specific name, such as Grace or John, but rather an identification or label. For example, a news release may say in the first sentence that two marketing employees have been promoted and in the second sentence give their names and titles. But if the president is retiring, his name will be given first because it has recognition among company employees and in the community.

—Charles Southwick, chief executive officer of Englewood Mills who began his career as a bookkeeper, will retire April 1 after 42 years with the company.

The *who* is Charles Southwick, specifically named because of the role he plays in the local business community. *What* represents the action. It can be simply stated in a verb. Consider this news lead:

—A Richmond, Va., man died Wednesday when he lost control of his car and it crashed into a bridge railing on I-95 South.

The verb "died" tells *what*. Similarly, in a letter to a high school's alumni, the verb tells *what:*

—Southeast High School's PTA is asking alumni to donate money to put at least two computers in every classroom by the end of the year.

What in the example is asking alumni for money.

When tells the audience the timeliness of the event being reported or the time frame of specific actions. Often it is one word. In most writing, *when* will go after the verb because the time element rarely is the most interesting information. Few leads begin with *when*. In the car accident example, "Wednesday" tells when the accident occurred. In the lead on the alumni letter, the time frame is less specific. But an alumnus reading the letter will know that the goal for installing the computers is December 31 of that year, so contributions should be made between receipt of the letter and well before December 31.

—The Wee Tots Day Care Center Board of Directors will meet Wednesday to decide whether to offer a summer camp program for older children.

Wednesday tells interested parents when a decision will be made.

Where gives the reader the geographic context of the story. In many cases that will pique audience interest because readers want to know about events that affect them. The closer the story is to the reader's backyard, the greater the interest will be.

Wire service and other stories in newspapers often start with *where* by using a *dateline,* the name of the city in capital letters, to let readers know immediately where the event occurred.

HOUSTON—NASA officials remained in a quandary about American astronaut Andrew Thomas's spacesuit and how to make one of the two suits aboard Mir a proper fit.

In stories without a dateline, the exact location would be the first word or words in the lead only when it offers some unusual aspect to the story. Usually the *where* is tucked elsewhere into the lead.

—A slice of history awaits you at the Tastee Diner in Silver Spring.

How expands on the *what* aspect. Look at the following lead from the *Washington Post.*

—A man was killed and his body crushed yesterday when a dumpster he and a woman companion were sleeping in was emptied into a trash compactor in the Hampshire Knolls section of Northeast Washington. The woman was seriously injured.

The lead tells *who, what, when,* and *where* but also talks about *how:* how the man died.

Why gives the audience the reason a decision or a change was made or is pending or the cause of an event. In the Richmond accident example, the audience knows why the man died: because he lost control of the car. In the alumni letter, alumni are asked to give money. Why? So the school can buy computers.

To reiterate: *how* and *why* will go in the first sentence or lead if there is some unusual aspect or if they are essential to understanding the message.

—Yelling to police that he would never be taken alive, a Washington fugitive raced his motorcycle through a police roadblock near Springfield and was shot to death by law enforcement officers Thursday.

Why and *how* the man drove through the roadblock are immediately clear to the reader.

Watch out for Too Much

Sometimes all elements fit concisely into a lead, as in the example about the Washington fugitive. But because all elements do not have to be in every first sentence, a writer can set up the point of the story using a few elements in the first sentence and explain the other elements in later paragraphs.

Consider this lead:

—A major housing development that preservationists believed had died last year has been resurrected by developers who say local planning officials are much more receptive to the revised version.

Are *who, what, when, where, how,* and *why* all answered in this first sentence? No.

Who: Developers.
What: Are resurrecting a housing development plan.
When: Implied now, but not stated.
Where: Implied in the county, but not specifically stated.
How: Not stated.
Why: Because planning officials seem more receptive.

The second paragraph of the story gives more explanation of *what* has happened, *when,* and *how.*

—Jonathan Gardner, one of the developers of the project, said a revised plan was submitted to the county planning board earlier this week. Developers resubmitted the plan after conversations last month indicated certain revisions could erase planning officials' objections.

The third paragraph answers *where* and gives more information, and the fourth paragraph moves into the controversy.

—The revised plan uses the same 300-acre site in southeast Granger County but has 46 fewer houses and relocates the swim and tennis club. Developers expect a public hearing to be set next month.

Preservationists have vowed to fight the renewed development efforts. They say the issues haven't changed despite what they call minor modifications in the original plan.

The first sentence, or the first paragraph, stands as the lead to the story. The other elements, particularly how developers decided to resubmit the plan and what changes were made, are later components of the article. The lead would have been quite complex if the writer had tried to include all the elements there.

A lead attracts readers to the story because it has other elements—beyond *who, what, when, where, how,* and *why*—that must be considered when the writer is structuring the first sentence. These other elements are called news values.

News Values

In structuring leads, writers are also guided by what journalists traditionally have called news values, or aspects of an event that make it worth knowing about. We can also define news values as qualities that are of interest to people or are satisfying in some way. These values or qualities carry over into any writing.

The traditional news values that journalism professors teach and that become second nature to reporters are prominence, timeliness, proximity, impact, magnitude, conflict, oddity, and emotional impact. Let's look at each of the news values and how they affect lead writing. Several of them are closely allied to the elements *who, what, when, where, how,* and *why* discussed earlier in this chapter.

Prominence

When the main character or characters in your story are well known, that is a signal to put those names in the lead. The routine becomes news, such as singer Michael Jackson becoming a father.

When Chelsea Clinton started college at Stanford University, all the major media covered the event. Because the president is a prominent figure, his daughter's first day as a first-year student became leading news. She was not just another kid starting college. Consider this lead from the *San Francisco Chronicle*:

—An exuberant Chelsea Clinton went to college yesterday, hurling herself into the new world of Stanford University, while her parents pulled themselves away from their only child for the first time in their lives.

People who are related to famous people are lead-worthy. Prominence extends even to pets, such as when what to name President Clinton's dog became news.

Timeliness

One adage in journalism is that old news ain't news. People want to know what is happening as soon as it happens. They want newness in the news. They want to know information they didn't know yesterday. They want timely, up-to-date news and depend increasingly on television, radio, and online services as initial sources of news information. Therefore, *when* an event happened is almost always in the first sentence of a story so that people will have a context for that event.

—The governor will honor five National Merit Scholarship winners from the state in a special ceremony at the Governor's Mansion Friday afternoon.

DALLAS—Lawyers for convicted murderer Karla Faye Tucker asked Gov. George W. Bush on Thursday to commute her death sentence to life in prison. She is scheduled to die Feb. 3.

Proximity

People are most interested about news that happens close to them. Audiences easily identify with stories with a geographic proximity, that is, those that occur in their own community, town, county, or state. They like to read stories about their neighbors' successes and even defeats.

Audiences are also interested in what happens to people from their communities in other locations. For example, people in Cleveland would want to know about an airplane crash in Washington State that kills residents from their city. A Cleveland newspaper might run this lead:

SEATTLE, Wash.—Two Cleveland businessmen were among 19 people killed early this morning when a jet struck a radio tower just outside Seattle.

The lead emphasizes Cleveland's loss while telling that the plane crash occurred. Writers call this localizing a message, or putting the local angle on a story that originated miles away, so that audiences can see how the message relates to them and their community.

News reports may also have an emotional or nonspatial proximity, whereby readers identify with a certain group of people. People who have suffered heart attacks are interested in articles about how other heart-attack victims have coped. People who live in a college town may be more inclined to read about stories originating from other cities with campuses, even if the cities are far away. Football fans anywhere could relate to the following Associated Press lead on the resignation of Barry Switzer, longtime head coach of the beleaguered Dallas Cowboys. The firing occurred just days before playoffs for Super Bowl XXXII.

—Barry Switzer resigned as coach of the Dallas Cowboys today, saying it was in the team's best interest to have someone else in charge.

"At this time, I believe a fresh start at this position will give the Cowboys their greatest opportunity to return to the top," Switzer said in a statement.

Impact

Audiences always want to know how they will be affected, whether by a road closing while a sewer line is being laid or by a sale at the local supermarket. Reporters often hear people ask, "But how does this affect me? What does this have to do with me?" High in any message should be an explanation of how an event affects individuals' daily lives or why they should be concerned.

When possible, the impact should be translated into tangible terms. For example, a water and sewer rate increase approved by the Little Rock Town Council Tuesday night will mean that the average resident will pay $3.52 a month more for service, bringing the average monthly bill to $31.96; when Congress passes legislation to reduce Social Security benefits, it will leave most recipients with $20 less a month. The impact of an earthquake is on the hundreds of people affected.

LOS ANGELES—Searchers pulled body after body from a crumpled apartment complex Monday after an earthquake that snapped freeways like matchsticks, left hundreds of thousands without power and water, and turned the nation's busiest highway network into a commuter's nightmare.

The impact of the earthquake that rocked Los Angeles was noted in the Associated Press lead: Hundreds of thousands had no power, and thousands of commuters had no roads to travel on.

Magnitude

Some folks like to distinguish between impact and magnitude in defining news values. *Magnitude* is defined as the size of the event. Death, injury, or loss of property are all elements of magnitude that attract audience attention. Large amounts of money, such as lottery winnings, as well as disasters, such as hurricanes, carry magnitude and are always big news. When a typhoon rips through the Philippines, the amount of damage inflicted and the speed of the winds are the magnitude of the storm. In an earthquake, the magnitude is the reading on the Richter scale.

Consider this lead, which has magnitude and an understood impact:

—Tuesday morning fifty-four school buses will drive more than 1,000 miles as they pick up 2,500 school children for the first day of classes this year.

The magnitude is represented in part by the 2,500 students, the 1,000 miles traveled, and fifty-four school buses. The understood impact of the first day of school is much broader, affecting any household in the county that has school-age children, or an employee of the school system, or an early morning commuter.

Conflict

Most news events reported contain some kind of conflict: contract disputes with striking workers, continuing struggles in the Middle East, the battles between neighbors in rezoning issues, or a grievance filed by an employee against a supervisor. People like to read about conflict. The extent of the conflict, either its size or its duration, will determine whether conflict is included in the lead of the message.

Conflict permeates the news. Doctors and medical ethicists debated the use of fertility drugs and selective abortion of fetuses in multiple pregnancies after an Iowa woman gave birth to septuplets. Consider the coverage of the continued strife in Northern Ireland. Or this lead by Susan Saulny from *The Washington Post* Metro section:

—Lawrence Downing likes to circle his eyes in dark colors with face paint and make designs on his cheeks, especially when he's at school and feels the need to stand out from the crowd.

But since November when the principal cracked down on "painting up," Lawrence has had to settle for heavy eyeliner and black lipstick to express himself.

Both the eyeliner and the lipstick are allowed at Loudoun County High School in Leesburg, where Lawrence, 16, is a sophomore. But every so often, they still get him into trouble.

Oddity

Editors often encourage writers to look for oddity or some unusual twist to a story, such as the police officer who responds to the accident call and discovers that one of the injured people is his son.

When a 60-year-old British woman gave birth to a baby boy, that made news. When the pope made the first papal visit to Cuba in January 1998, media covered the five-day trip and even anchored evening newscasts from the island country. Since 1976 when the U.S. Supreme Court reinstated the death penalty, states have been putting convicted criminals to death. In 1998 a woman was executed in Texas, the first there in 135 years and the second in the nation since 1976. The lead on the story focused on the unusual aspect:

HUNTSVILLE, Texas—Karla Faye Tucker, the first woman executed in Texas in 135 years and the second in the nation since the death penalty was reinstated 22 years ago, died by lethal injection Tuesday evening at the state execution chamber here.

Whenever a writer is working on a message that has an element of oddity about it, care must be taken to ensure that people are not portrayed as freakish or unnatural. For example, a story on the largest baby born in the county in thirty years may not need to be written at all.

Emotional Impact

Writers are recognizing more and more that people like stories that affect them emotionally and that have emotional impact. This news value also is called *human interest* and *universal appeal.* It is the quality that draws audiences to children, young people, and pets.

Think about your own interests. In looking at a page of a company newsletter, the photo of children and balloons at the company picnic will probably have more appeal than the picture of the president presenting a $5,000 check to the local PTA president.

Consider a story, with accompanying photographs, of children at a petting zoo:

> —The animals came by twosy, twosy, twosy—goats, sheep, ducks and a wallaroo.
>   And there were Jim and Angie, the monkeys; Goldie and Scarlett, the macaws; and Ralph, the chimpanzee.

People also like stories tied to love and romance. The article about a couple who both are line workers for a local utility company has great appeal. Including that aspect in the lead will attract readers.

Remember the Audience

In applying news values, writers must think about what is important to their audience. Knowing the audience determines the lead and also affects how the writer will rank information.

For example, a college community audience hears the mayor speak in a lecture series. What he says looks like this in the college newspaper's lead:

> —Students play a vital role in boosting the town's economy when they shop at downtown businesses, Mayor Leo Ryan said Wednesday.

The primary audience for the college newspaper is students.

What the mayor said has a different focus for the lead in the town's general-circulation newspaper:

—Town and college administrators need to develop a joint long-range plan that will address growth, particularly along the campus perimeter, during the next 20 years, Mayor Leo Ryan said Wednesday night.

A general-interest audience, primarily made up of town residents, would be more interested in what the mayor said that affected them directly.

Sorting It Out

At this point you are educated about the elements of a lead, but you still may be unclear about what goes first. That sorting process is learned best through practice.

Let's walk through the process.

You are a writer in a bank's corporate communications department. In three months, the company will open a fitness center for employees. The center will be in the old YMCA building next door to corporate headquarters.

You are to write a news release for the local newspaper. You have collected the needed information. Your list of elements looks like this.

Who: Amana Savings and Loan.
What: Will open a fitness center.
Where: Next door to corporate headquarters in the old YMCA.
When: In three months.
Why: To improve employee health. To provide a benefit to employees.
How: By renovating the old YMCA.

Now make a list of news values as they relate to the story. Ask whether each applies and if so, how.

Prominence: No.

Timeliness: Yes. Within three months.

Proximity: Yes. In downtown.

Impact: Yes. The renovation will mean local jobs and other economic benefits to the town. It will affect the lives of the company's 450 employees and the townspeople who have been wondering what will happen to the old YMCA.

Magnitude: Yes. The acquisition and renovation will cost the company almost $1 million.

Conflict: None internally. Shareholders approved the expenditure at the annual meeting. None externally. Town residents want the building saved.

Audience: Townspeople.

*Emotional
impact:*   Could be for people who remember using the old YMCA.

In writing the lead for the news release, you as the writer must consider the newspaper's audience—the townspeople—and ask, "What will they want to know first?" The answer is the timeliness of the renovation. The renovation is new news.

A first draft of the lead might read like this:

```
—Amana Savings and Loan will spend $1 million to renovate
the vacant YMCA downtown on Sycamore Street to create an
employee fitness center that will open within three months.
```

Here you have answered *who, what, when,* and *where.* You also have addressed the magnitude of the project.

The second paragraph will answer *why* and *how,* and the third paragraph will explain impact.

```
The bank will renovate the old YMCA building to provide a
convenient way for employees to remain physically fit, said
employee manager Kay Barnes. The bank will use the existing
layout and install new equipment and furnishings.

    The project will mean additional jobs during the
renovation and later when the center opens, Barnes noted.
```

General Rules for Leads

No matter what type of lead you choose to write, all leads have common features.

Leads should be short. As a guide, some writers use no more than thirty words. Many wire service stories have leads no longer than twenty words in the first sentence or paragraph. If one word or phrase works, use it.

—Native American.
Matthew Moore checked that box on his admission application to the University of Michigan two years ago, and got four years of free tuition worth $15,000 and a coveted student research job in a computer lab.

Leads should be concise and to the point. Writers must eliminate unnecessary words. Look at the following lead and see what has been eliminated in the rewrite and how the focus has changed:

—Two 14-year-old boys have been arrested and charged with breaking and entering and cruelty to animals after a local day care center was broken into Wednesday night and property vandalized, toys overturned and a pet rabbit, named Ray, killed with a nearby broom.

Rewritten:

—Vandals who broke into a local day care center Wednesday night, killed the center's pet rabbit with a broom, overturned toys and damaged property.
Two 14-year-old boys have been charged with breaking into Hillside Day Care Center and with cruelty to animals in the death of the center's pet rabbit, Ray.

Words should be precise and in the general vocabulary. Examples in the Native American lead are "box," "free," "job," and "lab." The words in the following Associated Press lead are precise and show the impact:

LAND O'LAKES, Fla.—When 3-year-old Mikey Spoul took his father's car for a joyride last month and explained "I go zoom," the act grabbed national attention and even became fodder for late-night show monologue jokes.
But nobody's laughing now. Mikey torched his bedroom curtains with a cigarette lighter and burned down his family's home, authorities said.

Leads should use active verbs. Consider the verbs in the lead example above: "grabbed," "torched," and "burned down," or the verbs in this lead:

—A Forest City man smashed the glass door on a Laundromat washing machine and yanked a 3-year-old child from the swirling waters Saturday morning.

Leads should be simple sentences, not rambling, convoluted sentences. No one wants to work too hard at understanding most communication. The writer has lost if the "huh?" factor enters in. That's when a person has to stop and reread a lead to understand what the writer is saying.

Compare the simple lead about the Forest City man in the Laundromat with this more convoluted lead:

—Under a handgun–control plan, announced by state and county grassroots organizations Monday, a person who sells a handgun to an unlicensed customer would be liable to a victim for three times his losses if that handgun is used to commit a crime.

Apply what you have learned about leads so far to untangle this report on controlling handguns. What's the point? Some grassroots organizations have come up with an idea for making handgun salespeople more responsible for crime.

What does the audience have to know? How about this lead:

—If a local citizens group gets its way, people who sell guns will help pay for the lives and property lost in handgun crimes.

Summary Leads

Writers base the structure of their leads on the type of story and the audience. Some information, such as police reports, lend themselves to summary leads. Other material works better in a descriptive or anecdotal lead.

The most common lead format is a summary lead that tells or summarizes the most important information:

—Four Northern High School students have received National Merit Scholarships.

—To reduce attrition, Telstar Corp. will build an on-site day care center that will enroll 125 children of its employees in May.

—The Republican Party is increasing its membership in Maryland, a state that Democrats once confidently claimed.

—Figure skater Michelle Kwan broke her own record Saturday night with eight perfect scores, reclaimed her national title, and earned her first Olympic berth on the U.S. team.

The summary lead serves the audience who skims newspaper stories, company newsletters, or handouts from school; who listens with one ear to radio news reports and one ear to the kids in the backseat of the car; or who casually tunes into the morning television news while getting dressed. Because of the crowded field of communication today, summary leads are used often to give people information quickly.

Summary leads are useful. They can be the introduction of a letter, the hook of a news story, the beginning of a news release, or the headline of a broadcast story.

Beyond One Paragraph

Although most summary leads consist of one sentence or one paragraph, they may be longer. Leads can be longer if they are clear and easy to understand.

Look at this lead from *The News & Observer* in Raleigh, North Carolina.

—On the big Monopoly board of radioactive waste disposal, Chem-Nuclear Systems Inc. seemed to have passed "go" last month.

That's when the company submitted a license application for its proposed radioactive waste repository in southwest Wake County and was expecting to receive a $2 million bonus from a state authority.

But the company might have skipped a few spaces. After thumbing through Chem-Nuclear's license application, the N.C. Division of Radiation Protection has determined that the 6,000-page document doesn't include at least 13 key pieces of information.

The writer sets up a complicated subject through a clever use of the familiar Monopoly game. Readers know in the third paragraph that there is a problem, a potential conflict. They are hit with an "oh, my" thought: How could a 6,000-page document leave out anything? Also note the use of the verb *thumbed*. The verb gives the sense of scanning the hefty document, and it makes readers curious to know whether a closer look would reveal more missing pieces.

A writer in a company's corporate communications department needs to tell employees about changes in the benefits package. She must do so in a way that is informative, pertinent, and clear.

—Long Branch Entertainment employees will see in their paychecks Feb. 1 some changes that represent good news and bad news.

The good news is the company's health insurance company has reduced the annual deductible from $500 to $250 per person per year.

The bad news is each employee with a family plan will pay $10.16 more a month in insurance premiums and employees with individual plans $6.32 more a month.

The three-paragraph summary lead contains information essential to employees: how the company's health insurance plan will change. The writer wanted employees to know right away that they were about to be hit in the pocketbook and why. Employees who want to know more about how and why the changes occurred will continue to read the message.

Multiple-Element Leads

The Long Branch lead on health care also illustrates how a writer presents more than one aspect to a message. Often a lead has multiple elements or more than one point it must convey to readers. A multiple-element lead summarizes information for readers and sets up what will be covered in the rest of the copy. It presents a challenge to the writer, who must be wary of complex or convoluted sentences. The best approach is to rank the elements, put the most important in the first sentence, and then create a second or third paragraph to present the other points.

—A group of University students has presented a list of concerns to Chancellor Paula Walls, asking foremost that the University allow 24-hour visitation in dormitories.

The letter, hand-delivered to Walls Wednesday, also asks the administration to name more minority students to campus-wide committees, to recruit minority faculty members, and to put a ceiling on student fees.

From this lead, readers have the most important information first: the list of demands and the high-priority demand. And they know the content and structure of the message.

Delayed-Identification Leads

Another type of summary lead is the delayed-identification lead. When an individual or individuals in a news story carry no prominence, their proper names are not given in the first paragraph. Rather, they are identified by a generic label: "An Orange County woman died when..." or "A Lockwood High School student has been named a National Merit Scholarship winner...." Immediately, in the next paragraph, the individual is named. If more than one person is in the lead or first paragraph, the individuals are renamed in that order in the next paragraph.

Consider this:

—An Orange County woman died Tuesday night when she lost control of her car and it overturned on Highway 125 near here.

Sarah Louise McFee, 29, of Rt. 6, Box 34, Lewisville, was dead on arrival at University Hospital.

Or this:

—One of two local fishermen who spent two days floating in life preservers in the Atlantic Ocean was released from the hospital Sunday, and his companion remained in good condition.

George Livermore, 37, of Cedar Grove left University Hospital after being under observation for two days. Colin West, 35, also of Cedar Grove, is expected to be released by the end of the week.

Other Lead Formats

Although the summary lead is the most useful, writers sometimes find other lead formats better suited to the kind of message they need to send. Some types of leads, such as anecdotal or descriptive, are popular in newspapers and magazines today. They can be risky because they don't hook readers soon enough. They must therefore be well written to entice readers to stay long enough to find out what the message is about.

In general, when using other lead formats, make sure you get to the point by the fourth paragraph. Otherwise, you may lose your reader. If you are writing for a newspaper, the story may have jumped or the end moved to another page before the reader ever gets to the point.

Let's evaluate some types of alternative leads.

Anecdotal Leads

Writers use anecdotal leads to put a human element into their messages. These leads can be particularly effective because they tell a story and have a plot themselves. Although they delay the point of the message, they set up complex problems and their effects on individuals. Writers must use the anecdotal example through the story, not solely as a hook that is dropped after the lead.

Consider this lead in *The Philadelphia Inquirer* by Pulitzer Prize–winning writer David Zucchino:

—Someone is knocking, quite gently, at the door.

"Who?" asks the gatekeeper of a shooting gallery near Cambria Street, where a man with a syringe tucked behind his ear is mixing heroin with water in a bottle cap.

A woman's voice answers, "Angela!"

The gatekeeper lifts a wooden barricade and the door swings open. A slender woman named Angela and her wild-haired friend Maureen bound through the breezeway, smiling and waving, intent on getting high. They have just spent $10 each at Fourth and Cambria Streets for two blue glassine bags of "Mercedes" heroin.

Soon needles are in the women's arms and heroin is coursing through their veins. Their heads droop and their eyes glaze and they are at peace. A few hours will pass before they must again shoplift to raise the cash to buy the drugs that lure them back to Cambria Street.

The daily journey of this pair of heroin addicts from their homes in New Jersey to a shooting gallery in North Philadelphia is a shopping trip. It is an expedition made thousands of times a year by thousands of

drug customers, whose cash lubricates the economy of a place some nar-
cotics officers call the Badlands.

The illegal drug trade pumps at least $250 million in cash a year into
a three-square-mile swath of North Philadelphia anchored by the Badlands, the Drug Enforcement Administration estimates.

(Reprinted with permission of *The Philadelphia Inquirer.*)

Zucchino takes seven paragraphs before he specifically tells us that his
story is about illegal drugs, although most readers have a good idea by the
second paragraph. The lead uses two women and how their lives are affected
by drugs. The simple writing and description are compelling and pull the
reader further into the story. Most writers would have made the point clear
by the fifth paragraph.

Descriptive Leads

Like an anecdotal lead, a descriptive lead puts emotion or a human element
into a message. It sets the scene for the reader. Consider *The Herald-Sun* lead
into this story:

DURHAM—A crowd of curious children and adults gathered on the
lawn and street in front of an apartment complex at 1108 Drew Street as
homicide investigators began their work once again Saturday afternoon.

At the top of the stairs, the body of a man in his late 20s lay half
inside an apartment, blood pooling beneath his head, a baseball cap still
clenched tightly in his hand. Blood streaks ran down the glass of the
open door.

But before officers could finish snapping photos and questioning witnesses, shots rang out from across the road on North Hyde Park Street.

Toddlers screamed and the crowd ducked for cover behind patrol
cars as several men ran out of an apartment, guns blazing as they fired at
random. Someone yelled, "Get the kids out of the street!" as people fled
inside, slamming doors.

The gun-wielding men jumped in a car and sped toward Alston
Avenue, scattering people caught in the street as they left.

Subsequent paragraphs identified who was killed and gives details of the
shooting.

Question Leads

Question leads should be avoided. They are rarely successful. In most cases, they are the lazy writer's way out, and they turn off audiences. In almost every case, they give the audience the option to turn elsewhere.

```
Who will pay to build nuclear power plants?
```

The reader might say, "Not me, and I don't care who pays." Think of another angle such as

```
The average electric consumer will end up paying the cost
for building nuclear power plants, a local watchdog group
stated today.
```

Occasionally a question lead can work, as in this one from the *Arkansas Democrat Gazette:*

—What's a prairie dog worth?
    Two to six years, Little Rock police say.

The reader at first mentally guesses a dollar figure, but then is surprised immediately that the correct answer is a prison term. The reader is hooked into the story on prairie dog–napping.

Quotation Leads

Such leads should be used sparingly because rarely does someone sum an entire speech or premise for a decision in one simple quotation. A quotation can be used if it is short, is relevant to the rest of the message, and does not need any explanation. It must be clear within itself. Look at this newsletter lead:

—"Taking advantage of the different opportunities available in the Scholars program is what made a difference in my academic career," said a University of Maryland senior who will attend Georgetown Law School next year.

The lead here is empty and nonspecific. The lead fails to point out that the senior is a semifinalist for a Rhodes scholarship, is the Student Government Association vice president, and was an intern at the FBI. A stronger lead would have focused on his accomplishments and linked them to his involvement in the Scholars program:

> —Randy Cates, a senior at the University of Maryland, is a semifinalist for a Rhodes scholarship, one of the most prestigious international academic awards; an FBI intern; and vice president of the student government association.
>
> He is also a College Park Scholar, and he says that award "is what made a difference in my academic career."

A partial quotation is used effectively in this example from the Associated Press:

> —Smoking and drug use among U.S. teenagers are increasing after a decade of decline, a study showed Monday, and its author warned that "the stage is set for a potential resurgence of cocaine and crack use."

Affective Leads

Many newspapers have developed a lead style that focuses on people. A story about a big social or economic problem can lead with one person to illustrate how individuals are affected. The lead makes readers feel the abstract on an interpersonal and even emotional level. The abstract then becomes real.

Look at these two examples. The first is from the Associated Press.

> KAJIADO, Kenya—Agnes Siyiankoi's husband used a wooden club the last time he beat her; she had to be carried to the hospital.
>
> After 13 years of abuse, the 30-year-old Maasai woman defied the tradition that she silently submit: She took her husband to court.
>
> The case is rare in a country where wife-beating is not only prevalent but also largely condoned.
>
> Siyiankoi is a member of the Maasai, a southern Kenyan tribe that views women as property, first of their fathers, then of their husbands.

Agnes Siyiankoi is the example that leads into the larger story subject: the treatment of women.

Patrice Gaines wrote in *The Washington Post:*

—Keith Ricardo Walker Jr. is an invisible man.

His life is not described by crime statistics. He does not use or deal drugs. He has never fired a gun or been fired at. He is not a high school dropout. He has never been to jail.

Walker, 20, is like the millions of young black men who do not distinguish themselves as either geniuses or felons but live ordinary lives—often against the same odds that have beaten their friends. In a city where so much is said about delinquent youth, the Keith Walkers go unnoticed.

Gaines's story is about young black men. Walker is just one of them.

The key to using the affective lead is to keep it short and get to the point right away. Writers must quickly reveal the social or economic issue the message is about. And they must use the individual throughout the story.

Direct Address Leads

The direct address lead talks straight to the reader or consumer. It usually gives advice or has a "hey, you" aspect to it.

—If you haven't had your car inspected this month, you need to do it soon. The fee for state-required inspections will double July 1.

—Wake up. You have only two weeks until April 15, the deadline for filing your taxes.

Staccato Leads

A series of single words identifies a staccato lead. It can be used for news, feature stories, or almost any kind of message.

—Popcorn. Peanuts. Candy.

All those good things you buy at the movies will cost you more in local theaters starting Sunday.

Choosing a Lead Type

In many cases the information will dictate the type of lead. A crime story, for example, generally will use a summary lead. A story on a city council meeting will need a multiple-elements lead to cover the council's different actions. Lack of prominence will dictate a delayed-identification lead. But sometimes a writer must ponder and decide which lead will set up the story best.

Look at this Associated Press lead about a 911 operator:

> NEW YORK—"You want the police to your house because your mother didn't come home?"
>
> It's nearly 7 P.M. on a Wednesday in the weeks before Christmas and somewhere in New York City, two scared young girls watch the clock, more frightened by the minute. They call 911 and reach Ivey Bruce.
>
> Her voice is soothing and steady. "OK, what apartment are you in? And what's the telephone number? And how old are you and your sister?"
>
> As she speaks Bruce types on a battered gray computer. The figures 10 and 11 appear on her screen, then "HOME ALONE." Another tap of a key speeds the girls' telephonic SOS to a police dispatcher in a nearby room.
>
> Bruce, a 45-year-old mother of two sons, nods as if to reassure the unseen child and then tells her police will be there soon.
>
> Like a novel half read, a mystery never solved, this story has no end for Bruce. After 14 years on the job, she knows that's as it must be.
>
> It's only suppertime in New York, and by the end of her 3:30 P.M. to 11:30 P.M. shift, this 911 operator will have heard accounts of panic and terror by the score.

The writer chose a long, anecdotal lead to set up a story about 911 operators. The story specifically follows one operator, Ivey Bruce, before it gives information about 911 services. By focusing on one typical call, the writer lets readers know how a 911 operator reacts to a call and interacts with the caller. The writer could have written a lead that said

> NEW YORK—The hectic and gargantuan New York City 911 service will field more than 10 million calls this year.

The system represents a lifeline found in 89 percent of the country. The operation rests largely with the 911 operators, who answer scores of accounts of panic and terror during their shifts.

Which lead works? The one with the human element will draw more people into the story than one that tosses out numbers. The faces behind the digits set up the story, and readers know by the end of the second paragraph that the key elements are 911, operators, Ivey Bruce, and calls.

Does It Work?

Once you have written a lead, scrutinize it, keeping in mind the guidelines in the leads checklist at the end of the chapter.

Consider this lead from a daily newspaper:

—Ten-month-old Betssie Martinez-Oidor's fever soared to 105 degrees Monday. Her mother, Isabel Oidor, called York Hospital. Oidor and her husband, Gabriel Martinez, told a Spanish interpreter they had never seen their baby this ill.

"They both got scared," interpreter Carmen Bones said. She told them to bring the baby to the hospital. They stayed until late Monday so the baby could be observed because of her fever. Betssie also had a runny nose, mild cough, and little appetite for her formula.

As the reader, what do you think the story is about? The lead says that the baby is ill with a high fever. Is the story about the effects of fevers on infants? No. See how far you have to read before you know what the story is really about.

Periodic doses of Tylenol® helped bring the fever down to 100.6 degrees by the time they returned Tuesday for a follow-up exam by Dr. Mary Barnes in the Mother/Child Clinic.

Applying her stethoscope to the baby's back and chest, Barnes ruled out bronchitis and pneumonia.

"I think the baby has the flu and an ear infection," Barnes said. "It's out there. There's so much of it around."

"Maybe she got it through me," the baby's father said to Bones in Spanish.

Betssie's parents have been ill with flu-like symptoms. They're far from alone. Pennsylvania is one of about 20 states experiencing an earlier-than-usual start to the flu season. The state's physician general, Dr. Wanda Filer, issued a statement that some flu cases of a Type A strain known as A/Nanchang have been confirmed in residents of several counties.

By paragraph 9, the story is clear: Pennsylvania is having a flu epidemic. All the discussion about the baby's illness makes readers wonder about fevers, immunizations, colds, or perhaps care for children. The example of the sick baby could be used, but readers need to know sooner what the actual topic is. Consider the rewrite:

—Ten-month-old Betssie Martinez-Oidor's fever soared to 105 degrees Monday, scaring her parents who took her to the hospital. Betssie has the flu. She is among the latest and youngest victims of this year's flu season. Pennsylvania is one of about 20 states experiencing an earlier-than-usual start to the flu season.

Then the writer can proceed with quotes from the parents and other details of the flu, its symptoms, and treatment.

Leads Should Do the Job

Remember to read through your stories carefully and ensure that your leads are honest: that they have set up for the reader what the story covers. Review the checklist below. Readers will be disappointed if they believe that a story is about one topic and discover that it is about another. Writers will lose credibility if they make false promises in their leads.

You can become a good lead writer, whatever the copy, by focusing on what is important to your audience, learning the guidelines of good writing, and reading good leads that are specific and present information accurately, clearly, and concisely. Look for such leads in everything you read.

The lead is the first step in writing your message. Completing the job will be discussed in Chapter 4.

Leads Checklist

Essential Lead Elements

1. I have looked at the facts and decided which are the most important.
2. My initial sentence is simple and complete.
3. My lead is accurate.
4. My lead is relevant to my audience.
5. My lead comes to the point, is well edited, and makes sense.
6. I have used understandable, fresh words and strong, active verbs.
7. My lead sets up the story.

Desirable Elements

1. I have emphasized the latest information.
2. I have included unusual aspects of the message.
3. If possible, I have used a local angle to show how the information relates to readers.
4. I have kept my lead short and readable—no longer than thirty words.
5. My lead attracts the audience's attention.
6. My lead summarizes the message.

EXERCISES

1. Read the following lead. Identify the elements and the news values present.

—A Forest City man smashed the glass door on a Laundromat washing machine and yanked a 3-year-old child from the swirling waters yesterday morning.

Sammy Smithers, 27, rescued Tammy Childers after she climbed into a washing machine and the machine started running. The child had some cuts and bruises and was listed in good condition at Mayview Hospital.

Elements

Who:

What:

When:

Where:

Why:

How:

News Values (identify only those present; not all will be)

Conflict:

Timeliness:

Proximity:

Prominence:

Magnitude:

Impact:

Audience:

Oddity:

Emotion:

2. Read the following lead. Identify the elements and the news values present.

The American Heart Association now offers a cookbook specifically designed to encourage children to discover the wonderful world of cooking and to develop healthy eating habits early in life.

The kid-tested and -approved *American Heart Association Kids' Cookbook* is geared to healthy children ages 8–12. The cost is $15.95.

Elements

Who:

What:

When:

Where:

Why:

How:

News Values (identify only those present; not all will be)

Conflict:

Timeliness:

Proximity:

Prominence:

Magnitude:

Impact:

Audience:

Oddity:

Emotion:

3. Read the following lead. Identify the elements and the news values present.

WASHINGTON—The Federal Reserve, concerned that the economic recovery may fuel inflation, took action that raised interest rates Friday for the first time in five years, signaling an end to an era of declining loan costs and sending a shiver through Wall Street.

Elements

Who:

What:

When:

Where:

Why:

How:

News Values (identify only those present; not all will be)

Conflict:

Timeliness:

Proximity:

Prominence:

Magnitude:

Impact:

Audience:

Oddity:

Emotion:

4. Read the following lead. Identify the elements and the news values present.

RENNES, France—Thousands of fishermen battled riot police Friday during a visit by Premier Edouard Balladur, prompting government promises to protect the ailing fishing industry from foreign competition.

   Authorities said 61 people—25 police officers and 36 protesters and bystanders—were treated for injuries they suffered in day-long clashes in Rennes.

Elements

Who:

What:

When:

Where:

Why:

How:

News Values (identify only those present; not all will be)

Conflict:

Timeliness:

Proximity:

Prominence:

Magnitude:

Impact:

Audience:

Oddity:

Emotion:

5. Read the following lead.

—Raymond Lineberger looked as if he were asleep. He was curled up on the sofa, his back to the television set tuned to a local game show. A red and green plaid blanket covered the lower part of his legs and his feet. He wore khaki pants and a red knit shirt.

A bullet had pierced the side of his head. Lineberger was dead.

Emma Jean Lineberger has been charged with first-degree murder in her husband's death.

What is the point of the story?

Has the writer considered the audience?

Rewrite the lead to focus on the point and what the audience needs to know.

6. Look at the information for the following two stories. List for each exercise *who, what, when, where, how,* and *why.* Identify the news values and where they apply, then rank them in order of importance. Then write the lead. You are to write only the lead, not the entire story, for each.

> A Super Bowl party was held yesterday in your town. In a fight during half-time, a guest pulled out a gun and fired shots. A mother of three children and her niece were shot and killed. They were in a house at 143 Elm St. with about 20 other guests and party-goers in attendance. They died instantly from the wounds. Police have a suspect but have made no arrests and have no motive.

Elements

Who:

What:

When:

Where:

Why:

How:

News Values (number them 1–9 in order of importance, 1 being most important)

Conflict:

Timeliness:

Proximity:

Prominence:

Magnitude:

Impact:

Audience:

Oddity:

Emotion:

Lead for Shooting

The Armored Car Co. has a plant in your town. It employs 350 people. It has been operating in the town for twelve years. It has been hit by recessionary times and has announced it will lay off half its workforce during the next six months. The company has plans to relocate or secure jobs for all displaced workers. A special committee has been established to work with laid-off employees. The company wouldn't say whether more employees eventually will be laid off.

Elements

Who:

What:

When:

Where:

Why:

How:

News Values (number them 1–9 in order of importance, 1 being most important)

Conflict:

Timeliness:

Proximity:

Prominence:

Magnitude:

Impact:

Audience:

Oddity:

Emotion:

Lead for Armored Car Co.

4

Beyond the Lead: Organization

Once writers have fashioned the lead, they face the task of organizing the rest of the message. They must decide what will come after the first sentences or paragraphs that hook the audience. The ranking decisions discussed in Chapter 3 that help them write the lead are invaluable in helping them develop the body of the message. Again, with audience needs and interests in mind, the writer outlines how the message will evolve.

As mentioned in Chapter 3, journalists have traditionally used the inverted pyramid form of writing to get to the point quickly and to set priorities for basic news stories. The principle behind the inverted pyramid style—to order information according to its value to the audience—is valuable in much writing today, whether it is for church newsletters, e-mail messages, Web pages, news releases, or magazine articles. The process of ordering information for the inverted pyramid involves critical thinking, an important skill for writers.

Different styles of writing may be more suitable for other audiences or for a particular medium. Students will find various organizational styles as they read print publications: newspapers, magazines, company newsletters. If you find yourself reading a story from start to end, clip it, and study it to identify the elements that pulled you into and through the message, and then save it. Some day you may want to adopt the style for a piece of your own.

This chapter discusses

- The inverted pyramid form of writing,
- News peg and nut graph,

- Other organizational styles, and
- How to unify writing.

The Inverted Pyramid

Leads must get to the point quickly, and messages must provide important information right behind the lead. Newspaper editors have recognized that need for decades. Henry A. Stokes, as an assistant managing editor for projects at the *Commercial Appeal* in Memphis, Tennessee, once wrote in a staff memo that reporters had to ensure stories attracted reader attention.

Stokes told staff writers that they were to "tell the news in an identifiable, functional format that guarantees the reader will receive the best information we can provide, written in a way that the reader can quickly and easily understand."

As a result, the newspaper adopted the four-paragraph rule: Tell the essential message in four paragraphs of reasonable length: the first four paragraphs of the story. Details that could be cut would follow.

The format that Stokes advocated was the inverted pyramid style of writing, long a standard in journalism. With the inverted pyramid, information in a message is organized in descending order of importance. The most important and compelling information comes first and is followed by information of lesser value. To be successful at using the inverted pyramid, writers must be able to evaluate and rank information, and they must know what is most important to their audiences.

This model shows how the inverted pyramid works:

Lead summarizes information. Next few paragraphs back up lead.

Next section provides background and additional important information.

Next section has information of lesser importance about the topics introduced in the lead.

Final section contains least important information, which could be cut.

In the inverted pyramid, the lead paragraph or paragraphs summarize the most important news values and elements and hook the audience. The next paragraph or paragraphs usually give additional crucial information that won't fit into the first paragraph. Background information comes next. From there, subsequent paragraphs develop the topics presented in the lead, introduce other important information, expand the significance of the information, and give details.

Each section will vary in length, depending on what the writer has introduced in the lead and whether he or she is building the message with quotations. A writer may devote four or five paragraphs to dialogue from a meeting before moving on to other actions set forth in the lead paragraph.

The inverted pyramid format helps a writer organize information logically, whether the topic is a single subject or has multiple subjects or elements. If the writer plans to develop several issues in the message, the summary multiple-element lead would set up the organization in the following way:

—The Rockland City Council voted unanimously Tuesday night to renew the city manager's contract for three years with a raise each year and to annex 325 acres south of Lewisville and Maxton roads.

Through the inverted pyramid, the writer sets up the order of importance in the lead and how the message will be organized. The most important item is the city manager's contract, which includes a pay raise. Because no one objected to the annexation of acreage, it carries less importance because it is not controversial. It can be discussed second. The important point, the action of annexation, is contained in the lead. The rest of the story follows the lead like this:

—In discussing City Manager Larry Morgan's new contract, council members agreed that Morgan had done an exemplary job in his six years as manager.

"We couldn't find anyone better," said Council Member Dick Haynes, who made the motion to give Morgan a 10 percent pay raise in the first year of the contract and 5 percent in the second and third years.

"We have maintained quality town services with only modest tax increases while Larry has been here," added Council Member Loretta Manson.

The council voted to annex the Heather Hills subdivision following a public hearing in which no one objected to the annexation plan. Residents who spoke said they wanted to come under the town's water and sewer services and to gain improved fire and police protection.

The inverted pyramid is more than just an organizational tool. It has been identified traditionally as a writing style that uses simple words, short sentences, and one idea to a paragraph. It also represents critical thinking: it forces writers to evaluate information and rank it in order of importance. Some critics have said that the inverted pyramid puts pressure on reporters to craft an attention-getting, information-packed lead, leaving them little time to follow through with a well-organized message. To be successful, writers must do both: write a compelling lead and organize a story logically. In reality, time constraints or deadline pressure may interfere with both functions.

Why the Inverted Pyramid for Media Writing?

Newspapers traditionally have used the inverted pyramid format for two primary reasons: to give readers the most critical material quickly so they can move to other stories if they wish and to allow a story to be cut easily from the bottom, leaving important information intact at the top of the story.

Many beginning writers question why they should follow the inverted pyramid style of writing when they plan careers in public relations, advertising, or marketing. They object to what they see as a rigid way of writing or formula writing—a basic format devoid of creativity.

At first glance, the objections seem valid. But as students use the inverted pyramid they will discover plenty of opportunities for description and for their own style to develop. As they will learn, the critical thinking that goes along with the inverted pyramid style fits the writing process outlined in Chapter 1. For the inverted pyramid, writers must gather information, list or rank information, write a draft, and rewrite.

John Sweeney, an associate professor in the School of Journalism and Mass Communication at the University of North Carolina at Chapel Hill, teaches advertising courses. He advises all students, no matter what their major, on the value of learning the inverted pyramid structure.

"Before you can develop your own style, you have to master the basics," he tells introductory writing students. "You have to be taught to be meticulous. To say it succinctly, concisely, precisely. You have to be able to distill information, whether it's a 30-second spot or a piece of newswriting or an ad distilled from a 100-page document on product data.

"Writing also has to have access: Anyone can read it and understand it," Sweeney advises. "You have to focus on what's key, get to the heart of the matter, and put the issue in perspective."

Online journalism has called for renewed interest in and use of the inverted pyramid. Online journalists know that as much information as possible needs to be seen on the home page, which is the first page of a Web site. Thus, news items appear only as leads or briefs on the home page, offering links to full stories. An online editor has to copy only an article's lead for the front page.

Online journalism uses news briefs, rather than full stories, to attract readers because research shows that readers presented with full stories often click away. Holding audiences is a priority in online journalism. In this new medium, the old standard for direct communication, the inverted pyramid, aids writers in conveying information quickly and succinctly. All media writers must recognize the logic of using the inverted pyramid in an age when busy consumers are bombarded with messages.

The Inverted Pyramid for Other Media

Research supports the belief that the inverted pyramid retains value today, when the majority of messages are becoming shorter and more direct. Consider broadcast messages, which usually begin with a short, catchy headline to grab the viewer's attention and then summarize the main points. Because broadcast news stories are short, it is imperative for TV and radio reporters to fit in as many compelling facts as possible in the few seconds allotted. The inverted pyramid allows for the speedy, information-rich writing that broadcast demands.

Corporate communication offices and nonprofit agencies, whether they are staffed by professionals or volunteers, more and more follow the traditional inverted pyramid style. It puts their agenda where readers and editors can see it. Even advertising depends on the inverted pyramid style, communicating to consumers in an abbreviated way a product's qualities and the reasons for buying it. On Web sites, as in brochures and magazines, brevity is essential: Every word and second cost the client money.

The inverted pyramid can fit most kinds of media writing and other kinds of writing in the real world—even the garden club's minutes. Although it works best in shorter pieces, it can be adapted for longer, more complex pieces, many of which use the inverted pyramid format early and then other organizational patterns later. For example, nondeadline pieces, such as feature stories and documentaries, attract readers best by getting to the point and summarizing first. Simple pyramiding in nondeadline writing can attract readers by creating a mood, setting the stage for more detailed information, or providing a memorable image.

Peter Baker of *The Washington Post* gets to the point quickly in his long feature about the president's aide, Stephen Goodin. Baker leads with two short sentences that sum up the news by comparing Goodin to a loyal canine companion. The remainder of the piece gives significant, colorful details with those of greatest news value cited earliest in the story, which follows here.

The President's Loyal Shadow

BY PETER BAKER

Washington Post Staff Writer

It only stands to reason that President Clinton would get a dog. He doesn't have Stephen Goodin around anymore.

Goodin would never put it that way, of course. He's far too steadfast, far too much of a believer. In fact, if Clinton really was looking for "one loyal friend in Washington," as his spokesman said about Buddy, the new White House Labrador, it must be because the fiercely devoted Goodin has just left the president's side.

For the last three years, the soft-spoken, 30-year-old Texan was Clinton's shadow, the sidekick who managed his round-the-clock schedule, who made sure his speeches were on the lectern when he arrived, who coughed up money for Girl Scout cookies if the president could not break a $20 bill, who placed a hand in the small of Clinton's back when it was time to go. His is hardly a household name, but since 1994, probably no one outside the first family has spent as much time with the leader of the free world.

"You kind of serve as the piece of his brain that he shouldn't have to use so he can think about policy or whatever," Goodin said the other day.

It is a strange and unique job, even in Washington. Officially, his title was as straightforward as its bearer: The President's Aide. Unofficially—and decidedly unglamorously—he was known around the White House as "the butt boy." There are a few reasons. One is the territory, typically behind the president. But more important, whoever is in that that role inevitably absorbs the full force of all the various presidential moods—and becomes an early-warning system for the rest of the staff.

"It's the wise White House staffer who checks with Stephen first" before approaching the president with an idea or question, said deputy press secretary Joe Lockhart. "You're walking into the Oval Office and it's a good thing to get a reality check."

It's natural when you spend that much time around someone to learn their body language," Goodin said. "It's like how do you know your girlfriend is mad at you without saying it?" There are those who have not followed Goodin's advice and paid the price. "It's a vindicating experience," he allowed with a sly grin.

After so many long days on the road and late nights in the West Wing, an exhausted Goodin finally stepped aside this month and took a less strenuous position as special adviser to the president. Kris Engskov, 25, an Arkansas native and popular aide in the press office, has taken over Goodin's former position.

Goodin lasted longer than most in one of the biggest burnout jobs inside the Beltway, yet a conversation with him leaves the impression of a

devotee who never lost the faith. He speaks of his boss with undiluted awe and admiration, and there is no discussion about the president's private side. For all of the many mysteries about the real Bill Clinton, this Clintonite plans no tell-all book.

Goodin's unflappability in the face of an occasionally volatile boss earned him many admirers in the White House, where it was known that his role was to take what came and keep it to himself.

"You are a sponge," said Andrew Friendly, Goodin's predecessor in the role. "Being the closest, sometimes when things don't go exactly as they should, you bear the brunt of the reaction. Nine times out of 10, it's not directed at us, but we happen to be the closest to him." (Still, Friendly added, Clinton's famed eruptions are somewhat overrated. "The president gets a bum rap; his temper's not that bad," Friendly said. When it does surface, he added, "it's short-lived.")

While unwilling to divulge any Clinton secrets, Goodin's proximity to the president's sessions with world leaders would make him privy to volumes, and he vividly recalls some of the remarkable events he witnessed up close: the funeral of Richard M. Nixon attended by five living presidents; the White House event where he lent his tuxedo bowtie to Israel's Yitzhak Rabin just weeks before Rabin was assassinated; the president's first trip to war torn Bosnia, where the dress code was flak jacket instead of dinner jacket; the visit to Poland, when Clinton stood in the same place where the Warsaw Pact was signed and welcomed the ex-communist nation into NATO.

And there was the night that Clinton accepted renomination at last year's Democratic National Convention, where Goodin found himself on stage alongside all manner of political luminaries, except he was sitting on an upside-down trash can calling into a radio because the TelePrompTers were blinking in and out.

"I know this sounds hokey, but I don't mind being corny: This is what America's all about," Goodin said. "I mean, I'm nobody and I got to follow the most powerful man on the planet around."

With glasses, long sideburns, a soft accent and genial disposition, Goodin grew up in Gainesville, Tex., where he lived in a mobile home. His parents were both registered nurses who entered the marriage already with children, creating what Goodin calls a "Brady Bunch" family of six (he would be Peter, the middle boy).

He studied psychology at the University of Texas at Austin, where his only intersection with politics was his 1990 graduation, when President George Bush delivered the commencement address. Ultimately, though, he caught the political bug himself. An internship on Capitol Hill led to some campaign work and the Democratic National Committee, and finally to the White House.

As Clinton's personal assistant, Goodin would arrive each morning at least a half-hour before the president's day began to review the schedule and map out the possible pitfalls. Organization was key and it clearly is one of his strong suits. Indeed, he arrived for an interview about himself with two pages of handwritten talking points, his outline neatly organized into Roman numeral sections and alphabetized subsections ("I. American Dream; A. humble background...")

Whether in Washington or on the road, Goodin would keep Clinton informed on who was in the audience he was about to address, stay on top of what was next on the calendar and ensure the president's briefing materials included everything he should have. When the president worked the rope line at some event, Goodin collected the books, baseball caps and photographs that people wanted signed and made sure they later were returned to their owners. Whenever Clinton lingered too long—and that was often—it fell to Goodin to politely tug him away.

Of the many lessons Goodin learned during the last three years, though, one is that being an elected official is too all-consuming. Running for office, he has decided, is not for him. Yet for all of their face time, that is not something he chose to confide in Clinton.

"That," Goodin said, "is the thing that would disappoint him the most."

Organizing a Story

The basic work of organizing a message in inverted pyramid style is done when you use the steps outlined in Chapter 3 for writing leads. The writer first identifies news values and the elements to structure a lead. News values and elements introduced in the lead will be developed in greater detail within the message. The writer will use the remaining news values and elements in subsequent paragraphs based on ranking information that is important to audiences.

For example, a news value, such as oddity, may be referred to in a lead but must be developed fully later in the message. Remember the lead in Chapter 3 on the couple who got married as they were skydiving? Although readers have the basics from the lead about how the wedding happened, they may want more information about why skydiving was important to that particular couple. The body of the message answers that question.

—A Hollywood, Fla., man and woman exchanged wedding vows at 1,300 feet as they plummeted to earth hand-in-hand under silver parachutes five miles west of here Wednesday afternoon.

Grace Mason and John Kempner met while skydiving at a local club and decided it would be the most significant way to start their married life together.

"Skydiving brought us together," said Grace Mason Kempner after the ceremony. "It seemed to be the appropriate way to tie the knot."

She learned to skydive while a student at Dade Community College. Her husband was a paratrooper in the Army. They have known each other two years and have been jumping partners for the last six months.

Each wore a silver jumpsuit, but the bride carried a nosegay of white satin roses.

Applying News Elements and News Values

It's important here to note a difference between paragraphs in an essay for an English composition or literature class and paragraphs in even long forms of media writing. In an essay or composition, a paragraph can be a whole presentation or argument on a topic. But in mass communication, a paragraph is identified as a single unit of timely information. It is a solitary fact, thought, or "sound bite" from the larger message. When a writer is concerned with transmitting information quickly, his or her ideas about paragraphing change.

Journalists rarely use the word "paragraph." In the newsroom, a paragraph is a "graph." This abbreviated word symbolizes the abbreviated form that paragraphs take in news stories. A graph generally still will have several sentences, but on occasion it may be one sentence long and transmit a single news element or news value.

Let's consider a message about the community theater in a town called Rockland. You are to write a news story about auditions for an upcoming production. The elements *who, what, when, where, how,* and *why* can be easily listed:

Who: Rockland Theater.

What: Will have auditions for the play "Gypsy."

When: 7–9 P.M. Monday and Tuesday.

Where: The theater at 211 W. Sycamore St.

How: People will read a piece of their own choosing, then one impromptu piece from the director.

Why: So the play can be produced.

Look at the news values we discussed in Chapter 3 and determine which ones apply here. The magnitude of the production and the timeliness of the pending auditions are relevant; news values such as conflict, oddity, and impact may not exist. Prominence is a factor if the lead role will be held by a well-known stage actress and local residents will have the chance to act with her.

You might write this lead:

```
—Local residents can audition 7 to 9 P.M. Monday and
Tuesday for parts in the Rockland Community Theater's
upcoming production of "Gypsy" with television and film
star Salma Hayeck.
```

The lead identifies the elements *who, what,* and *when,* as well as the news value of prominence. To handle the overflow from the lead, you must add a second paragraph to answer *where* and to show impact:

```
—Auditions will be at the theater at 211 W. Sycamore St. and
led by Director Neal Folger. He is looking for 16 local actors.
```

Anyone interested in auditioning has the basic information from the first two paragraphs. In subsequent paragraphs you will expand on the lead, noting that the production also will require a 30-member chorus and explaining what people will have to do during the audition.

You would continue the story:

—Local residents wishing to audition must prepare a song and a part to read, said Folger. Each audition is not to exceed five minutes.

People interested in being in a 30-member chorus need prepare only a song not to exceed three minutes. They will audition with the music director, Carole Banner.

You have determined that the audience would be most interested in the requirements for auditioning and how to audition. If aspiring actors could not meet the requirements, they would have no need to read further.

Those who are potential actors would want to know more about the selection process and when rehearsals would start. In the final paragraphs, you would state

"We will let people know by Friday if they are selected," Folger said. "Rehearsals will start the next week."

The community theater produces six shows each year. One in the fall and one in the spring have professional actors or actresses.

"Having professional talent promotes the theater and makes the acting experience much more exciting for our local talent," Folger said. "We have had wonderful success in the past, and we expect the same for 'Gypsy.'"

In the last paragraph, you would use the director's quote to wrap up the message and look to the future.

Breaking It Up

Let's look at the story and see how the information was ordered and why.

Local residents can audition 7 to 9 A.M. Monday and Tuesday for parts in the Rockland Community Theater's upcoming production of "Gypsy" with television and film star Salma Hayeck.

The lead tells *who* can do *what when* and *why.* It also includes the news value prominence of Salma Hayeck, which might attract some people to audition.

Auditions will be at the theater and led by Director Neal Folger. He is looking for 16 local actors. Local residents wishing to audition must prepare a song and a part to read, said Folger. Each audition is not to exceed five minutes.

Graph 2 expands the first graph by telling where folks can audition and what is required during the auditions for the major roles.

People interested in being in a 30-member chorus need prepare a song not to exceed three minutes. They will audition with the music director, Carole Banner.

Graph 3 continues to expand the information, giving details about auditions for lesser roles.

"We will let people know by Friday if they are selected," Folger said. "Rehearsals will start the next week."

Graph 4 moves to the next step after auditions: when people will be notified and when rehearsal begins.

The community theater
produces six shows each
year. Two, one in the fall and
one in the spring, have
professional actors.

Graph 5 provides background on the
theater and its productions.

"Having professional talent
promotes the theater and
makes the acting experience
much more exciting for our
local talent," Folger said.
"We have had wonderful
success in the past, and
we expect the same for
'Gypsy.' "

Graph 6 is a follow-up quote to
graph 5. A quote also makes a good
ending.

Another Approach: The Second-Day Story

In the story just given, you have followed a traditional inverted pyramid
format to announce the auditions. The story represents what could be
called a first-day story. In looking at newspaper clips about the Little Theater, you believe another story is warranted. So you decide to do what is
called a second-day story that gives new information and also includes background from the first-day story.

The lead and message might go something like this:

—When Director Neal Folger starts auditions for the season
opener of the Rockland Community Theater in early August,
most board of directors members will be crossing their
fingers for a smooth year.

The board hired Folger, the former director of the
River Road Theater in Danville, a year ago, and soon the
theater was embroiled in controversy. Last year's season
opener of "Grease" showed nudity when three performers

dropped their pants as part of a song on mooning. This year's season opens Oct. 15.

"We felt we went through a wringer right off the bat last year," Board Member Mary Tyson said today. "Although some people like Neal's productions, most people in our community prefer more traditional entertainment. Nudity just has no place on our stage."

Board Member Justin Fellows said the board hoped for a successful season with less turmoil than the previous year.

"We think Neal is quite talented, but we are just a community theater, and we want fun, not indignation," he said.

Folger said he was surprised at the reaction to "Grease."

"I certainly learned what this community will accept on stage," he said. "This year we intend to produce shows that keep people fairly well covered."

Fellows added the board hoped Folger's appealing season lineup will attract a substantial audience to the Rockland Theater.

The director will have auditions for "Gypsy" from 7 to 9 P.M. Monday and Tuesday at the theater at 211 W. Sycamore St. Folger is looking for 16 actors who will play opposite television and film star Salma Hayeck in the season's opener.

Local residents wishing to audition for the major roles must prepare a song and a part to read, said Folger. Each audition is not to exceed five minutes.

People interested in being in a 30-member chorus need prepare only a song not to exceed three minutes. They will audition with the music director, Carole Banner.

People will be notified by Friday if they have been chosen, Folger said, and rehearsals will begin next week.

For the second-day story, you opted to put controversy in the lead. The second graph gives readers background on how the controversy occurred. The lead notes conflict, so readers expect to read comments from both sides, which you include. In graphs 3 through 8 come the quotes from Tyson, Fellows, and even Folger that balance the story. Readers interested in auditioning will continue to read the message to find out information about the auditions, which are mentioned in the lead. The specific times are included in graph 9, and audition information is in graphs 10 and 11.

Again as the writer, you followed the inverted pyramid style of writing, ranking the material in a way that is important to your audience. You set up the lead about auditions and controversy. The need for answers to the controversy will come first, followed by information on the auditions—information that has been reported.

In stories that are continued over several days, such as reports of the death of Diana, Princess of Wales, in August 1997, latest information will go at the beginning. Once the most relevant and up-to-date information is shared, then writers will include background. After initial stories about Diana's death, subsequent accounts during the next week began with the condition of the driver, the possibility of another car that could have contributed to the accident in the tunnel, reaction of the British royal family, funeral services, and other developments as the investigation continued. Each story contained background that explained when, where, and how Diana died, but each day the background information became a shorter part of the story. Writers followed the inverted pyramid in their reports.

Getting There

Communicators first must be able to master the traditional before they can be avant-garde. Mastering the inverted pyramid style of writing gives any student journalist or communicator the basic plan for writing messages that focus on what is important and emotionally compelling for the audience. The style organizes information so that it is accessible, appealing, simply stated, and easy to understand.

On the practical level, mastering the inverted pyramid style also means throwing out the clutter that plagues most beginning writers. It means writing and rewriting and cutting unnecessary words to make the message cleaner and clearer.

Many writers abhor such admonitions to cut and tighten. They wonder how their writing will have any style or be differentiated from anyone else's. For routine assignments, it won't. But the personal style, such as that in the article about the Rockland Community Theater's upcoming season, can be added to make messages more appealing—as long as the message still remains uncluttered.

Look again at the Peter Baker story about the president's sidekick. It's simple and direct, but it has clear hallmarks of Baker's style, such as varied sentence length and description. Also look at how organization helps the reader move through the article.

News Peg and Nut Graph

Newspaper reporters talk about the "news" peg when developing stories. The peg, just like a peg on the wall where you hang a coat, is what a writer hangs the story on. It is the reason for writing the message. In our Rockland theater examples, the news peg in the first-day story is the auditions; in the second-day story, it is the residents' concern and hope for a smooth season.

Every piece of writing—whether it appears in print, is aired, or is shared—has a news peg. Writers, no matter what their skill or medium, have a reason for composing a message. That reason is spelled out in the *nut graph:* the paragraph that defines the point the writer is making. The rest of the message expands and clarifies the singular idea in the nut graph.

The nut graph should be in the first four to five paragraphs, and sometimes it is more than one paragraph. Writers who put the nut graph any lower risk losing audiences who want to know the point of the message quickly. In some cases, the lead serves as the nut graph, particularly if it is a summary lead. Audiences who hear a summary up front know why the story was written. When writers use anecdotal or descriptive leads, as described in Chapter 3, they must summarize and focus the message for audiences after drawing them in. In longer pieces, such as those described in the following section on other organizational styles, the nut graph becomes more crucial. A story may have a descriptive lead, such as the example in Chapter 3 about men beating their wives. The nut graph—here graph 3—tells what the story is about:

KAJIADO, Kenya—Agnes Siyiankoi's husband used a wooden club the last time he beat her. She had to be carried to the hospital.

After 13 years of abuse, the 30-year-old Maasai woman defied the tradition that she silently submit: She took her husband to court.

The case is rare in a country where wife-beating is not only prevalent but also largely condoned.

Siyiankoi is a member of the Maasai, a southern Kenyan tribe that views women as property, first of their fathers then of their husbands.

Look at the stories that follow. Identify the nut graph or nut graphs, and see how quickly each appears.

Chelsea Moves to College Dorm, Clintons Feel the Pain of Empty Nest

BY V. DION HAYNES

Chicago Tribune

President Clinton was smiling as he sat through various welcoming speeches at Stanford University on Friday, but he had a pained look on his face.

Sitting with his arms around his daughter Chelsea, the president and First Lady Hillary Rodham Clinton shared bittersweet moments as the time neared for them to say good-bye to their only child.

Like many other parents, the Clintons felt the pride of seeing their child take her first steps into adulthood yet endured the pain of letting her go. Indeed, the Clintons will have to adjust to a 3,000-mile separation from Chelsea as well as their new status as empty nesters.

The 17-year-old Stanford freshman with the corkscrew curls and infectious smile isn't the first president's child to go off to college. Allan Hoover, son of President Herbert Hoover, attended Stanford in the 1920s; Jack Ford, son of President Gerald Ford, enrolled at Utah State University in the 1970s; and President Jimmy Carter's son, Jeff, attended Georgetown University in the 1970s.

Chelsea, Class of 2001, is the First Child to engage in this rite of passage amid so much fanfare. On a glorious, 80-degree day, Chelsea made her college debut before 13,800 students and 300 reporters.

The arrival by Air Force One and the Secret Service brigade notwithstanding, the Clintons are attempting to provide a normal college experience for Chelsea.

On Friday morning, the president lugged his daughter's suitcases and boxes into her sparsely furnished dorm room. He even brought his tools just in case.

Chelsea, wearing bell-bottomed blue jeans, chatted with her roommate and started arranging her belongings. The first lady greeted the roommate's mother and other parents.

The trio spent the rest of the day attending receptions and orientation meetings with the 1,659 other freshmen and their parents. Then in the early evening, as required by Stanford, the Clintons said farewell to Chelsea and went to a parents' reception.

As has been the case throughout his presidency, the Clintons kept the private moments involving their daughter to themselves. Though the president was quoted this week in Washington as saying, "I'm happy and sad at the same time," the Clintons held no press conference and made no public statements at Stanford.

Attempting to ensure that her daughter will not be hounded on campus, the first lady issued a plea to the media to give Chelsea space.

At least one publication—the *Stanford Daily* student newspaper—will honor those wishes. The paper won't follow her or cover her activities unless she is involved in a newsworthy event. Moreover, the editor has notified staffers that she won't tolerate anyone spying on Chelsea and feeding tidbits about her to the outside press.

Stanford officials share the responsibility of shielding her from the media spotlight. On Friday, they sealed off most campus activities. Kept open was an afternoon orientation session, where Chelsea and other freshmen were officially welcomed by university President Gerhard Casper, a longtime professor and administrator at the University of Chicago, and other dignitaries.

Some students soon were buzzing about Chelsea sightings.

"She's very nice and friendly; she was saying hi to everybody," said freshman Tim Yuen, 17.

Upperclassmen predicted Stanford would return to normal routine once the satellite trucks and journalists leave. Senior Steve Chappel said students are accustomed to famous people and will treat Chelsea like everyone else.

"We've had many other big names here—(actor) Fred Savage and Tiger Woods, to name a few. There's always a bit of hoopla at the beginning," said Chappel, 20, an electrical engineering student.

"Once they made friends and settled in, the hoopla went away. I'm sure it will be the same with Chelsea."

(Reprinted with permission of the *Chicago Tribune.*)

Police rescue Fla. woman, 80, put off bus for holding puppy

PAT LEISNER

Associated Press

TAMPA, Fla. – The bus was a greyhound, but the driver was no dog lover.

An 80-year-old woman returning home from her birthday party was kicked off a bus at a rural truck stop late at night because of her birthday present: a tiny puppy named Cookie.

Dogs aren't allowed on Greyhound, and the driver refused to make an exception, leaving Antonia Sanabria at the side of the road about 80 miles from home in Tampa at 3 A.M. Friday. Sanabria had boarded the bus Thursday night in Panama City after visiting her daughters.

A security guard summoned by the bus driver called Marion County sheriff's deputies—adding to her fright.

"When the bus pulled away and I saw all those policemen, I was scared," Sanabria said. "I thought they were going to put me in jail. I don't know, I was crazy with fear. I've never gone to jail."

What could have become a terrifying ordeal for the woman, who uses a crutch and has trouble hearing and seeing, instead became an inspiration.

After getting her a sandwich and something to drink, police from different jurisdictions teamed up to ferry Sanabria all the way from the Ocala area to her Tampa doorstep in five different patrol cars.

"I've never seen so many people so nice with me—an old lady. They gave me love, respect, attention," she said. "Love has a lot of names—compassion, respect, friendliness."

As soon as she got home, all Sanabria wanted to do was sleep, which she did with her new 7-week-old Pekinese pup. When she woke up she found a bouquet of roses with a card that read: "We want you to know there are still some nice people in the world," from Hillsborough sheriff's deputies in Tampa who coordinated the relay.

Greyhound apologized and gave her a refund Saturday. The unidentified driver, a 20-year Greyhound veteran, was suspended pending investigation.

"It's unfortunate that a lady of this age and condition would have something like this happen to her in the middle of the night," said George Gravley, a Greyhound spokesman.

Sanabria's daughter, Sally Creel of Panama City, was outraged, saying, "What a low life thing to do."

But after the police rescue, her mother was far from bitter.

"It was a birthday I'll never forget," Sanabria said.

(Reprinted with permission from the Associated Press.)

The nut graph in the Chelsea Clinton story comes in paragraph 5, where it is stated that Chelsea Clinton is a college freshman. Other clues to the story's content are evident in the first four paragraphs. In the Greyhound story, the nut graph is graph 3, stating why Sanabria was left along the highway in the middle of the night.

Other Organizational Styles

Although the inverted pyramid works for much writing, you may find other formats that are better for a particular message because of the event being reported. Some formats use the inverted pyramid format to introduce material, then move into another organizational pattern.

Chronological Format

In some cases, making the decision about how to organize a message is easy. Chronology—telling events in the same order in which they occurred—often can meet audience needs. A news story about a bank robbery, for example, would have a summary lead telling that the robbery occurred, where, and when. Then events would be revealed chronologically. The writer would organize the rest of the story by using time elements, as in the following article:

—A masked woman robbed the First Guaranty Savings and Loan on Main Street shortly after 9 A.M. today and escaped into a thickly wooded area nearby. Police have made no arrests.

The robbery occurred when the woman entered the bank and approached a teller. She handed her a note asking for money and saying she had a gun in the sleeve of her sweatshirt.

Although the teller did not actually see a gun, she gave the woman an undisclosed amount of cash. The woman put the money into a purple sack, ran from the Savings and Loan, and disappeared in the woods behind the bank's parking lot.

At 6 P.M., police were still looking for the suspect, who was described as a white woman in her mid-20s. She weighs about 150 pounds and stands about 5 feet 6 inches. She has shoulder-length blonde hair. She wore a purple sweatsuit and had pulled a stocking as a mask over her face. Bank employees could not describe her facial features.

Here the lead, or first paragraph, states *who* did *what where* and *when* and the latest information. Graph 2 shows how events unfolded. The last time element tells readers the status of the investigation at the newspaper's deadline.

While some messages can be developed chronologically, organization generally is not that simple. Not all messages involve action that evolves over time. For example, a high school principal writing in the school newsletter cannot use chronology to inform teachers about changes in ordering classroom supplies. Although teachers may be interested in the events that led up to the changes, they want to know the specific changes immediately. That is when another format is needed.

Hourglass Format

Some writers have adapted chronological development to longer stories in what they call the hourglass format of writing. A summary lead followed by the inverted pyramid style gives readers the most important information in four to six paragraphs, allowing them to stop at the end of the inverted pyramid segment. Then the writer sets up more information with a simple statement by a source: "Maynard described the events this way."

Beyond the transition statement, the message unfolds chronologically. Writers can use the style for many kinds of stories, such as telling of the search for a lost child, recounting a day in the life of a popular singer, or bringing out the details of a baseball game. Many stories on the death of Princess Diana appeared in 1997. Writers used the inverted pyramid format up front, updating the story, then developed the message chronologically using the hourglass format with details of the accident.

Electronic media writers often use the hourglass format. For example, a local television station aired a story about a crime that police had been unable to solve. After noting the latest information, the reporter said, "Here's how police have recreated the sequence of events." The details that followed were a chronological account of the crime. The story ended with the reporter showing the local telephone number for Crimestoppers.

Mapped Format

Assistant Professor Jacqueline Farnan and newspaper copy editor David Hedley discussed another variation on the inverted pyramid style called the mapped format. They noted that the inverted pyramid becomes confusing for longer pieces, but they believed it serves as a way to introduce the most important elements of the message.

The term *mapped format* describes the technique of indicating points of interest within the message, just as a map includes highlights for its readers. The mapped format benefits topics that are of mild interest to readers, such as business and government. It also aids readers in finding information that is of particular interest to them in longer stories.

A mapped message is organized into sections. The first is the inverted pyramid lead. Subheads in a subject–verb–object sentence help readers, especially those who just scan stories, define categories of information. Farnan and Hedley say the mapped format "conveys news in a form that is easy to grasp for disinterested scan readers and easy to follow for interested readers." Readers can quickly find the segments of information that most benefit or appeal to them.

The mapped format can also help the writer organize. Let us assume you are writing a story on the cost of funerals and the alternatives to traditional burial. Your research finds categories of information: reasons why funerals are expensive, caskets and their costs, funeral home expenses, cost of burial plots, cost of cremation versus burial, memorial services, and how to cut costs. After drafting the lead, you can group categories of information under subheads, which help organize the story and readily identify parts of the story for readers.

Dennis B. Roddy of the *Pittsburgh Post-Gazette* wrote a lengthy story about Dianna Green, a vice president for an electrical utility company. You may remember the lead from Chapter 3. Here are the first seven paragraphs.

> Meticulous to the end, Dianna Green organized her suicide with corporate precision.
>
> Notes were addressed to each sibling, handwritten with the green ink that had been her hallmark when signing official documents for Duquesne Light Co., where she had been a top vice president for nine years.
>
> Nearby was a will, assembled in longhand, dividing her real estate and stocks, and leaving $10,000 each to several of the charities with which she filled what little personal time she had. Also on hand were the series of increasingly urgent letters from the New York attorney Duquesne Light had hired to persuade Green to sign a severance agreement, give up any rights to sue and leave quietly.
>
> "The company prefers to settle this matter in an amicable fashion; however, if I don't hear from you by 5 P.M., Tuesday, April 22nd, the

company will proceed in a manner to protect its interests," attorney Irene C. Warshauer wrote.

Warshauer had even included a draft of an announcement by Duquesne Light President David Marshall, announcing "with great sadness that Dianna Green is leaving the company at the end of the month to begin pursuing other career interests that she has had for many years."

It was now April 25. The severance agreement rested, unsigned, near the suicide notes. At the bottom of Warshauer's final letter, dated April 21, Green had written: "Thank you for making my last days on earth a living hell."

Dianna Green, vice president for customer operations for the region's largest electric utility, lay in her bed, a .25 caliber pistol in her mouth and pulled the trigger.

(Copyright, *Pittsburgh Post-Gazette,* 1998, all rights reserved. Reprinted with permission.)

Roddy's story continues with details about how Green's corporate life fell apart after officials discovered her master's in business administration did not exist. To aid readers with the long story, editors developed a mapped format. Subheads guided them to aspects of Green's career, her style, and the question of her educational degrees.

Newspapers are not the only medium to use mapped formats. CNN News Online uses subheads in its full stories to break up text and to assist readers in finding information.

Numerical Format

A writer may organize a message numerically or by points. For example, a city council votes on three issues: water and sewer rates, a rezoning application, and the town manager's contract. The writer would list in the lead the actions taken and the votes, thereby setting up the three points to be expanded in the body of the story in that order.

Writers covering a speech will often use a numeral or point-by-point format that follows the organizational structure of the speech after summarizing the speaker's remarks. For example, a speaker discusses three major risk factors in heart disease. The writer notes the three risk factors in the lead: risk factor one, smoking; risk factor two, lack of exercise; risk factor three, lack of a well-balanced diet. The points serve as transitions from the lead to the sections of the message.

The reporter's story might read:

—Cardiovascular disease is the No. 1 cause of death in the United States, but it can be reduced with lifestyle changes such as no smoking, regular exercise, and a well-balanced diet, the chairman of the American Heart Association's Wayne County chapter said Tuesday.

Gus Rivas said Americans should pay attention to the risk factors at an early age and get children to be aware of healthy lifestyles.

More than 3,000 children smoke their first cigarette every day. This number will translate into more adults who are at risk for cardiovascular disease.

"Children consume more than 947 million packs of cigarettes in this country," Rivas said. "More than 25 percent of high school students who smoke tried their first cigarette while in the sixth grade."

Youngsters need to exercise, he noted. Studies show that today's youth do not get enough regular exercise.

"Riding a bike, walking, even doing household chores can establish fitness patterns," Rivas said.

A well-balanced diet low in fat is essential to reduce the risk of heart disease, Rivas said. About one out of four children is obese, and obese children are at a risk for obesity as adults.

The writer followed the lead, using the three points or risk factors as a way to organize and unify the story.

Brights

All short articles are not news. Some news stories can be written so that they become a *bright,* that is, a short news-feature no more than five paragraphs long and with a twist at the end.

Consider the following bright that resulted from a routine police report of a missing man:

PHOENIX—Tammy Plumb called police when her husband didn't return from a one-day hunting trip. Four days later, Jesse Plumb was found by an army of searchers—unharmed, but feeling sheepish about a tryst with another woman.

Plumb might be billed $13,000 for the mountain search, which involved a helicopter, dogs and more than 40 deputies, sheriff's Sgt. John Kleinheinz said.

Tammy Plumb has moved out.

Unifying Writing

Any story, memo, news release, broadcast piece, or e-mail message needs unity to be a coherent and complete piece. Each paragraph in a written piece must follow the preceding paragraph logically. Each paragraph must build on previous information. Each section of the piece must fit the subject or theme. Unifying writing takes careful thought and planning, and it requires rewriting or reorganizing after a draft is done.

Transitions and repetition of certain words are ways to unify writing and to get readers from the beginning to the end. The first two or three paragraphs set up many of the unifying elements, for example, people, places, things, controversy, or chronology.

Repetition of Words

Some writers are uncomfortable repeating words in their writing. They pore over the thesaurus or dictionary, looking for synonyms that may not be as good as the word itself repeated. Repetition is okay. Repetition offers unity in a message and gives readers familiarity. Repetition is also clearer: Readers are not stopping to match synonyms and words.

The topic will determine the words repeated. A memo that covers changes in employee benefits should use the word "employee" throughout rather than switching from "worker" to "staff" to "professional" to "craftsman." The same applies in writing about an organization; "organization" or the organization's name can be used throughout rather than "group," "agency," or "company."

Transitions

Transitions are cues for readers. Transitions set up changes in location, time, and mood. They keep readers from getting lost or confused.

A simple sentence or word may be needed as a logical bridge from one section of the message to the next. Any transition should wrap up the previous thought and introduce the next one.

"We must continue our efforts to reduce teenage pregnancy, and our programs are aimed to do that," the governor said.

While the governor defended his policies, others in state government cited lack of action on welfare issues for his dwindling popularity.

The second sentence indicates a shift from the governor's words to those of state government officials.

Most writers are accustomed to simple words or phrases as transitions. Look at some words and phrases that give readers certain information about where a story is going.

A change in opinion: but, on the other hand, however

Clarification: in other words, for example, that is, to illustrate, to demonstrate, specifically, to clarify

Comparison: also, in comparison, like, similarly, on the same note, a related point

Contrast: but, in contrast, despite, on the contrary, unlike, yet, however, instead of

Expanded information: in addition, an additional, moreover, in other action, another, further, furthermore, too, as well as, also

A change in place: above, higher, beneath, nearby beside, between, across, after, around, below

Time: while, meanwhile, past, afterward, during, soon, next, subsequently, until then, future, before, at the same time

Look at how a few transitions work. In developing a story chronologically, time serves as a transition. Look at the First Guaranty bank robbery story earlier in this chapter. The time elements pull the reader from shortly after 9 A.M., when the robbery occurred, until 6 P.M., when the woman still had not been caught. In other stories, time-oriented words and phrases could be "at the same time," "later that day," "Tuesday," and "last week."

A story about voter reaction on election day uses polling sites around town as geographic transitions: "Voters at Precinct 35 (Town Hall) said . . . ,"

"Those voting at Precinct 15 (Main Street Presbyterian Church) said...,"
"Precinct 2 voters (Blackwell Elementary School) said...." Other geographical phrases would be "on the other side of town," "at his father's 25-acre farm," "next door," and "at the White House."

Tone to Unify a Message

Knowing audiences will help the writer determine what tone to set in organizing and writing a message. The tone or mood of a story can act as a unifying device. A PTA newsletter editor knows that her audience is busy, fast-moving, and distracted by children, work, day-to-day routine, and a deluge of media bits. She knows her audience is in need of quick information about kids and school. She must write lively copy with short, pithy sentences and paragraphs. Active parents need newsletter copy that looks like this:

> Spring cleaning may leave you with trash and treasures.
> Please donate them to Southview School's Trash and Treasure
> sale! This year's sale is planned for May 9.
>
> Doris Tucker will begin receiving donations April 26
> at her home, 322 Dale Drive. For more information, call
> 499-2342.

In contrast, a newsletter for adults 50 years and older requires a more serious, thoughtful tone as well as some humor and nostalgia amid careful, complete news updates and obituaries of members. Its readers have interest in stories. An article might begin this way.

> On November 12, Seniors Together lost one of our great
> members and friends, Gladys McKenzie, who gave endlessly of
> her time to us and our organization. We share in the grief
> of her family but feel blessed that we had the chance to
> know Gladys.
>
> Gladys became such a part of our volunteers and
> outreach to our members who were homebound. She joined the

```
organization eight years ago and always had a smile and
willingness to put in the extra time where needed.
```

A writer's knowledge of audiences will determine the mood or tone that will best maintain interest and retain it throughout the message.

Quotations to Unify Stories

Quotations can be effective transitions throughout writing. They add liveliness and an emotional element, allow people to speak directly to readers and listeners, and help them feel more connected to personalities and events. They can supplement facts and add detail. News stories and news releases should have a good balance between direct and indirect quotes. Information on direct and indirect quotes, attribution, and punctuation of quotes is given in Chapter 10.

Look at *The Washington Post* story on Stephen Goodin earlier in this chapter. Writer Peter Baker uses quotes to illustrate Goodin's feelings about working for the president. The quotes allow readers to get inside Goodin's head, and they add a liveliness to the story. Quotes bridge information within the story.

As you can see from the Baker and also the Dion Haynes story on Chelsea Clinton in *The Chicago Tribune,* quotations are good endings for stories. They can refer to the lead and wrap up a piece, they can leave the reader looking to the future, or they can add a touch of humor. But sometimes writers have to be careful in using a quote at the end. If the story is cut from the bottom, readers should miss only a chuckle, not important information.

Unifying Devices in Practice

Let's go back and look at the second-day newspaper story on the Rockland Community Theater. What are the unifying devices? First, see what the lead set up.

—When Director Neal Folger starts auditions for the season opener of The Rockland Community Theater in early August, most board of directors members will be crossing their fingers for a smooth year.

Broadly, the lead hints at a controversy and lets readers know that board members will be quoted. Words that are established for repetition are "theater," "board," "directors," "year," "Folger," "audition," "director," and "season."

The board hired Folger, the former director of the River Road Theater in Danville, a year ago, and soon the theater was embroiled in controversy. Last year's season opener of "Grease" showed nudity when three performers dropped their pants as part of a song on mooning. This year's season opens Oct. 15.

The second paragraph spells out a controversy and describes what occurred. Words repeated for unity are "board," "Folger," "director," "theater," and "season." We are also given a time element: last year and this year.

"We felt we went through a wringer right off the bat last year," Board Member Mary Tyson said today. "Although some people like Neal's productions, most people in our community prefer more traditional entertainment. Nudity just has no place on our stage."

Graph 3 uses a quotation from a board member. Readers expect to hear from at least one. The quote gives board members' feelings and why the nudity was a problem. Repeated are the themes of last year's controversy, nudity, and the director.

Board Member Justin Fellows said the board hoped for a successful season with less turmoil than the previous year.

Graph 4 introduces another speaker and reiterates last year's controversy and the upcoming season.

"We think Neal is quite talented, but we are just a community theater, and we want fun, not indignation," he said.

Graph 5 gives readers more information about the director and repeats the idea of a community that disapproves of nudity on stage.

Folger said he was surprised at the reaction to "Grease."

Graph 6 is a complete sentence and a new graph, which lets readers know that a change in speakers has occurred, and a defense is coming. It continues the unity through the words "Folger" and "Grease."

"I certainly learned what this community will accept on stage," he said. "We intend to produce shows that keep people fairly well covered."

Graph 7 repeats "community" and begins the transition from last season to the current season's offerings.

Fellows added the board hoped Folger's appealing season lineup will attract a substantial audience to the Rockland Community Theater.

The Fellows quote in graph 8 completes the transition from last year to the current year. It also repeats the words "Fellows," "board," "Folger," "season," and "theater."

The director will have auditions for "Gypsy" from 7 to 9 P.M. Monday and Tuesday at the theater at 211 W. Sycamore St. Folger is looking for 16 actors who will play opposite television and film star Salma Hayeck in the season's opener.

Graph 9 introduces the new information about the auditions. Again, the familiar words are there: "director," "audition," "theater," "Folger," and "season."

Local residents wishing to audition for the major roles must prepare a song and a part to read, said Folger. Each audition is not to exceed five minutes.

People interested in being in a 30-member chorus need prepare only a song not to exceed three minutes. They will audition with the music director, Carole Banner.

People will be notified by Friday if they have been chosen, Folger said, and rehearsals will begin next week.

Graphs 10, 11, and 12 are complete ideas about different aspects of the auditions. Graph 10 begins with information about the major roles, whereas graph 11 is about the lesser parts. Each uses words such as "audition," "Folger," "director," and "song" as unity. The last graph wraps up the story with an indirect quote that looks to the future.

News versus Feature

Students may wonder where the feature story fits in the discussion of print formats. Most articles printed today are news-features or features. Traditionally, writers have used one value to distinguish news from features: timeliness. Features have a timeless quality: They can be published any time and remain useful and entertaining. News, however, must be printed immediately. A story about fashions is a feature; the death of a nationally known fashion designer is news.

Because electronic media have assumed the role of breaking news, newspapers and magazines have taken on an explanatory role. Their job is to flesh out the headline on television or radio and to provide the substance and follow-up. To make the story different, writers have adopted more feature formats, using anecdotal and descriptive leads before getting to the nut graph or the actual news. The example of the 911 operator in Chapter 3 shows how a feature approach can be adopted for a news story.

Writers call the news-feature approach soft news. It doesn't carry the hard-hitting lead: City Council voted 5 to 3 Wednesday night to raise property taxes 3¢ per $100 valuation. The lead instead focuses on someone affected:

—Darcy Little has lived on Southbend Street for 35 years. Each year she fears what increased property taxes on her two-bedroom home will do to her fixed income.

Her fears were realized Wednesday night when city council voted to raise property taxes. It means Little will pay $235 a year more and raises doubts that she will be able to remain in her home.

Students will find that they use news and feature formats in whatever career they choose in print journalism. Newspaper reporters, magazine writers, freelance writers, newsletter editors, novelists, columnists, and others rely on the organizational styles discussed here to produce messages.

Writing formats change. Newspaper reporters, for example, have adopted more narrative styles of writing, using anecdotal and descriptive approaches.

Some editors believe that style will attract more readers; others say the style will pass. Time will be the test of whether new formats attract and retain audiences.

But no matter what style or format they use, and whatever medium they work for, print journalists follow the same writing process outlined in Chapter 1. Some, such as magazine writers, have time to put their work aside before editing. Newspaper reporters who work under deadline pressure, however, find that they compress the stages. They may have little time for extensive rewriting and editing. Those tasks may fall to others in the newsroom, such as metro editors and copy editors, with whom writers share their work. In any case, the written piece proceeds through those stages before it is published for audiences.

The Professional Writer

The examples in Chapters 3 and 4 give you, as a student journalist, a peek at the kinds of careers you can pursue as a writer: newspaper reporter, magazine writer, novelist, columnist, or even online news editor. Other chapters will pose additional opportunities, such as wordsmithing as a copy editor, analyzing information as a database journalist, or producing a company's Web pages.

Throughout the text, the need for good writing skills in any of those professions will be stressed over and over. But basic skills aren't enough. All writers, regardless of which medium will publish their work, must be accurate in gathering and printing information. Editors at all levels can improve their copy, but no editor will know whether the information is correct. The reporter must accept the burden of accuracy. Failure to check and double-check facts can result in libel suits for newspapers and destroyed credibility for writers. Once a writer has ruined his or her reputation, it may be impossible to regain believability.

The writer also must bear responsibility for gathering information ethically. Students who want to be successful must be scrupulously honest and adhere to a personal code of ethics. Sources must know when they will be quoted, and writers should not accept gifts for information. Unlike doctors and lawyers writers cannot be barred from practice for performing their jobs in an unethical manner. Again, what suffers is their reputation—and that could cost them jobs and income.

Many organizations assist students and other writers in adhering to professional standards and learning more about mass media issues that relate to the print field. The American Society of Newspaper Editors and the Newspaper Association of America have Web sites that have extensive information about print media and links to other useful sites, including lists of other pertinent journalism organizations.

Organizations such as the Society of Professional Journalists (SPJ) have developed codes of ethics for journalists as guidelines for behavior. News outlets generally have ethics statements for their reporters and writers to follow. For example, a publication may not buy a travel story if the writer received a free trip from the resort featured in the piece. Newspaper reporters may be banned from accepting anything from a source, even a cup of coffee, or from entering certain writing contests that award money.

Students starting out in the profession may find it helpful to join professional organizations such as SPJ, which has a valuable Web site and links to helpful sources. Groups exist for different types of writers and are noted in Chapters 11, 12, and 13. Organizations hold workshops to keep writers up to date on trends in the field and can even provide writers a sense of belonging, particularly freelance writers, who work on their own. Professional contacts help individuals who want to make career moves. Students should become aware of groups and people who can guide them in attaining a rewarding and satisfying professional life.

Code of Ethics

Society of Professional Journalists

Preamble
Members of the Society of Professional Journalists believe that public enlightenment is the forerunner of justice and the foundation of democracy. The duty of the journalist is to further those ends by seeking truth and providing fair and comprehensive account of events and issues. Conscientious journalists from all media and specialties strive to serve the public with thoroughness and honesty. Professional integrity is the cornerstone of a journalist's credibility. Members of the Society share a dedication to ethical behavior and adopt this code to declare the Society's principles and standards of practice.

Seek Truth and Report It

Journalists should be honest, fair and courageous in gathering, reporting and interpreting information.

Journalists should

Test the accuracy of information from all sources and exercise care to avoid inadvertent error. Deliberate distortion is never permissible.

Diligently seek out subjects of news stories to give them the opportunity to respond to allegations of wrongdoing.

Identify sources whenever feasible. The public is entitled to as much information as possible on sources' reliability.

Always question sources' motives before promising anonymity. Clarify conditions attached to any promise made in exchange for information. Keep promises.

Make certain that headlines, news teases and promotional material, photos, video, audio, graphics, sound bites and quotations do not misrepresent. They should not oversimplify or highlight incidents out of context.

Never distort the content of news photos or video. Image enhancement for technical clarity is always permissible. Label montages and photo illustrations.

Avoid misleading re-enactments or staged news events. If re-enactment is necessary to tell a story, label it.

Avoid undercover or other surreptitious methods of gathering information except when traditional open methods will not yield information vital to the public. Use of such methods should be explained as part of the story.

Never plagiarize.

Tell the story of the diversity and magnitude of the human experience boldly, even when it is unpopular to do so.

Examine their own cultural values and avoid imposing those values on others.

Avoid stereotyping by race, gender, age, religion, ethnicity, geography, sexual orientation, disability, physical appearance or social status.

Support the open exchange of views, even views they find repugnant.

Give voice to the voiceless; official and unofficial sources of information can be equally valid.

Distinguish between advocacy and news reporting. Analysis and commentary should be labeled and not misrepresent fact or context.

Distinguish news from advertising and shun hybrids that blur the lines between the two.

Recognize a special obligation to ensure that the public's business is conducted in the open and that government records are open to inspection.

Minimize Harm

Ethical journalists treat sources, subjects and colleagues as human beings deserving of respect.

Journalists should

Show compassion for those who may be affected adversely by news coverage. Use special sensitivity when dealing with children and inexperienced sources or subjects.

Be sensitive when seeking or using interviews or photographs of those affected by tragedy or grief.

Recognize that gathering and reporting information may cause harm or discomfort. Pursuit of the news is not a license for arrogance.

Recognize that private people have a greater right to control information about themselves than do public officials and others who seek power, influence or attention. Only an overriding public need can justify intrusion into anyone's privacy.

Show good taste. Avoid pandering to lurid curiosity.

Be cautious about identifying juveniles, suspects or victims of sex crimes.

Be judicious about naming criminal suspects before the formal filing of charges.

Balance a criminal suspect's fair trial rights with the public's right to be informed.

Act Independently

Journalists should be free of obligation to any interest other than the public's right to know.

Journalists should

Avoid conflicts of interest, real or perceived.

Remain free of associations and activities that may compromise integrity or damage credibility.

Refuse gifts, favors, fees, free travel and special treatment, and shun secondary employment, political involvement, public office and service in community organizations if they compromise journalistic integrity.

Disclose avoidable conflicts.

Be vigilant and courageous about holding those with power accountable.

Deny favored treatment to advertisers and special interests and resist their pressure to influence news coverage.

By wary of sources offering information for favor or money; avoid bidding for news.

Be Accountable

Journalists are accountable to their readers, listeners, viewers and each other.

Journalists should

Clarify and explain news coverage and invite dialogue with the public over journalistic conduct.

Encourage the public to voice grievances against the news media.

Admit mistakes and correct them promptly.

Expose unethical practices of journalists and the news media.

Abide by the same high standards to which they hold others.

(Reprinted with permission of the Society of Professional Journalists, adopted September 1996.)

Moving on with Writing

Writing is a series of choices—choice of language, pertinent facts, introductions, organizational pattern, tone, quotes, and topics—and all need to be made in an informed way, based on what writers know about their audiences.

Books and other writers can give you tips on how to organize your writing. The best way to learn is to apply the techniques through your own efforts. Do not let organization just happen. Make an outline. Consciously apply a certain organizational style to your writing. Let someone else read your piece to see whether it makes sense.

Good organization helps you reach your audience. Look at the Associated Press story. The reporter uses all the strengths of simple writing, repetition for unity, and quotations as transitions to pull readers through an emotionally compelling story that could have been just another routine drug bust story. The following chapters will guide you further in knowing your audience and writing for it.

Crime, Fear, Poverty All Part of Life in America

Young Woman's Eyes Reflect Despair of Violent Nation

BY JULIA PRODIS

Associated Press

DALLAS—Her eyes are the color of earth, and as vacant as the lot next door.

She's sitting on a concrete step holding a baby that's not hers. Her 16-year-old friend is lying face down on the sizzling sidewalk beside her, his arms arched awkwardly behind him, his hands cuffed in plastic police ties. A girlfriend is similarly contorted at her feet.

"What's your name?" a policewoman asks this hot August day in Dallas.

In a low, slow whisper, she answers, "Latasha."

"La-what?"

"La-Tasha," the thin, moonfaced 19-year-old says with slightly more effort, her blank gaze never looking higher than the holster holding the officer's 9 mm semiautomatic.

Minutes ago, eight muscular members of the Dallas drug enforcement squad, wearing black boots and bulletproof vests, had stormed the faded yellow bungalow behind her. It took two heaves of "the slammer" to break down the door, blocked only by an empty bookcase.

Shrieks from inside, then blurs of motion as the young man bolted out the rear and the woman ran toward the back fence. Latasha Smith never said a word, and the baby didn't cry.

She has the dull look of someone who had seen this rerun too many times. Her look of despair, so deep it turns everything gray, is the same look that flattens the faces of the young and hopeless in poor, violent American neighborhoods everywhere.

Neighborhoods where crack heads fear friends and neighbors more than the cops. Where homes are so filthy detectives can't pick up evidence without something crawling on it. Where neighbors scatter when someone screams for help.

For Americans who say crime is their gravest concern, these calloused Latashas and their criminal friends stir angry fear. But for Latasha, it's just another day.

The baby with cocoa skin and heavy brown hair spits up on Latasha's chest as she rocks negligibly back and forth. Indifferently, she wipes his face with her droopy white tank top.

"Who's payin' for that baby?" the policewoman asks.

"It ain't MY baby," she retorts.

"It's my baby," says the 16-year-old boy, squirming awkwardly on the sidewalk. As he strains to lift his head to speak, the pebbles clinging to his cheek dribble to the ground.

Latasha tells the officer she has three children of her own and she's on welfare. She quit the last job she had washing dishes because she didn't like it. Her children are scattered with relatives and friends today.

"Did you grow up like this baby is growing up?" the reporter asks.

"My daddy shot my momma dead when I was 2." She speaks flatly, like a kid bored with homework. She was raised by her grandfather.

She doesn't explain why she is at this house that isn't hers holding somebody else's baby.

An undercover officer recently bought drugs at this house. The police had come back to clean it up and close it down—one of nearly 400 Dallas dope houses stormed this year.

After running background checks on the three, the sergeant in charge decides to arrest the handcuffed youths on drug charges and ticket Latasha for failing to appear in court after being cited for driving without insurance.

"Do you ever dream of a better life?" the reporter asks.

She shrugs.

She doesn't watch the van carry her two friends away. She just sits in front of the house with the For Rent sign and the broken door, holding someone else's baby, and stares blankly at the vacant lot next door.

(Reprinted by permission from the Associated Press.)

EXERCISES

1. You are a reporter for the *Rockland Chronicle*. You have picked up the following police report—written last night—from the Town Police Department. Write a message with a summary lead, then develop the message in chronological order.

Report: Tony's Restaurant Robbery

Investigating Officer: Sgt. Rodney Carter

At 10:00 P.M. a robbery at Tony's Restaurant was reported. Owner, Tony Hardy said that he was working late preparing the payroll when a man wearing a stocking mask entered the back door of the kitchen at about 8:40.

Hardy said that the man told him to go into the office and open up the safe. Hardy took almost $3,000 out of the safe and put it into a blue, waterproof sack.

The restaurant closes at 9 P.M. Hardy said he thought the robber knew he was there alone, but that he didn't think the robber was a Rockland resident.

Hardy said he got a good look at the man: a stocky white man, about 5'6", and round-faced. He estimated the man's age to be 24. Hardy said the man's shoulders were so broad that he might have been a weight lifter. Hardy suggested that if the thief wanted to lock him up somewhere, the storage closet off the kitchen was as good a place as any. The thief agreed and locked him up there. The thief wrapped a clothes hanger around the door. He told Hardy he had a partner, and that Hardy wouldn't live to see his family and relatives if he came out of the closet before 15 minutes had passed.

Hardy said he waited the 15 minutes even though he
didn't believe the story about the partner, or at least a
partner who would be stupid enough to hang around for 15
minutes. He had no trouble getting out and then called the
Rockland Police.

We have some leads on the suspect and the investigation
is continuing.

2. From the following information, write a summary lead for the *Rockland
   Chronicle* that focuses on *who, what, when,* and *where* plus human interest.
   Then develop the message chronologically.

From the Rockland police chief, Ralph Robinson, you learn
the following:

Two sisters were playing at a Laundromat about 5 P.M.
yesterday. The girls are the daughters of Nancy and Phillip
Childs of Rockland. The girls were with their aunt, Janice
Childs. The 3-year-old, Jennifer, climbed into one of the
washing machines. Her sister, Elizabeth, 7, closed the
door. The machine started filling up with water. When she
realized the washer was running, Elizabeth ran to get her
aunt. Ms. Childs tried to open the washer door but could
not, because the washers are equipped with automatic locks
on the doors.

Robinson said the girl was trapped in the washer for
more than five minutes before she was rescued. He said a
customer had put coins into the machine before the little
girl crawled inside, but the customer hadn't used the
machine because he thought it wasn't working.

On the telephone you talk to Paul Hecker of 601 Arbor Drive in Rockland. He was on his way home from work and stopped at the Glen Rock Shopping Center to buy groceries. He heard screams coming from the Glen Rock Laundry and Dry Cleaner. He ran inside the Laundromat to see what was going on. Ms. Childs ran up to him and asked him to save the child. She asked if he had any tools, so he ran back to his toolbox in the back of his truck and got a hammer. Hecker said he took the hammer back inside and smashed the glass in the washing machine door. He then reached in and pulled her out.

A Rockland Hospital spokesperson said Jennifer was admitted yesterday afternoon and was listed in good condition. Her parents could not be reached for comment.

3. You are to write a message with a summary lead. Think about the latest information for the summary lead. Then organize the story using the hourglass format of writing. You will need to merge the two accounts of the event into one chronological account. Be sure to attribute information when it is quoted.

Middleton Police Chief Ralph Poe held a press conference at 7 P.M. last night. He said an emergency medical service team had come to an alley beside the downtown Pizza To Go restaurant yesterday afternoon after a neighboring businessman reported that there was a man in the alley who appeared to be injured.

The man, Henry Donovan, 39, of Rt. 2 Box 8 in Middleton, suffered from multiple gunshot wounds, Poe said. Paramedics took him to Memorial Hospital, where he was pronounced dead on arrival, Poe said.

Donovan's ex-wife, Regina Donovan, 34, manages the Pizza To Go restaurant and lives at Rt. 3 Box 254-A,

Middleton. She and Henry Donovan, a truck driver for Keller Trucking Company, were divorced in August 1990. He came to the restaurant yesterday afternoon to pick up their two children for a visit. Donovan arrived at the restaurant at 2:30 P.M., Poe said.

Poe said Mrs. Donovan called police at 3 P.M. and told them she thought an armed man was in the restaurant, possibly holding her children hostage.

Poe said he called in police officers, who stationed themselves at the front and back doors of the restaurant to prevent the gunman from exiting. County sheriff's deputies were also dispatched to the scene. Upon arrival, they searched the building and found no gunman. The two children, Henry Donovan, Jr., and Helen Donovan, were next door at Belinda's Bakery and were unharmed.

Police have charged businessman Bill Buchanan with first-degree murder.

After an investigation, police determined that Buchanan shot Donovan in the restroom of the Pizza To Go, then pulled his body out the back and put it in the trunk of his car, parked in the alley.

Ms. Donovan said she was sweeping the sidewalk in front of the building when she heard the shots. She realized her children were inside and said she panicked and ran to a neighboring business to call police. While she was calling police, Buchanan went back in the Pizza To Go, got the two children and took them to the bakery next door, Poe said in the news conference.

When police and county sheriff's deputies arrived, they found no one. After the police left, Buchanan dragged the

body out of his car and put it into the alley. He then
called police about 4 P.M., pretending that he had found it.

"It appears Mrs. Donovan had been dating Buchanan and
had recently broken up with him, saying she was considering
a reconciliation with her husband," Poe said.

Buchanan is being held in the Suffolk County jail
without bond. He was arrested Wednesday afternoon. His
first court appearance for a probable cause hearing will be
Monday.

4. You are to write a message based on the following information. Write a
summary lead, then organize the story point by point. Your audience is
Rockland residents.

Topic: Mobile Crime Watch
In charge, Ross S. Frick, crime prevention officer,
Rockland

Frick gives the following information: "When we
realized breaking and entering was up 45 percent, we knew
we had to do something to offset that increase. So we are
establishing the new Mobile Crime Watch. One of the things
I always hear about neighborhood watch in Rockland is that
nobody is in the neighborhood during the day. We need more
people involved in reporting crime during the daytime.

"To accomplish this will take three parts. In the next
two weeks the Police Department will train 65 Power and
Light employees and local cable franchise employees during
one-hour sessions. Postal workers will be trained next. All
of these people are out in the community anyway. Many of
them have portable telephones so they can report things. In
the past they might have seen things and didn't report them
to the police. Mobile watch participants won't be surrogate

police officers. We don't want them to take any action whatsoever except go to a telephone. We don't want them to approach people or ask questions.

"Then we will notify residents of neighborhoods where we are starting the Mobile Watch programs so they will be aware that extra eyes on crime are in their neighborhoods. We will notify residents through flyers placed in mailboxes.

"As the final part, we hope within six months to set up a reward and award program for Mobile Watch members—the employees and residents—who help us be successful in catching criminals."

From background information, you learn that a Power and Light employee was working on a telephone pole in our county and saw people breaking into a house. He plugged his phone into the wires and police arrested the subjects.

Nearby Middleton started a similar program, called Eyes on Crime, five years ago, and it has worked. The town has shown a decrease in all crimes except rape and murder.

REFERENCES

American Society of Newspaper Editors Home Page. Available at: http://www.asne.org.

Jacqueline Farnan and David Hedley, "The Mapped Format: A Variation on the Inverted-Pyramid Appeals to Readers" [abstr]. Paper presented at the Association for Education in Journalism and Mass Communication Conference, Atlanta, Ga., August 1993.

Fred Fedler, *Reporting for the Print Media*. New York: Harcourt Brace Jovanovich, 1989.

Lionel Linder and Colleen Conant, "Newswriting for the Commercial Appeal," inhouse publication, 1989.

Newspaper Association of America Home Page. Available at: http://www.naa.org.

Richard Shumate, "Life after Kovach," *Washington Journalism Review,* Vol. 14, No. 8, September 1992.

Society of Professional Journalists Home Page. Available at: http://www.spj.org.

5

Saying It Straight

For years, writing coaches at newspapers and magazines have worked to distill a set of qualities in writing that will catch and hold readers. Many people, such as Roy Peter Clark at the Poynter Institute in St. Petersburg, Florida, have spent a great deal of their professional careers analyzing the qualities of good writing. Authors such as William Zinsser, best known for his book *On Writing Well,* offer advice on how to strengthen and improve prose. Even communication researchers, charged with finding out what makes publications sell, have considered what qualities are valued in messages.

The research shows that the most effective writing is simple and forceful; that is, it says it straight without flourishes and pomp. This chapter

- Looks at three essential qualities in writing: accuracy, clarity, and completeness,
- Reviews five broad rules for good writing,
- Examines sentence structure, and
- Offers specific tips to improve writing.

Watchwords of Writing

No message will succeed if it does not have three essential qualities: accuracy, clarity, and completeness. We know from the discussion of audiences in Chapter 2 that they can be fickle; once they are lost, they may not return. Writing that is accurate, clear, and complete has a better chance of holding audiences, particularly those who may be clicking through a Web site or leafing through a brochure.

Accuracy ensures the credibility of all writing. When the audience catches a misspelled name or an erroneous date, it doubts the accuracy of the information that follows. An audience that cannot trust a communicator will abandon him or her.

Clarity means the writer uses language that an audience understands. Simple language is preferred over complicated words. Jargon and technical language are avoided. The message comes through.

Completeness answers an audience's questions. A message that is complete satisfies the audience and does so quickly.

Let's look at each element more closely.

Accuracy

Good communication of any kind always contains accurate information. Accuracy is comforting to audiences, who want to depend on information. Errors can occur at any stage in writing: gathering information through research and interviewing, transcribing notes, calculating figures, and creating the copy (when typos can occur). To ensure accuracy, writers must use good information-gathering techniques. They must obtain information only from reliable sources, then check and recheck it against other sources. Chuck Stone, syndicated columnist and university professor, notes, "If your mother says she loves you, check it out." If you find a discrepancy or an error and you don't have time to check it, follow the adage, "When in doubt, leave it out."

We are all prone to committing errors sometimes. Just because a well-known person recites a fact or the fact is found in a computer database does not mean it is correct. The potentate may be in error, and human beings type information into databases. Name spellings, middle initials, street numbers, birth dates—seemingly trivial details—become of monumental importance once they become part of a message. Such details may be accurate in notes but then may be transcribed erroneously into copy.

If messages are wrong, people are misled. Writers and audiences rarely forget the mishap when a name is misspelled or an address is wrong. Inaccuracies in messages lead to distrust among audiences—and they can lead to libel suits. Once audience members are misled by a source, they have difficulty trusting it again.

Inaccuracies can damage good will. In an "About Town" column in a small town, a local writer reported that "Bob and Mary Allison" had been on vacation in Bermuda. Mary, indeed, had enjoyed her trip; Bob had been dead eight years. Publication of their names in tandem was a sad event for everyone in the neighborhood, especially the embarrassed writer.

Clarity

A message will have impact if it is clear and straightforward so that everyone in its audience can understand it. "Send a check for $75 by February 1 if you want to ski with the Seniors Club in February" makes the requirement clear. The writing is direct and uses simple, to-the-point language.

A message needs to be so clear that no misunderstanding or confusion can possibly result. A university-wide e-mail note about a memorial service for a popular librarian who died described the church as "the Baptist Church on Michigan Avenue near Howard University." Unfortunately, more than one church fit that description. Because the message was unclear, several people missed the memorial service, a one-time event.

Completeness

Useful messages also are complete, giving sufficient information for real understanding and guidance. A news story that leaves out an important fact can be misleading and even harmful.

In December 1997 Michael Kennedy died in a skiing accident in Colorado. Early news stories along the East Coast identified him only as the son of the late U.S. Attorney General Robert Kennedy and nephew of President John Kennedy. The information was true but incomplete: Michael Kennedy was the brother of Maryland's living and popular lieutenant governor, Kathleen Kennedy Townsend. Complete information changed the story dramatically, particularly for East Coast audiences.

Keys to Good Writing

Researchers, language professionals, and experienced writers agree on five basic tenets of good writing. Anyone can apply the rules while writing and editing.

Good Writing Uses Short Sentences

Most readability experts argue that regardless of age, education, or economic status, people prefer and understand writing that uses short sentences. Human beings have little patience with long, complicated sentences that tax their brain power. Of course, not all sentences should be short; readers would be bored, so sentence length should vary. A short sentence can have impact. A long, complex sentence can set up an idea for the audience or create a mood, and a short sentence can follow immediately, almost as a punch line. Get the point?

A study at the American Press Institute showed that reader understanding drops off dramatically if sentences exceed twenty words, and comprehension continues to drop as sentences grow longer. Only about one of twenty people studied could clearly comprehend fifty-word sentences, a common length in newspapers and in academic writing.

Short-term memory rarely exceeds fifteen seconds, which may not be enough time to read one of the many fifty-word sentences in traditional magazines and newspapers. Consider this lead from the *Washington Post*.

> TOKYO, Jan. 29—It surely won't be smooth and it probably won't be pretty, but the process of change—political, economic, and social—will continue apace now that Prime Minister Morihiro Hosokawa won passage tonight of the most far-reaching package of electoral reform Japan has seen since just after World War II.

By the time many readers have reached the end of that fifty-word sentence, they may have forgotten the beginning!

The English language is based on a pattern of simple, subject–verb–object constructions. Most are short. Because people learn and use English this way in everyday life, they prefer this pattern in messages.

Readers would be more likely to warm up to a straightforward approach to the Japanese electoral reform, such as this one:

> TOKYO—The Japanese Parliament passed tonight the most far-reaching package of electoral reform the country has seen since just after World War II.
>
> Passage signifies continued change—political, economic, and social—for the Japanese people, a process that won't be smooth.

Regular readers of *The Washington Post,* however, are used to the style of long lead sentences. The style fits the *Post's* audience. The style would not be suitable for many other audiences.

Journalism Professor Fred Fedler of the University of Central Florida says that simplicity makes stories more interesting and forceful. He cites as an example a prize-winning story by World War II journalist Ernie Pyle; the average sentence length was 10.6 words.

Good Writing Uses Short Words

Perhaps your high school English teacher praised you for using "penurious" rather than "stingy," or "inebriated" rather than "drunk." Then you were expanding your vocabulary, but now your audience will thank you for choosing the simpler word.

Just as they do with long sentences, readers and listeners become tired and discouraged when they face too many complex words—usually those exceeding three syllables. To be sure, you can use commonly known, longer words such as "responsibility," "establishment," "participate," and "governmental." Be sure, however, that the longer words are a better choice than a shorter version, such as "duty," "founding," "join in," or "federal" or "state."

When writing, select the simplest word possible to convey the meaning. For example, in a police story, avoid saying that the two men had an "altercation." Use the word "fight." Instead of "finalize," choose a word such as "conclude" or "finish." Rather than "exasperate," use "annoy" or "bother." Instead of "terminating" this paragraph, we will "end" it.

Good Writing Eliminates Wordiness

"You can almost detect a wordy sentence by looking at it—at least if you can recognize weak verbs, ponderous nouns, and strings of prepositional phrases," Claire Kehrwald Cook writes in her book *Line by Line: How to Improve Your Own Writing.* Her advice gives writers clues about where to find wordiness and where to improve sentence structure.

Author William Zinsser notes that the secret to good writing is to strip every sentence to its cleanest components. Writers must detach themselves from the information and chisel it to the bare essentials. Writers must throw out extra words and phrases—even extra sentences and paragraphs. An old adage advises, "Two words are never as good as one." Consider the simple word "new." When used in the following sentence, it is unnecessary: "Crews expect the new building to be completed within two months." All buildings under construction are new. Leave the word out.

Audiences can find the facts only when excess is trimmed. Sparse writing is more professional, more informative, more objective, and more likely to be read. Writer Stanley Elkin describes the process of eliminating excess in writing:

> *"[It's] a kind of whittling, a honing to the bone, until you finally get whatever the hell you're looking for. It's an exercise in sculpture, chipping away at the rock until you find the nose."*

Wordy writing is likely to be redundant or repetitious. No writer needs to say that a fire "completely destroyed" a downtown block; if it was destroyed, the destruction was complete. This classic often appears: "Jones is currently the manager of consumer services." "Is" means "now," and "now" means "currently." Kill the word "currently." Think about other phrases such as "past history," "acres of land," "4 P.M. in the afternoon," "at 12 midnight," "dead body," and "totally incomprehensible."

In seeking wordiness, look specifically for unnecessary adjectives and qualifiers. For example, a project cannot be the "most" unique. "Unique" means one of a kind. Qualifiers such as "very," "truly," and "really" can generally be cut without damage to copy.

Sometimes a statement or entire paragraph that repeats a speaker's direct quotes can be deleted.

> —Jones said he was delighted that the school would receive $40,000 to use for purchasing audiovisual equipment materials for the library.
>
> "I am just delighted that we will have the $40,000 to buy audiovisual equipment for the library," Jones said.

Delete the first paragraph. It does more than serve as a transition to the direct quote—it steals it.

As in art, too much embellishment in writing only detracts and distracts. Consider the effectiveness of the following message before and after its extra words are deleted:

> —Ninety-two years ago, the Tung Wah Dispensary attempted to cure the ailments and afflictions of the San Francisco Chinatown community

from its humble outpost at 828 Sacramento Street. When the institution realized that its cramped quarters were counterproductive to the logistics of health care, it expanded its services and relocated to 835 Jackson Street, eventually being renamed the Chinese Hospital.

Simplified, the history looks like this:

```
Ninety-two years ago, the Tung Wah Dispensary treated
sickness in San Francisco's Chinatown from its humble
outpost at 828 Sacramento Street. Cramped quarters and
expanded services led to a new location at 835 Jackson
Street, the building that eventually was named the Chinese
Hospital.
```

Without its embellishments—"ailments and afflictions," "institution," and "counterproductive"—this message is much more readable and just as informative.

Good Writing Avoids Jargon or Technical Language

In our high-tech society, so much jargon exists that it is difficult to tell what is jargon and what is plain English. Few people recall that "input" and "output" originated in computer jargon. The same is true of the terms *bottom line* and *in the red*. These familiar terms are still questionable in good writing.

Examples of jargon abound in everyday life. Parents received an annual report from the elementary school. In listing the objectives for the year, the report stated

```
Objective Three: The mean score for the kindergarten
program will increase from 5.1 to 5.4 as measured by the
FPG Assessment Report. The lead teacher for
developmentally appropriate practice coordinated the
efforts of our kindergarten teachers to enable our program
to meet this objective.
```

For parents, what does this say? Not much. What is a mean score? What is the FPG Assessment Report? What is developmentally appropriate practice? When people see or hear such words, they stop. Confusion sets in. Parents just want to know how their children are doing in school.

Why Is Jargon Such a No-No?

First, it makes too many assumptions about audiences. Technical language reserves a message for insiders: those who are familiar with the lingo. "Outsiders" who could benefit from the information may be put off. For example, an art exhibit notice that contains artistic jargon may scare away potential visitors to the gallery. Technical terms may create a feeling that the gallery is reserved for an elite group. As a result, an audience may feel excluded or perceive the message as exclusive. For the same reason, it is also wise to avoid foreign words and phrases in published writing—unless those words are commonly used, such as voila!

Second, jargon is precise only to the insiders who use it. Once again, consider the word "input," which may be anything from telephone conversations to cash contributions. A more specific term is better.

Third, jargon usually is ambiguous. The "bottom line" mentioned in a school newsletter may mean many things: expenditures, income, or both; parent satisfaction; student learning outcomes—or almost anything. Skilled writers avoid vagueness by avoiding jargon.

Of course, whether writers use jargon or technical language depends on the audience. If they are writing for a medical publication whose audience is nurses and doctors, the language can be more specific to that profession.

Too often, though, messages for general audiences or lay people are filled with educational, legal, economic, or medical jargon. Some technical language because of its use has become more understood by the general public, such as SAT scores for Scholastic Aptitude Tests and AIDS for acquired immune deficiency syndrome. But language too often goes unexplained.

A problem related to jargon is the use of institutional language: abstract terms and phrases that may communicate well in a specific workplace or institution but that lose meaning for a general audience.

For example, medical professionals use the term "treatment modalities." That terminology is nonspecific and lacks meaning and interest, even to a well-educated general audience. Treatment modalities should be named in terms an audience can understand: a series of shots, an antibiotic for ten days, physical therapy for several months.

In a report an academician wrote, "Shrinking and unstable sources of funding lead to short-term dislocations."

What he meant was a lack of consistent and adequate funding interrupts research.

Many institutional words began as one part of speech and have been transformed into another. Teacher may ask parents "to conference" at 4 P.M.; the vice president may decide "to host" a reception. In good writing, parents will meet with teachers, and the vice president will greet guests at the reception.

It is easy to find words to substitute for institutional terms, and the simpler words are always more specific. Some general, ambiguous terms found frequently in workplaces are "input" and "facilitation." Input may mean discussion or suggestions; facilitation may be planning or sponsoring an event. Good writers find out what is meant by such terms, and they substitute simpler language.

Some terms cannot be avoided, such as the nation's gross national product (GNP). Writers must explain such words adequately when they use them. As *The Associated Press Stylebook* explains it, "The gross national product is the total value at retail prices of all the goods and services produced by a nation's economy in a given time period."

Although jargon is conversational, it rarely is efficient in writing. When talking, you can be sure how much your audience knows about your topic; you can supplement messages with hand gestures, facial expressions, and other visual aids; and you can clarify or define confusing terms if your audience looks puzzled or asks questions.

But when you are writing, your text stands alone and must be absolutely clear. Your goal as a writer is to eliminate misunderstanding, and eliminating jargon and technical language is a giant step toward that goal.

Good Writing Comes to the Point Quickly

Chapter 3 focused on the need for writers to come to the point quickly. Perhaps this is the most problematic of writing challenges. A writer may not want to come to the point because the point is unpleasant: A company has lost money or laid off employees. A popular program has been discontinued. But audiences see through attempts to delay bad news, and they interpret them as sneaky ways to hide information. However unwelcome the message, direct communication conveys a feeling of openness and honesty.

Some writers fail to come to the point because they are in "writer's mode," self-indulgently crafting a long introduction to the main points rather than getting to those points. Readers of nonfiction are after information rather than art, and they consider the most direct messages to be the greatest masterpieces.

Still other writers have trouble coming to the point because they do not know what the point is. Critical thinking—deciding on the main goal in communicating—precedes every writing task. To come to the point, writers must know their audiences and analyze information carefully enough to know the point that audiences will want to know.

Writer and filmmaker Nora Ephron tells a story about her high school journalism teacher. In one lesson, he taught his class to recognize main points by telling them their faculty members would be attending a major conference the next day. He asked them to write a news story about it.

In the students' articles, the introductory paragraphs summarized the facts: All teachers would travel to a nearby city and hear famous speakers. After collecting the papers, the teacher threw them away and told the students, "The point is that there will be no school tomorrow."

Ephron says she never forgot the point:

It was an electrifying moment. So that's it, I realized. It's about the point. The classic newspaper lead of who-what-when-where-how and why is utterly meaningless if you haven't figured out the significance of the facts. What is the point? What does it mean? He planted those questions in my head. And for the first year he taught me journalism, every day was like the first; every set of facts had a point buried in it if we looked hard enough. He turned the class into a gorgeous intellectual exercise, and he gave me enthusiasm for the profession I never lost. Also, of course, he taught me something that works just as well in life as it does in journalism.

These rules of good writing may be familiar to you already. But a little redundancy and repetition are like a drill to set indelibly in writers' minds the importance of copy that says it straight. Experienced writers know that in simplicity lies beauty and power.

Words

Three of the five good writing tenets just given—short words, avoidance of wordiness, and avoidance of jargon—focus on words, the basic unit of any oral or written message. A good writer needs knowledge of language, a good vocabulary, and the sense to know when a word is inappropriate or unnecessary.

The Power of Little Words

Most of the little words in our language come from the original language that was spoken in England before Roman and French invaders added their vocabulary to the mix. The English common folk retained their own words for everyday things, and they borrowed from Latin and French only when they had to.

As a result, the things nearest and dearest to us still are called by their original English names: home, fire, food, and mother, for example. And it is these words to which English-speaking people still respond emotionally. The word *home* has much stronger emotional appeal than the cooler, more technical word *domicile,* which is borrowed from Latin. Likewise, *food* sounds good; *nutrients,* a Latin-based word, is another matter.

How Little Words Are Successful

Professor and writing coach Carl Sessions Stepp says that people respond to small words because they usually are "first-degree" words, or words that are immediately understood. Everyone has a single, readily available mental picture of "home," along with a host of meanings and feelings associated with that mental picture. But few people can respond so completely to "domicile." The writer who uses "mother" taps the audience's rich reserves of emotion and information.

Stepp points out that larger, multisyllabic words, many of which have origins in other languages, are "second-degree" words. Such words are abstract rather than concrete. They produce no immediate images in the minds of readers or listeners and are often ambiguous when other information is given. Take, for example, the word *nutrition.* Does it mean food substances, or measures of vitamins and minerals? It is a second-degree word because the audience needs more information for full understanding.

Consider other second-degree words, such as facility and output. Compare them with these first-degree words: school and grades.

Stepp argues that writers are more likely to appeal to audiences if they choose first-degree words and avoid second-degree words. In writing, we deal with many second-degree words that are part of science, technology, education, and almost every other field. Writers need to remember to define such words in first-degree terms whenever possible, as in this sentence:

```
Nutrition—the kinds of foods patients eat every day—is the
topic of a workshop for nurses at Sibley Hospital April 14.
```

Little words are more heart-warming and more easily understood. They also save space, time, and the reader's energy. They are more readable. And audiences respond to readable copy with overall approval, giving high marks to writers and to the entire publication.

Let's revisit the Associated Press article about the Dallas drug bust that follows. The language could not be much simpler. Most fifth-graders could read the story with very little trouble.

Crime, Fear, Poverty All Part of Life in America

Young Woman's Eyes Reflect Despair of Violent Nation

BY JULIA PRODIS

Associated Press

DALLAS—Her eyes are the color of earth, and as vacant as the lot next door.

She's sitting on a concrete step holding a baby that's not hers. Her 16-year-old friend is lying face down on the sizzling sidewalk beside her, his arms arched awkwardly behind him, his hands cuffed in plastic police ties. A girlfriend is similarly contorted at her feet.

"What's your name?" a policewoman asks this hot August day in Dallas.

In a low, slow whisper, she answers, "Latasha."

"La-what?"

"La-Tasha," the thin, moonfaced 19-year-old says with slightly more effort, her blank gaze never looking higher than the holster holding the officer's 9 mm semiautomatic.

Minutes ago, eight muscular members of the Dallas drug enforcement squad, wearing black boots and bulletproof vests, had stormed the faded yellow bungalow behind her. It took two heaves of "the slammer" to break down the door, blocked only by an empty bookcase.

Shrieks from inside, then blurs of motion as the young man bolted out the rear and the woman ran toward the back fence. Latasha Smith never said a word, and the baby didn't cry.

She has the dull look of someone who had seen this rerun too many times. Her look of despair, so deep it turns everything gray, is the same look that flattens the faces of the young and hopeless in poor, violent American neighborhoods everywhere.

Neighborhoods where crack heads fear friends and neighbors more than the cops. Where homes are so filthy detectives can't pick up evidence without something crawling on it. Where neighbors scatter when someone screams for help.

For Americans who say crime is their gravest concern, these calloused Latashas and their criminal friends stir angry fear. But for Latasha, it's just another day.

The baby with cocoa skin and wavy brown hair spits up on Latasha's chest as she rocks negligibly back and forth. Indifferently, she wipes his face with her droopy white tank top.

"Who's payin' for that baby?" the policewoman asks.

"It ain't MY baby," she retorts.

"It's my baby," says the 16-year-old boy, squirming awkwardly on the sidewalk. As he strains to lift his head to speak, the pebbles clinging to his cheek dribble to the ground.

Latasha tells the officer she has three children of her own and she's on welfare. She quit the last job she had washing dishes because she didn't like it. Her children are scattered with relatives and friends today.

"Did you grow up like this baby is growing up?" the reporter asks.

"My daddy shot my momma dead when I was 2." She speaks flatly, like a kid bored with homework. She was raised by her grandfather.

She doesn't explain why she is at this house that isn't hers holding somebody else's baby.

An undercover officer recently bought drugs at this house. The police had come back to clean it up and close it down—one of nearly 400 Dallas dope houses stormed this year.

After running background checks on the three, the sergeant in charge decides to arrest the handcuffed youths on drug charges and ticket Latasha for failing to appear in court after being cited for driving without insurance.

"Do you ever dream of a better life?" the reporter asks.

She shrugs.

She doesn't watch the van carry her two friends away. She just sits in front of the house with the For Rent sign and the broken door, holding someone else's baby, and stares blankly at the vacant lot next door.

Language can be a little grander and still be simple. Consider this excerpt from Wallace Stegner's book, *Crossing to Safety.*

Sidney Lang looks at the door that is the only break in the wall of shingles facing him. Hoping that Charity might have been watching for him, he waits for it to open. But the longer he waits, the more he is convinced that that door has not been opened in years. It looks rusted shut and mossed over. A plank walk leads around the cottage on the right-hand side. To welcome him from there, Charity would have to come out in the rain.

For a few minutes more he waits, imagining her under a big umbrella, dazzling the downpour with her smile. She does not appear. No one appears. He hears only the steady patter and rustle and drip of rain in the wet woods, and the gush of water from the downspout at the corner. The woods around him are an intense, wet green. Even the air is green.

Eventually, reluctantly, he reaches his slicker from the back seat, shawls it over head and shoulders, opens the door, sets his L. L. Bean moccasins down on the drenched grass, and is committed. Hunching, he hurries around the house on the slippery walk. From around the corner he hears the steady sound of a woman's voice.

Stegner uses words that are simple, descriptive, and familiar to create a picture of the rain-drenched woods and Sidney Lang's uncertainty about what kind of welcome he will receive from Charity.

The Right Word

Wordsmiths such as the late Theodore Bernstein and the late John Bremner have long decried the lack of precision in language. Bremner lamented what he called "the surge of literary barbarism" in English usage. Both stressed the importance of knowing language and definitions. In his book *Words on Words,* Bremner wrote

To love words, you must first know what they are. Yes, words are symbols of ideas. But many words have lives of their own. They have their own historical and etymological associations, their own romantic and environmental dalliances, their own sonic and visual delights.

To language craftsmen like Bremner, writing is a love affair with language.

A careless writer describes a basketball player as "an intricate part of the team." Perhaps his footwork is intricate, but what the writer really meant to say was "an integral part of the team."

A letter from a university provost to a newspaper columnist thanked her for "the prospective" she gave to a local issue. The provost meant "perspective."

In a news story, a student quoted a professor as saying, "The meeting will be a great opportunity for faculty members to mingle with their piers." Professors overboard!

Language needs to be specific and correct. Television personality Archie Bunker spouted malapropisms: words that didn't say what he meant. Oriental was ornamental, and distinguished was extinguished. We laughed. As writers, we do not want our audiences laughing at us—unless we mean for them to chuckle.

Similar Words

Words that sound alike are troublesome for writers. Among the most common homonyms are principal and principle, affect and effect, its and it's. Such words are particularly troublesome today, when writers depend heavily on computer spell-checkers. Few programs will know the difference between "naval" and "navel" or "stationary" and "stationery." The resulting confusion can be misleading and embarrassing. Writers must be comfortable in reaching for a good dictionary or other reference book to check correct spelling and usage. Other references, such as those listed at the end of this chapter, are valuable for writers who are choosy about words. Appendix C discusses spelling in the computer age.

Writers should pay heed to synonyms. Many writers haul out the thesaurus when they are weary of using a word too often. But a synonym may not be specific. One editing teacher advises against using a thesaurus and prefers a dictionary. Remember that repetition of a word or words throughout a message is acceptable. Repetition can unify a message. Use the word *bank* throughout a news release about the opening of a financial institution's 78th branch bank. It unifies the release, and bank is more specific than facility.

Word Choice

While taking care with word usage, writers should strive to choose words that are universally accepted and understood. If they are unsure about a word or its use, they should consult a stylebook or a dictionary. *The Associated Press Stylebook,* for example, adds cautionary notes about how specific words included in its entries should be used. The note might warn that the word is offensive or derogatory. Dictionaries will include in the definition whether the word is below the normal standard for literate writing. Dictionaries also will indicate spellings of words and correct usage, as in the case of homonyms.

If a dictionary or a stylebook warns against usage of a word, as profanity perhaps, writers should use it only if they have a compelling reason. They may also have to explain in a note at the beginning of the article or the broadcast that the message contains offensive language. Using profanities and vulgarities is discussed more fully in Chapter 10 on quotations and attribution.

Sentences

Sentences should be complete. Each must have a subject and a verb and must state one complete idea, thought, or meaning. Granted, some writers use short but incomplete sentences for emphasis, such as "The day he left was cold and in the dead of winter. January 22, to be exact." Sentence fragments or stray phrases generally have little place in straight writing, and beginning writers should avoid using them.

This is a fragment: "January 22, to be exact."

This is a sentence: "The day he left was cold and in the dead of winter."

This is a sentence: "That day was January 22, to be exact."

Sentence Types

Grammarians define different types of sentences on the basis of structure.

- A simple sentence is one independent or main clause. It can have more than one subject and verb, object, and modifying phrase.

  ```
  Five people died Wednesday in a skiing accident in
  France.
  ```

```
A local businessman has won a national award for
implementing an innovative employee benefits program.
```

- A compound sentence has two or more simple sentences that may be joined by a conjunction such as "and" or "but" or by punctuation such as a semicolon.

```
Fire destroyed a historic landmark in downtown Midland
Tuesday, but the owners said they will rebuild the
bookstore on the site.
```

```
Many people have changed their diets to cut out high-
fat foods; others have ignored warnings that a high-fat
diet can cause heart disease.
```

- A complex sentence has at least one independent or main clause and other clauses that are dependent on the main clause.

```
When the school board meets Monday night, it will vote
on a controversial multicultural plan that some
elementary school students' parents fear will focus on
sexual orientation as well as on ethnic diversity.
```

- A compound-complex sentence is a compound sentence with at least two independent clauses and one or more dependent clauses.

```
The Democratic candidate for lieutenant governor has
raised almost $600,000 for his campaign, which has been
hard fought against the Republican incumbent, and he
expects supporters to contribute even more after he
completes a three-day tour across the state.
```

Vary Sentence Types

Good writers use a variety of sentence types, but they prefer the simple sentence. A good guideline is to use many simple sentences and to use compound sentences formed from short simple sentences.

Writers use complex sentences because of the need for attribution, amplification, and identification. But they work hard to avoid compound-complex sentences, saving them to express ideas that are difficult to state any other way.

Here's a good example of effective sentence variety from a *USA Today* story about young adults in Iran:

> —Suddenly a parade of BMWs screeches to a halt in front of a ritzy apartment building.
>
> Out jump dozens of young women, with only their faces showing over their black full-length veils.
>
> They enter blowing kisses to the well-groomed crowd, and they race toward a back room, giggling.
>
> Minutes later, they emerge in revealing bustiers, leather miniskirts, black high heels, gold earrings, and lots of Chanel No. 5.
>
> "Everything you see in a Los Angeles club you see here," says Hooman, 27, a Western-educated importer.

Notice that the first two sentences are simple and the third is compound. The fourth also is a simple sentence; even though it is a long list, it is easy to read because of its simple structure. Only the last sentence is complex, integrating three separate thoughts: You see many things in a Los Angeles club, you see those things here, and the attribution by Hooman, an importer.

Studies show that people of all ages and levels of education prefer simple sentences, in which subjects come before verbs and verbs before the remainder of the sentence. A series of simple sentences relaxes your readers or listeners and prepares them to encounter something more complex when it occurs in your text, as it inevitably will.

Look at the sentence variety in the story by Alison Delsite of *The Patriot-News* in Harrisburg, Pa. She uses a mix of complex sentences and simple sentences. Paragraph 4 is one complex sentence. But in the next paragraph a series of short, simple sentences carries the action.

Life-Saving Tickets Win Fame, But No Fortune

BY ALISON DELSITE

The Patriot-News

Patrick Gayle's lottery tickets weren't losers after all.

Not only did they help deflect a bullet and possibly save the Harrisburg man's life, they brought him a few days of fame and, maybe, a little extra cash.

Gayle was interviewed on CNN. Crews from TV's "Hard Copy" taped a segment outside the Allison Hill convenience store where he was shot.

He was interviewed for publications nationwide, including *The National Enquirer* and a lottery magazine in Florida. He did radio shows. "I told them, 'I feel blessed,'" Gayle says.

On April 23, Gayle was walking into a Regina Street store to play the Daily Number when he was struck by a bullet during a shooting that police say was a continuation of the long-standing Allison Hill-Uptown rivalry.

The bullet was deflected by a cigarette lighter and a wad of tickets in his shirt pocket. The lighter shattered. The tickets were tattered. The shirt had a hole in it. He wasn't injured.

The *Patriot-News* story about the shooting made the Associated Press' wire. Since then Gayle's phone has been ringing.

Edward Meyer, vice president for exhibits at Ripley's Believe It or Not, said Ripley's intends to do a cartoon on Gayle and hopes to purchase his tickets. For now, they are evidence, in the custody of Harrisburg police.

Meyer wouldn't say how much Ripley's would pay. "Probably a couple hundred dollars. Stories like this are right up our alley," he said. "We'll make it worth his while, but not make him rich." Gayle, a forklift driver, said he spends $40 a day on the lottery.

Meanwhile, the phone in Patrick Gaylor's home in Swatara Twp. also has been ringing.

It seems callers—including ones from TV's Montel Williams and Maury Povich shows—unable to find Gayle's number, have called Gaylor's instead.

"They ask, 'Are you the person who was shot and saved by a pack of lottery tickets?'" said Gaylor. "No," he laughs. "But I hope he makes a lot of money off it anyway."

(Reprinted with permission of *The Patriot-News*.)

Common Sentence Errors

In constructing sentences, some writers forget the rule of parallel structure. In writing, all parts of any list or series must be parallel—that is, if the first element in the list starts with a noun, all others must be nouns as well. For example, the structure of this sentence is not parallel:

```
Previous legislative agendas included the Family
Preservation Act, child protective services, and
extending to school boards the right to ban corporal
punishment.
```

Nouns in the list, "act" and "services," are not parallel with the verb form "extending." The sentence should be rewritten to read

```
Previous legislative agendas included the Family
Preservation Act, child protective services, and the right
of school boards to ban corporal punishment.
```

When writers start with a specific verb form, such as an infinitive with "to," they must keep the same format. The structure of the following sentence is not parallel:

```
The banquet is an occasion to reward corporations for
"family friendly" policies and recognizing volunteers and
the media.
```

It should be rewritten to read

```
The banquet is an occasion to reward corporations for
"family friendly" policies and to recognize volunteers.
```

Another common sentence error is the incorrect placement of modifying phrases or clauses. Such misplaced elements can lead to humorous and misleading sentences, such as the following:

```
After wheeling me into the operating room, a mask was
placed over my face.
```

```
The bank makes low-interest loans to individuals of any
size.
```

```
Mrs. Rogers was arrested shortly after 3 P.M. at the home
where the couple lived without incident.
```

Once spotted, modifier problems are easy to repair. Good writers train themselves to check modifier placement: Did the mask really wheel me into the operating room? Does the bank discriminate based on height and weight? Did the couple really live in the house without incident? The questions can be cleared up by quick rewriting:

```
After I was wheeled into the operating room, a mask was
placed over my face.
```

```
The bank makes low-interest loans of any size to
individuals.
```

```
Mrs. Rogers was arrested without incident shortly after 3
P.M. at the home where the couple lived.
```

A good sentence can never be interpreted to mean more than one thing. Linguists say it has a "single reading"—meaning that the reader never needs to go back and read it again to understand it. If the reader goes back, it should be to savor the quality of the writing. Good writing aims for a single reading, so that readers move unobstructed through messages to meaning.

Paragraphs—Short Paragraphs

Words become sentences, and sentences become paragraphs. English composition books devote entire chapters to the topic of writing good paragraphs.

But, as mentioned in Chapter 4, when writers are concerned with transmitting information quickly, their ideas about paragraphing change. A paragraph is a whole presentation or argument on a topic in an essay for an English composition or literature class, whereas in mass communication, a paragraph is a single fact, thought, or "sound bite." That single thought or idea may take several sentences to explain. In newswriting, paragraphs are often short to break up blocks of gray copy. Just as they do with short sentences, writers should vary their paragraphs.

Effective use of three graphs instead of one is shown in this sports story by *USA Today* writer Chuck Johnson:

> —Some major league players are in line to get rich quick over the next 10 days.
>
> The filing period for salary arbitration runs today through Jan. 14. A total of 113 players are eligible. Salary figures will be exchanged Jan. 18, and arbiters will hear cases Feb. 1–20.
>
> Atlanta, Montreal, St. Louis and Kansas City, with eight players each, have the most eligible to file.

Newspaper and magazine writers start a new graph to signal a new fact or a change of speaker—and sometimes just to give the reader a break. Readers appreciate white space in a publication, and frequent "graffing," as it is called, gives such visual relief by making space—literal and figurative—between ideas.

New Speaker Equals New Paragraph

One of the most useful functions of frequent graffing is that it effectively signals a change of speakers. Notice how *Washington Post* writer Paul Taylor moves smoothly from one quote to another, just by starting new graphs:

> —"Political advertising is so wretched that most of it wouldn't be approved by our own self-governing boards," Alexander Kroll, chairman and chief executive officer of Young & Rubicam, said at a recent ad industry luncheon here.
>
> "I think we need to ban political ads," Jay Chiat, chairman and chief executive officer of Chiat/Day/Mojo, which creates ads for Nissan and Reebok, said in an interview.

"The worst thing that has ever happened to the advertising business is political advertising," said Malcolm MacDougall, chairman of the Mac-Dougall Co.

With quotations, the short bursts provided by one-sentence graphs add a lively, conversational air to newswriting and hold the audience's attention. "New speaker, new graph" is a writer's rule that can add clarity to all writing.

Most writing can benefit from shorter paragraphs. Bite-sized paragraphs may not be appropriate in all settings, but leaner paragraphs tend to streamline messages of all kinds and to save time and space, the most precious resources in any mass medium.

Where We Are

For many beginning writers, thinking about rules stymies them from the start. But let's summarize what we have said so far about good writing.

1. Good writing uses short sentences.
2. Good writing uses short words.
3. Good writing eliminates wordiness.
4. Good writing clears away redundancy, jargon, and institutional language.
5. Good writing comes to the point quickly.
6. Good writing has a mix of sentence types.
7. Good writing has short paragraphs.

When listed, the rules seem more manageable.

The Way to Clearer Writing

Writing often moves from the general to the specific, and this chapter is following such a path. At the outset, we discussed broad principles of accuracy, clarity, and completeness. We then looked at the basic tenets of good writing and the components of any piece of writing: words, sentences, and paragraphs.

Now for the specifics. Additional guidelines can help you say it straight. Keep the guidelines in mind as you write, but do not be so tied to them that you stop after every sentence to analyze whether it meets the standards of good writing. Go ahead and write, then go back and apply the guidelines in editing.

Write the First Draft As You Would Say It

Writing coach Robert Gunning said writers should write the way they talk. He argued that all writing would improve if people simply talked and wrote down what they said. Gunning was onto a great idea: First drafts are most effective when a writer puts down on paper what he or she would tell someone about a topic. Most people talk in subject–verb–object order that is easy to understand. The result is text that is conversational, uses simple language, and is easy to revise into a well-organized written message.

Author Tom Wolfe made his fiction writing career by writing the way he talked. You can see his colorful style in the following section.

Colorful Description

In his speech to the American Society of Newspaper Editors, Wolfe noted the phenomenon of the "trophy" wife, what the successful chief executive officer believes he deserves as a perk. He described the courtship ritual, adding his characteristic style, this way:

> . . . the sight out on the discotheque floor of the 57-year-old CEO with his trophy wife-to-be. He's wearing his hard-finished worsted navy blue chalk-striped suit. He's wearing his medium spread-collar white shirt . . . and he's wearing his hair combed back over his ears in little sloops known as the 57th Street biggie look. His trophy wife-to-be, his lemon tart, is out there, and she's wearing a pair of Everlast boxing trunks. She's got on a man's strap style undershirt. She's got a hairdo that looks as if a Snapper lawnmower's gone over her head . . . .
>
> And he's beaming at her with red eyes through these walnut shell eyelids. . . . He's desperately trying to do the robot or the eel or the sadomacho until the onset of dawn, saline depletion, or myocardial infarction—or whichever comes first. And after all, why shouldn't he? Because what are Mom and the Cutlass Sierra

and Buddy and Sis up against a love like this? That first night on the disco floor,
she wore a pair of boxing trunks while leather punks and painted lulus, African
queens and sado Zulus paid her court. I grow old, the 1990s way. Deaf but from
a Max Q octophonic beat. Stroked out but on my own two feet. Disco macho for
you, my new cookie.

Don't Begin at the Beginning

After seeing a four-car collision, the typical observer arrives home and blurts
out, "I saw an incredible wreck on Highway 501. Four cars collided; all the
drivers were injured, and one car burned." Only then will the observer back
up and give background: "I was in the left lane, coming home from the
mall," and so on.

Like urgent conversation, writing needs to jump straight to the point,
then fill the reader in—just as we discussed in Chapter 3 on writing leads.
This technique gives writing a conversational tone and at the same time gets
to the ever-so-important point of the message.

Starting with salient facts is a natural way to tell about important information. Unfortunately, it is a form that most people forget after years of
reading stories and writing essays, both of which usually start with formal
introductions. If your goal is to say it straight, say it—your main point—soon
in your message. Suspenseful beginnings work best in drama.

Writing and Editing: Two Compatible Tasks

When you spill out your conversational first draft, write it without stopping
to edit. Mixing writing and editing wastes time and effort. If you edit as you
go (and most amateurs do), you may fuss over a sentence that you eventually
eliminate. At the very least, you will interrupt your own thought processes and
conversational flow. So write first. If you pause to ponder sentence structure or
information, that's okay. But do not wander or stray from the effort.

Some beginning writers lack the confidence to sit down and write. But
author Joel Saltzman points out that we all are more competent wordsmiths
than we think:

When you're talking, odds are that 98 percent of the time you don't even think
about grammar. You're doing fine and it's just not an issue. . . . I am suggesting

*that you don't worry about it right now; because the more you worry about gram-
mar, the less you're going to write.*

After you finish your outpouring of prose, let the copy cool by taking a
short break before you begin to edit. This separates the writing and editing
processes and allows you to see your copy in a different way. If you edit or
rewrite immediately after your draft is finished, you will read what you think
you wrote rather than what is actually on the page. More about the editing
process is covered in Chapter 6.

Stick with Subject–Verb Order

Most human languages prefer to place subjects before verbs, and English is
no exception. Curious people want to know who did something, then what
they did (and to whom or what). Keep these audience interests and preferences in mind when you write. Subject–verb–object order generally gives
the sentence action.

```
A man wearing a stocking mask robbed the University dining
hall late Tuesday night and locked the dining services
manager in a closet.

A massive earthquake registering 6.8 on the Richter scale
rocked Japan early Tuesday morning.
```

Readers get confused if subjects and verbs are scrambled, regardless of
how artistic the result may be.

```
"Came he swiftly to her bower?"
```

Not in the information age.

Choose Active Verbs

We learn that verbs are action words, but not all verbs are active. Some show
no action at all, such as the verb "to be" in all its forms (is, am, are, was,
were, be, being). Such verbs are less interesting and harder to picture than
active verbs.

Writers prefer active verbs because they contain more information and sensory detail. "He was president" is vague compared with "He dominated the country as president." Good writing is filled with active verbs that evoke images in the mind of the reader or listener.

```
Lightner whacked the ball with such force that it sailed
over the outfield wall—his first home run of the season.

Babies cried, children clamored, balls thunked into
holes, tickets ching-ching-chinged into eager
hands, the noise competing against the Chuck E. Cheese
theme song in the background.
```

Choose the Active Voice

When writers use active verbs, they write in active voice.

"Lightner hit the ball." The subject, Lightner, performs the action. The object, the ball, receives action. This sentence format is called active voice, and it is the natural order of English. "A man wearing a stocking mask robbed the University dining hall" carries more action than "the University dining hall was robbed by a man."

Every now and then, a sentence has no obvious subject and must be written in another format, called the passive voice. Take, for example, this sentence: "The law was changed several years ago." It is in passive voice. The recipient of the action, the law, has been moved into the subject position—probably because a long legislative process kept the writer from isolating a single person or session responsible for changing the law.

Research shows that people prefer active sentences over passive ones. The sentence "Congress passed the bill" is easier to read and comprehend than its passive equivalent, "The bill was passed by Congress." Skilled writers prefer the active voice and use passive sentences only when necessary. In our example about Lightner, a passive structure would hardly have the same impact: "The ball was hit by Lightner."

Sometimes writers use passive sentences for emphasis: "The anticrime bill was passed by Congress." Here the writer wants to focus on the provisions of the bill rather than on Congressional action and writes the lead accordingly.

Generally Put Time Elements after the Verb

Because verbs are stimulating to readers, they should come before less interesting elements. Audiences need to know when something happened, but they can wait to find out. The time element, a necessary but often dull part of a message, can be relegated to a place after the verb. Some writers prefer to put it immediately after the verb. Here are a few examples:

```
Former Mayor Barry Anderson was married Tuesday morning in
a small private ceremony.

Grant applications requesting up to $100,000 for research
on learning disabilities may be submitted through June 15
to the National Institutes of Health.
```

Sometimes, however, the time element carries importance and needs to go elsewhere—even first in the sentence.

```
Wednesday a 14-year-old youth collected $125,000 that he
found in a paper bag a year ago. The money was never
claimed.
```

In this example, the beginning and end of the sentence set up the time span: On Wednesday the youth cashed in after waiting a year.

```
Beginning this weekend the city planetarium will offer
extra weekend shows to expand its offerings for people who
work and school children.
```

Right away, people know that an event is coming soon.

Be Specific Rather Than General

Always give the most specific information you can. Significant details enlighten and delight readers and pack information into a few words. Instead of saying that model and actress Elizabeth Hurley went shopping, tell what she bought: cosmetics. What kind? Inquiring minds want to know! Instead of saying that a reporter had a messy desk, try

```
On his desk Howard had a can of unsharpened pencils and two
potted ferns, both of them dead.
```

Watch out for words that have almost a generic quality, such as facility. Be specific: bank, gymnasium, recreation center, high school. Use the specific noun.

Author Tom Wolfe has a marvelous talent for combining simple words into run-on, colorful, entertaining description, as you have just seen in the excerpt from his speech to the American Society of Newspaper Editors in 1990.

Appeal to the Senses

An audience, whether it is reading or listening, still can use the full range of senses as it absorbs information. That means writers must pay attention to their senses when gathering information. Writers can report the facts or describe the scene without being subjective—a fear that many beginning writers have and that keeps them from being descriptive in their writing.

Writing that appeals to the senses—that creates mental pictures, aromas, and sensations—is more memorable and more appealing; it transports the audience to the scene of the message. Once captured, the audience is likely to remain in the writer's world long enough to get the message.

Through writing that appeals to all the senses, *Washington Post* feature writers Patrice Gaines and DeNeen L. Brown take readers to an inner-city housing project in the following passage:

> Three days after lethal gunfire exploded at a nearby schoolyard and two hours before the mayor was to visit, maintenance men and female prisoners were cutting grass, trimming trees, and picking up litter at Fort Dupont Dwellings, a cluster of scarred, two-story brick buildings with Plexiglas windows.
>
> A school-crossing guard and some mothers who had just walked their children to school Tuesday morning were amused by all the raking, sweeping, and grooming. They found it especially comical—worthy of

loud, cynical laughter—that workers were cutting grass in front of buildings where no one lived.

"They do nothing until somebody gets shot, then they pacify us with two days of cleaning up," said a 53-year-old grandmother. For 28 years, she has lived in this apartment complex that was built in the 1940s to be a stopover for families expected to move out and up.

Fort Dupont Dwellings was home to Launice Smith, the 4-year-old girl who died yesterday after being shot in the head Saturday afternoon at a pickup football game at Weatherless Elementary School. The 300 block of Ridge Road, where Launice lived, is called "Little Vietnam" by some because of the popping sounds of gunfire nearly every night.

The reader sees the scarred buildings and dim Plexiglas, hears cynical laughter and gunshots, and even smells the freshly cut grass. No one would doubt the authenticity of the writers' description, which sets the scene and mood for the audience.

One need not be a feature writer to use sensory appeal. It works well in everyday forms of communication, such as directions to the company picnic. Instead of "turn right two blocks after the fork in the road and proceed to 1511," how about:

```
Look for a grove of tall pines two blocks after the fork in
the road; turn right and go to the red mailbox marked 1511.
You'll smell pungent smoke from Marvin's famous barbequed
ribs.
```

With such sensory appeal, it's doubtful that anyone will get lost.

Use Statistics Sparingly and Powerfully

We live in an era when numbers make powerful messages: A basketball arena will cost $121 million. A pharmaceutical company will lay off 1,600 workers.

Audiences become insensitive if they are bombarded by alarming numbers, regardless of how striking those numbers may be. Statistics of any kind should be delivered one at a time in good writing. Never let two numbers touch in written copy; avoid putting numbers close to one another except in direct comparisons:

> Women work 88 hours per week doing home and workplace
> chores, whereas men work about 60.

Another good rule of thumb is to limit yourself to no more than three numbers in any one paragraph to avoid overwhelming your reader or listener. In a business story, for example, numbers can be confusing, so spread them out and keep them simple.

> British Airways has become the largest carrier at Gatwick
> airport outside London, serving one-fourth of the
> airport's passengers. The airline company ticketed 7.4
> million passengers in 1997.

> British Airways' business was way ahead of the next highest
> carrier, Monarch Airlines, at 2 million passengers, and
> Britannia Airways at 1.8 million.

Professor Philip Meyer, who has been a consultant at *USA Today*, suggests that in any statistical report one or two numbers stand out as being crucial. The important numbers should appear early in your message, and others may be summarized in lists or tables outside the written text.

Translate Statistics into Everyday, Tangible Terms

People have little intuitive understanding of large numbers. The citizen who learns that a sports arena is to cost $121 million is left with many questions: Is that a good price for an arena? How many new schools would that buy? How much will my county taxes increase?

Good writers provide an understanding of big numbers in several ways. One way is to compare one number with another:

> The $121 million price tag compares with the $58.2 million
> cost of an arena built in 1989 in Springfield.

Another way to present numbers is to give them in terms the average person deals with each day. Few of us can visualize $121 million, but many people can understand a 3.5 percent tax increase to fund the stadium.

The clearest way to present costs is to use an individual citizen as an example:

```
A person owning a home with a tax value of $154,000 will
pay about $200 more each year in taxes to finance the
arena.
```

Such writing allows the audience to understand personal gains or losses that may be obscured in reports of large numbers.

Double-check Your Math

Many writers jokingly say they went into communications because they could not do math. But any writer needs to use numbers and must be sure they are correct. Errors can be embarrassing.

In a news story about salary increases at city hall, a reporter looked at the current year's salary for the city attorney: $65,000. The proposed salary for the next fiscal year was $69,000. The city attorney would get a 5 percent pay increase, she wrote. The actual increase was 6 percent. The reporter erroneously divided the difference of $4,000 by the new salary rather than the current salary. Other city employees were upset that the city attorney was getting 5 percent compared with their 2 percent. When the real difference eventually was published, the unhappiness grew. (And the city attorney expressed his anger that the figures were published at all, forgetting that the salaries of public officials are public record.)

When in Doubt, Leave It Out

Unless you are able to check the accuracy of a spelling or a surprising fact, leave it out or hold publication until you can check it. Accuracy is linked, in the minds of audience members, with quality—with company quality, publication quality, and writer quality. Your reputation is riding on what you write.

Some errors are painful to people in the community. A university magazine noted offhandedly that a famous scientist had discovered a new kind of plant. His research assistant, who in fact had made the discovery and received credit for it in scientific journals, called the reporter to correct the error. Few people will ever see a small correction notice, but people such as the offended research assistant will remember the slight for years.

Multiple copies of a mistake are always embarrassing, whether in an office memo or a front-page story. Such mistakes also may lead to legal problems. Appendix A gives libel guidelines for writers.

Rewrite Long Introductory Phrases

Audiences are eager to get to the point, and long introductory phrases slow them down. Long phrases also interrupt the subject–verb–object pattern that readers and listeners prefer.

Avoid:

```
Because the Redskins had been waiting all season for a
victory, several players refused to be interviewed.
```

Prefer:

```
Several Redskins players refused to be interviewed after
waiting all season for a victory.
```

Eliminate Long Strings of Prepositional Phrases

Any group of two or more prepositional phrases makes a sentence seem to meander rather than flow. Too many prepositional phrases strung together within a sentence are undesirable but easy to fix. Prepositional phrases are among the movable parts of any sentence; they also may be placed in new (short) sentences.

Avoid:

```
The school's marching band will appear in a series of
performances on three consecutive Tuesday afternoons on
```

```
the athletic field near the gymnasium on the school campus
beginning this Tuesday.
```

Prefer:

```
The school's marching band will present a series of Tuesday
afternoon performances beginning this week. The band will
play on the athletic field near the gymnasium.
```

Look for unnecessary prepositional phrases everywhere in writing. Take

```
Marilyn Jacobs, one of the writers of the letter, said the
group wants action immediately.
```

and edit it to read:

```
Marilyn Jacobs, who helped write the letter, said the group
wants action immediately.
```

Avoid Making Everything Look IMPORTANT

Some writers like to add emphasis by underlining text or by using capital letters, exclamation marks, and even quotation marks. Frequent use of such elements detracts from professional polish. Once in a while, everyone needs to add emphasis. Save it for when it *"REALLY"* counts. In some messages, such as e-mail, emphasis can be interpreted as anger, exasperation, and even sarcasm.

Avoid a message that looks like this sentence:

```
If you don't get your information sheet in today, you WON'T
be in the new directory AT ALL.
```

Try:

```
If you don't get your information sheet in today, you won't
be in the new directory.
```

Clear Out Euphemisms

Most of us were taught to use euphemisms in polite conversation—to say "expecting" rather than "pregnant," "plump" rather than "fat," and "passed away" rather than "died." In fact, we like euphemisms because they are handy substitutes for embarrassing words. In media, straight talk is preferred.
    Avoid:

```
The guard said that two residents of the correctional
facility had gone to "their just reward."
```

Prefer:

```
The guard said that two prisoners had died.
```

Using the straightforward words "prisoners" and "died" instead of the longer euphemisms keeps the sentence short and the reading easy.
    Good writing requires specific information. Most euphemisms are designed to be imprecise—to mislead or give false comfort. Never forget that "protective reactions strikes" are "bombings" and that "peacekeeper missiles" are "nuclear warheads." Both terms came into vogue with the politically correct language. Politically correct terms generally are longer and less accurate than the synonyms they replace. For example, a drunk is a "person of differing sobriety," and a loser is an "individual with temporarily unmet objectives." Writers have to draw the line between what is acceptable taste and what is a surrender to faddish writing. Those who are not in the politically correct circle may wonder what on earth the writer is saying. Once euphemisms are removed, the meaning is clear and timeless.

Keep Writing Readable

Readability is defined most simply as the level of difficulty of a given message. Readable, or high-readability, writing is easy to understand. Several ways to measure readability have been found, most of which are based on (1) sentence length and (2) concentration or number of multisyllable words.
    One common readability measure is the Fog Index, developed in the 1940s by Robert Gunning for United Press International wire service. Despite its age, the Fog Index is still used as a measure of readability. To compute a Fog

Index, (1) calculate the average number of words per sentence in a given message and (2) count the number of difficult words, or those with three syllables or more, in a 100-word sample from the message. Add these two figures together and multiply by 0.4.

The resulting number—the Fog Index for the writing in question—corresponds to the number of years of education a reader would need to read and understand the copy. For example, a publication with an average of 22 words per sentence and 15 difficult words in the 100-word sample would have a Fog Index of 14.8. That means its readers would require some college education to read the piece comfortably.

Let's see how that works on the Patrice Gaines piece about Fort Dupont Dwellings. Seven sentences have 199 words or an average of 28 words per sentence. Words with three syllables or more in the first 100 words number 6. Add 28 to 6 and multiply by 0.4; the answer is 13.6. The Gaines piece does not have high readability because of the long sentences. Only six of 100 words have three or more syllables, so her preference for simple words keeps the readability between high school and college level. That is consistent with *The Washington Post*'s overall style.

Most readability experts agree that clear writing is geared to the eleventh- and twelfth-grade level. Even people with a great deal more education seem to be most comfortable reading at this level. Journalism Professor Fred Fedler notes that most wire service copy is written at about the tenth-grade level. Many grammar-check software packages have readability measures that automatically tell writers the readability of any piece.

The Wall Street Journal's Fog Index routinely falls into the eleventh- to twelfth-grade range, despite the complicated nature of financial reporting. A clever marketing strategy is operating here: Dow Jones knows that to make business reports palatable, they must be readable.

Be Aware of Misinterpretations

As writers edit their copy they need to be aware of all possible interpretations of what has been written. They need to know an audience's language tastes for effective communication. Language choices can alter meaning for the reader or put a different slant on a message—often a slant that the writer never intended. Sometimes the results are comical, such as a ship was "birthed" instead of "berthed" at a nearby naval station, or a mother who wants "piece of mind." Think about the sentence, "Donations may be given by church members of any size." The size of the donations, not of church members, is the issue.

A prepositional phrase in the wrong place can change the meaning. Lacey Smith died of a head wound at Memorial Hospital at 4 P.M. Wednesday. What the writer meant was that Lacey Smith died Wednesday afternoon at Memorial Hospital after suffering a head wound. Smith had the head wound before arriving at the hospital; Smith was not wounded by hospital personnel. "The thief was muscular with a round face about 5 feet 3 inches tall." How tall was the thief?

Watch out for Language Trends

Writers should avoid popular trends in writing. As we noted earlier in the discussion of avoiding euphemisms, the politically correct movement substituted a myriad of words and phrases for ones that had been part of common language. In many cases, the new language was wordy and less precise.

The use of such "pop" language excludes segments of the audience that may not be cued to the lingo. Certainly language evolves. Each time a new edition of Webster's dictionary comes out, new words are included. Many of us can remember when "ain't" was not in the dictionary. Dictionaries list and define words that are common in the English language, but a dictionary is just one of many sources writers use.

One trend that has caused extreme pain to language experts is the conversion of nouns to verbs. Host has become "to host," and conference has become "to conference." With computer use increasing, the media use soon will be standard. Many computer terms already are accepted usage, but some writers still cringe when they hear words such as "input."

Another trend that offends many writers is the addition of "-ize" to create new words: prioritize, finalize, maximize, accessorize. Again, although the words have found their way into everyday usage, language professionals try to find better and more accurate verbs.

How the Rules Apply

Overwhelmed by so many rules? Keep them in the back of your mind while you do the most important task of all: Write! Then go back to your draft and apply the principles. Remember: You'll never need all the rules at once.

For practice, let's take a real-life letter, with names and places changed, that defies the guidelines in this chapter. It is neither clear nor correct; it is wordy and indirect. In short, it's a mess.

```
Mr. and Mrs. Joe Dighton
103 Roberts Road
Silver Springs, Md. 20901

Dear Joe and Patti:

I do hope you enjoyed your recent visit to THE CLIFFS
retirement community and THANK YOU for taking the time to
look at our community. I thoroughly enjoyed visiting with
you and Patti last evening and do hope you folks will
decide to become a part of "Our Family."

While Rand McNally has named us the second best place in
America to retire because we have the 20th lowest cost of
living, third best health care and ranked us a bargain in
housing costs. They also ranked us as the Nation's safest
community, boasting a practically nonexistent crime rate.
Nestled in the foothills of the Blue Ridge Mountains in
Swain County, North Carolina, and surrounded by two scenic
rivers and a national forest is a location that provides
the best of GOD's creation for spending lazy days of
fishing, swimming boating, hiking or hunting. If you prefer
our tennis/swimming complex or 18-hole championship golf
course designed by Dan Birch is most enjoyable.

Our developer has endeavored to create a community for
middle class America based on traditional family values
centering on a family atmosphere and our backgrounds are
varied from physicians, engineers, farmers, government
employees, retired military and the list goes on . . .
```

```
If I can be of further assistance or you have friends—or
know of someone—looking for what we have to offer please
give me a call.
```

```
                    Sincerely,

                    Donna Sales

                    Marketing Director
```

Needless to say, Joe and Patti were unimpressed by the letter from The Cliffs. What can you fix, now that you have all this chapter's advice on writing? Can you help Donna Sales to "say it straight"?

Here's a list of some problems with her letter:

- Too much is made IMPORTANT by Overuse of Capitalization.
- Donna has made an error in logic: The letter is to both Joe and Patti, but the writer stumbles in saying, "I enjoyed talking with you and Patti."
- Too many statistics are mentioned too quickly, and they do not appear in parallel form. Also, they are not comprehensible: Is the resort 20th from the highest cost of living—meaning that it is expensive— or is it 20th from the lowest cost?
- Joe and Patti's hometown, Silver Spring, is misspelled in a way that most Silver Spring residents find particularly tiresome. (Silver Springs is a place in Florida where people ride in glass-bottom boats.)
- Most sentences begin with long introductory phrases.
- Most sentences are too long, complex, and confusing.
- The second paragraph is too long.
- The letter is wordy throughout and has a Fog Index of 14.8.

You may want to add to the list, but let us focus on simplifying the language, shortening the sentences, lowering the Fog Index, and clearing up the confusion. Here's a rewritten version:

```
Patti and Joe Dighton

103 Roberts Road

Silver Spring, Md. 20901
```

Dear Patti and Joe:

I hope you enjoyed your recent visit to The Cliffs. Thank you for taking time to look at our community. I enjoyed visiting with you both and hope you will decide to become part of The Cliffs family of residents.

Rand McNally has named us the second best place in America to retire to because of our reasonable costs for high-quality health care and housing. It also has ranked us the nation's safest retirement community.

The Cliffs, nestled in the foothills of the Blue Ridge Mountains in Swain County, N.C., is bounded by two scenic rivers and is next to a national park. This is an ideal location for retirement, providing the best of God's creation for your days of fishing, swimming, boating, hiking, or hunting. You may also enjoy our tennis and swimming complex or our 18-hole championship golf course, which was designed by Dan Birch.

Our developer has created a community with traditional family values and a warm, family-like atmosphere. Our residents have varied occupational backgrounds, including medicine, engineering, farming, and military and government service.

Please give me a call if I can answer your questions about The Cliffs, or if I can help any of your friends who are looking for what we have to offer.

> Sincerely,
>
> Donna Sales
> Marketing Director

If Patti and Joe had received the revised letter, they might have given The Cliffs another look.

The long sentences are divided, and the long paragraph splits naturally into two. The result is a more inviting letter. The new Fog Index is 10.9, which Gunning would applaud. Most important, The Cliffs appears to be a well-run enterprise. And the only difference is in the writing.

Consider this newspaper story:

A Grove City–area woman has been accused of rigging her ex-husband's washing machine in hopes of torching him and his trailer for the insurance money.

State police at Mercer last week arrested Valerie Norine Lagun, claiming the 43-year-old had hoped to kill a semidisabled Thomas Lagun in May when he turned on his washer. She was charged with attempted murder, attempted arson and recklessly endangering another person.

Free on $10,000 bond, Mrs. Lagun is again living with her 57-year-old ex-husband at her home at 458 Blacktown Road, Pine Township, detective Robert Lewis said Tuesday.

"They're still using the washing machine," Lewis said.

According to court papers at District Justice Larry Silvis' Worth Township office, Mrs. Lagun told police she conspired with another man in the plot. She agreed to pay him half of the $5,000 from Lagun's life insurance policy and $10,000 from their renter's insurance.

Police didn't name the man—described as an acquaintance of Mrs. Lagun—because he hasn't been charged, Lewis said. Police know of his whereabouts but are still gathering evidence in hopes of charging him, Lewis said.

According to court papers:

Mrs. Lagun told police she took the man to Lagun's trailer at 169 Jamison Road, Worth Township, after dark.

Once inside, the man wired three bottles containing gasoline to the washing machine. A flip of the washer's switch should have ignited the fire.

"It could've exploded and probably killed him if it blew up. The potential was there," Lewis said.

Lagun discovered the gasoline after an electrical breaker tripped when he attempted to use the machine, according to court papers. He reported the incident to police, and Mrs. Lagun confessed July 24.

She told police she was surprised the explosive didn't work, but happy that her ex-husband wasn't killed, according to court papers.

Mrs. Lagun has a preliminary hearing at 1 P.M. Jan. 8 before Silvis.

The story has compelling interest: potential death, oddity in alleged method of killing someone, human interest because the ex-husband and wife are still living together despite the charges, and the twist about the washing machine.

Consider this rewrite that includes most of the original information. But it is rewritten to apply good writing rules and reorganized in an hourglass format to pull readers through the story and reward them at the end:

A Grove City–area woman has been accused of rigging her ex-husband's washing machine to explode, killing him and destroying his trailer so she could collect the insurance money. But that's not where the story ends.

Valerie Norine Lagun, 43, was arrested last week by police who claim she had hoped to kill semidisabled Thomas Lagun in May when he turned on his washer. She was charged with attempted murder, attempted arson and recklessly endangering another person.

Mrs. Lagun is free on $10,000 bond and has a preliminary hearing at 1 P.M. Jan. 8 before District Justice Larry Silvis.

According to court papers, Mrs. Lagun told police she conspired with another man and agreed to pay him half of the $5,000 from Lagun's life insurance policy and $10,00 from their renter's insurance.

The man—described as an acquaintance of Mrs. Lagun—hasn't been charged, detective Robert Lewis said Tuesday. Police know of his whereabouts but are still gathering evidence and hope to charge him.

Mrs. Lagun told police she took the man to Lagun's trailer at 169 Jamison Road, Worth Township, after dark. The man wired three bottles containing gasoline to the washing machine. A flip of the washer's switch should have ignited the fire, according to court papers.

Lagun discovered the gasoline after an electrical breaker tripped when he attempted to use the machine, according to court papers. He reported the incident to police, and Mrs. Lagun confessed July 24.

"It could've exploded and probably killed him if it blew up. The potential was there," Lewis said.

Mrs. Lagun told police she was surprised the explosive didn't work, but happy that her ex-husband wasn't killed, according to court papers.

Despite the charges, Mrs. Lagun is again living with her 57-year-old ex-husband at her home at 458 Blacktown Road, Pine Township.

And, noted detective Lewis, "They're still using the washing machine."

The following exercises will require you to apply the guidelines in this chapter, just as we did in The Cliffs and the above newspaper examples. When you have completed them, take a message you constructed during the last week and rewrite it to be clearer and simpler. Chapter 6 will review the steps of editing to make the task more manageable.

EXERCISES

- Change the words used incorrectly in the following sentences.

  1. The perspective budget for the coming year will include raises for the city's firemen.
  2. An incoming ice storm will effect whether we can drive to work tomorrow.
  3. The state historical society will reenact signing the state constitution in the Capital.
  4. The country's navel force has been reduced.
  5. His desire for money is his principle guiding force in business.
  6. The coach said the team ignored his advise to make it a passing game.
  7. Jiminy Cricket said Pinocchio should let his conscious be his guide.
  8. The engineer eliminated the High Road sight because it sloped to much.
  9. Returning the stolen car to it's owner is the best decision.
  10. The most affective writing follows good writing principals.

- Edit the following sentences to make them shorter and to the point.

  11. In order to expedite the delivery, the company will add a third delivery truck for its routes on Monday.

12. We will have pizza for dinner whether or not you choose to come.

13. She is presently employed as the assistant to the president, but she expects to make a decision whether or not to change jobs by the end of the year.

14. If they are willing to pay the difference between the economy pack and the family pack, customers will learn that the family pack will save them more money in the long run.

15. Students voted Thursday to conduct a poll to determine the status of living conditions in dormitories.

16. Clarendon Park residents will march Saturday to protest the city council's decision to annex the neighborhood over residents' objections.

17. If the school maintains lines of communication and makes the alumni feel as if they are still a part of the school even though they have already graduated, the school should have no problem reaching its fund-raising goal.

18. The residents of the neighborhood said they would petition the city council to reconsider again the decision to allow beer sales before 11 A.M. on Sunday morning, which would be against the wishes of many church-going citizens.

19. Fifteen scholarship winners, who were chosen because of their high academic achievement, will be given $15,000 in scholarship money to use at the college of their choice after they graduate from high school.

20. Child-care experts disagree over whether or not children should be spanked as part of a parent's disciplinary techniques or whether or not putting children in a time-out away from activities is punishment enough.

• Correct the grammar and punctuation problems in the following sentences.

21. He will likely have the money to attend the fund-raising gala and becoming a sponsor.

22. The organization's goals are to educate the medical community about the disease; attract 400 new members this year; support those who have the disease and encourage more research.

23. As an environmentalist, his efforts focused on the University's South Loop Road plan to save trees, green space and the University's student–family housing development.
24. She paid $35—half the savings in her piggy bank, for the Rush t-shirts at the concert.
25. Setting the meeting for 2 P.M., the time should be agreeable to all participants.
26. The committee of financial consultants and economic experts have to develop a plan to reduce the corporation's debt.
27. Irene uses coupons when she goes to the grocery store; saving $3 to $4 each trip.
28. It is a difficult plan for a politician to explain to their constituents.
29. The program offers workshops for child day care teachers on positive discipline as well as conducts community issues forums and workplace seminars.

- Edit to eliminate redundancy.

30. Susan is currently director of marketing sales.
31. He served as past president of the Rotary club.
32. The elementary school will need twenty-five acres of land for a multipurpose building, playground, and ball fields.
33. Fire completely destroyed the town hall in the month of June.
34. The future outlook for the economy indicates interest rates may rise slightly.
35. The circus will be at 3 P.M. Sunday afternoon and 7 P.M. Sunday night.
36. Due to the fact that more than two-thirds of the people did not respond, the picnic will be canceled.
37. She climbed up the tree in order to get a better look at the defendant.
38. John went on to say that any student's effort should be recognized.
39. The Broadway show will close down six months after it first began.

- Edit the following story to eliminate redundancy and wordiness. Simplify words where possible.

A group of local parents have asked the administrators of the town recreation program to close a town swimming pool unless safety conditions at the pool are improved next summer.

Parents said they are particularly upset over the drowning death of a 5-year-old boy in the shallow end of the pool in August.

In a letter addressed to the assistant town manager, Renee Lovelace, the parents also said that they were concerned because the pool had too few lifeguards and because they felt lifeguards needed to improve the treatment of children.

"We are especially upset about the treatment of children at the pool last summer," said Irma Middleton, one of the writers of the letter. "We would rather drive our children to other pools than have them go to a pool where they are not safe."

The letter said that the town needs to hire a pool manager who is a strict disciplinarian. The town also needs to hire more lifeguards.

The letter writers also noted that when the child drowned to death last summer, three lifeguards were at the pool but only two on duty.

"There's no earthly reason why a child should drown in a pool with lifeguards on duty," said Middleton.

Lovelace said the town would take under consideration the parents' concerns. She was in agreement that more lifeguards should be hired, she added.

The town's pools are scheduled to reopen after Memorial Day weekend.

- Correct any punctuation problems in the following sentences:

40. "I'm very impressed with Clinton," said Judy Aronson, a post-doctoral fellow at UNC Hospitals, "he seems like he's thought things out."

41. Retired nursing assistant Phoebe Alston feels the campaign had too much mudslinging.

42. People were asked, whom did they vote for and why.

43. Greg Dreher, 18, a University freshman said he was voting for Bush because he thought the economy would suffer at the hands of Clinton and other Democrats.

44. Tracie Ray, 20, a junior from New Jersey, said the committee of young Republicans had their obvious favorite.

45. Heather Jones, a sophomore from Broadway, said, "I'm not happy with the campaigns at all and I voted for Clinton because he maintained a sense of honesty in the campaign."

46. People came out to vote in high numbers, and poll workers said they had to remain long after the polls were closed.

47. Martha Ellison said, "Voting is a privilege. I have never missed a vote, and I hope I never will."

48. A low voter turnout is not understood in countries where people have just received the vote said the media analyst.

REFERENCES

Henry Beard and Christopher Cerf, *The Official Politically Correct Dictionary and Handbook*. New York: Villard Books, 1992.

Theodore M. Bernstein, *Dos, Don'ts and Maybes of the English Language*. New York: The Times Book Co., 1977.

John Bremner, *Words on Words*. New York: Columbia University Press, 1980.

E. L. Callihan, *Grammar for Journalists*. Radnor, PA: Chilton Book Company, 1979.

Claire Kehrwald Cook, *Line by Line: How to Improve Your Own Writing*. Boston: Houghton Mifflin, 1985.

Fred Fedler, *Reporting for the Print Media*. New York: Harcourt Brace Jovanovich, 1989.

Robert Gunning, *The Technique of Clear Writing*. New York: McGraw-Hill, 1954.

Nora Ephron, "Writers' Workshop," video series produced by South Carolina Educational Television, 1980.

Norm Goldstein (Ed.), *The Associated Press Stylebook and Libel Manual*. New York: The Associated Press, 1997.

Lauren Kessler and Duncan McDonald, *When Words Collide*. Belmont, CA: Wadsworth Publishing, 1992.

Ernie Pyle, *Here Is Your War,* New York: Pocket Books, 1945.

Wallace Stegner, *Crossing to Safety*. New York: Penguin Books, 1987.

Carl Sessions Stepp, excerpt from videotape, "Taking Charge of Your Local Paper," National Rural Electric Cooperatives Association, Washington, DC, March 1993.

Tom Wolfe, excerpt from transcribed speech to American Society of Newspaper Editors, Washington, DC, April 1990.

William Zinsser, *On Writing Well*. New York: Harper & Row, 1976.

6

Editing and
Polishing Writing

Dear God, I like the Lord's prayer best of all. Did you have to write it a lot or did you get it right the first time? I have to write everything I ever write over again. Lois.

So goes a letter in *Children's Letters to God,* a collection by Stuart Hample and Eric Marshall. Lois has learned a lesson early and is way ahead of many writers. Many student or beginning writers assume that a writing job is finished once they get a message down on paper. But experienced writers know that writing is only a first step, and a small step at that.

The first writing is called a first draft because whatever is written initially—be it a letter, a memo, a news release, a televised announcement, an online news brief, or a radio ad—is never as clear and polished as it could be, and it is never the finished copy.

A first draft is a rough, almost private stage of writing. North Carolina novelist and English professor Doris Betts tells students, "Handing in your first draft is like passing around your spittle"—in other words, unprofessional and offensive.

Between the first draft and the finished product comes editing. The first draft should be as good as you can create it. Just because you will edit does not allow you to be sloppy or careless on the first go-round. Editing will refine and improve that first effort.

This chapter looks at

- The steps of editing,
- The importance of style,
- Basic style rules, and
- Copyediting symbols.

Editing, Editing, Editing

All writers must know how to edit. As Claire Kehrwald Cook notes in her book, *Line by Line: How to Improve Your Own Writing:*

> *In correcting your own work, you have a free hand. You don't need editorial delicacy and diplomacy. You only need editorial skills that will enable you to look objectively at what you have written. If you can master them, you can do more to improve your writing than anyone else can.*

As a writer you are responsible for editing and revising your own work, even if you work on a newspaper staff or in a large corporate communications office where others also will edit your work. You are the originator, the one who must shape and streamline the initial draft. The draft must be clear, accurate, and complete when it leaves your hands.

An editor can catch inconsistencies and grammatical errors and can ask questions to make the draft more complete. But an editor may not know enough about the subject to find all inaccuracies, or may be harried because of a deadline and not have time to correct all flaws. Eventually, you may be an executive who must communicate policies to staff members, or you may be the sole information specialist within a nonprofit organization. No one else is likely to fix your writing and improve it.

As you gain experience as a writer, you also will be asked to revise the work of others. You may be promoted to an editing position or solicited by others who know less than you do about good writing skills.

Editing is hard work, and it is time-consuming. It can be creative and satisfying. But, in any case, it has to be done.

William Strunk wrote *The Elements of Style,* a brief but pointed book on how to improve writing. Much of the material is still pertinent more than seventy years after it was written. Strunk's student, E. B. White, remembered the book from class and in 1935 had it published. White, who wrote the foreword, never forgot the advice of his mentor. He once told an interviewer that he rewrote essays as many as fourteen times before they were published. He spent three years writing the popular children's book, *Charlotte's Web,* and almost twelve years writing *Stuart Little.*

Anyone who reads *The Elements of Style* can see that each word is carefully selected to say just what Strunk and White mean: There's no fat and no redundancy. Despite its age, the little book's wisdom and guidelines are invaluable to anyone who wants to be a serious, competent writer and editor.

The Steps of Editing

Writers should consider editing as a process. Specific tasks allow writers-turned-editors to be focused and thorough in the editing process. Of course, writer–editors approach a 6-inch story quite differently from a 40-inch feature. Sometimes, on first reading, an editor will decide the story needs substantial revisions; other times, only minor changes will be needed. That decision comes in the first step of the editing process and will determine how much time needs to be devoted to editing.

Writers who use computers should edit at the computer screen. They may not have time to print out a draft and edit on paper. Editing on screen saves times and allows the writer to use computer tools, such as a spelling checker, to help in the editing process.

Editing follows basic steps:

• Read the written piece from start to finish to get the sense of what you have written. You may fix any minor errors, but at this point, determine whether substantial or minor changes are needed. You may move directly into reviewing for accuracy and language, including spelling and grammar, and the final read-through. Or you may have underlined sections and noted questions that need attention.

• If the piece is in need of substantial reworking, you may determine that more research and rewriting is required. That work would come in the second step of editing.

• Once the content is okay, writers and editors must check for accuracy, an intense, time-consuming job. In a professional office, writers have help from editors or fact-checkers. But regardless of who helps, writers ultimately are responsible for the accuracy of their work.

• Next, review language. Are words simple, clear, and direct? Are sentences active and easy to read? Is the message free of grammar and spelling errors and bias? Remember that jargon and institutional language are rampant. This step is also when you tighten writing. If an article needs to be shortened, writers often can do that by substituting one word for a phrase, eliminating redundancies, and reducing long titles or numbers of prepositional phrases. Such fine-tuning improves writing and replaces cutting complete paragraphs.

• After the revisions are completed, read the story again. Check carefully any sections that have been changed. Often, writers make new errors when they revise. The last stage is a final read-though for overall quality and reader appeal. This stage is what some people equate with the term *editing.* It is the final cosmetic once-over where the writer-editor is pleased with the story. If not, then the editing steps should be repeated.

If you have been editing on the computer screen, you should do one final step: Run the computer's spelling checker. It will catch spelling errors and also flag repeated words and missing spaces. Such errors are often overlooked.

Some writers may question the sequence in editing. But the reasoning is quite simple: It is efficient. If reviewing for language came first, sentences that had been corrected for spelling and grammar could possibly be deleted during later content editing. It's far better that the sentences go first. More important, the most critical tasks are done first in case the writer-editor runs out of time. For example, it is more important to write a compelling lead than to smooth out a transition. And it is more important for the piece to be complete and accurate than free of spelling errors.

Editors should be flexible as they edit. If they see a problem that needs to be fixed, regardless of the stage, they should address it then. Editors who wait may forget to make the repair.

A Closer Look

The steps of editing have been outlined only to show why editing and revision are necessary. Let's look at what each step does.

Reading the Copy

Read through the entire piece uninterruptedly as if you were a consumer who had never heard of the subject. This is usually a step most writers skip; yet it is critical for them to step back and see the message as a whole, as audiences will see it.

"But why should I read my own writing before I start to make changes?" a student writer may question. "I collected the information. I wrote it. I know what is there." Within that statement lies the danger. Because a writer may be so familiar with a topic and its components, he or she may overlook whether the meaning is clear to someone new to the subject.

In the first step, the ideal scenario is to put away a piece of writing for a few days and come back to it. Then you can look at it with a fresh eye: with the eye of an editor rather than the eye of a writer. But you may not have that luxury. If you are pressed for time, get up, walk around, have a snack, and get some fresh air. Then return to your writing. You will see it from a new perspective.

Read aloud to slow down and to hear what you have actually written—not what you think is there. The most common errors detected by reading aloud are awkward language, inadequate explanations that confuse the meaning, and too much prose on a particular topic.

As you read and detect weaknesses, you can make simple notes in the margin, such as "fix," "delete," or "explain." You will find, after your first reading, that you are eager to get on with improving your writing.

Examining Structure

If your piece needs substantial revisions, you may need to consider again the audience and ask, Does the message attract audience attention and meet audience needs? Does the lead adequately set up the article? Are all the points raised in the lead answered in subsequent paragraphs? Is the lead itself interesting and written in a way to attract an audience into the message?

Remember from Chapter 3 that the lead gives the audience specific cues about the substance of the message. To maintain your credibility with your audience, you do not want to promise a certain message in your lead and then not deliver it.

To hold the audience with the message, a writer must look at the overall organization and ask

- Is the message developed logically? Do facts follow in a clear sequence?

- Is the transition from one point to another effective? Each paragraph should be tied to the previous one.

- Are paragraphs organized so that each contains one thought or idea? Readers will be confused if too many thoughts are packaged into one paragraph. Start a new paragraph—basically a unit of organization—with each new quote or each new idea.

- Are there statements or sentences that stop you because they are out of context?

- Do all the quotes add to the message? Would it be better to paraphrase or omit some?

Again, the answers to these questions may require rewriting.

To determine if you need more information, ask

- Is the message up to date? Are the latest statistics used? For example, a television news story on accidental deaths attributed to alchohol must have this year's figures on reported cases, not figures from two years ago, or even last year. Your audience wants to know how serious the situation is today. If those numbers aren't available, you need to say so, and why.

- Are any questions raised that aren't answered? Each message must be complete. A news release that says a company is privately held must define what privately held means. A message that is written and not aired may need some description so readers can mentally picture the action.

The answers to the questions in this step of editing are guidelines for how much reporting and rewriting must be done so that copy is complete and flows smoothly and logically.

Checking for Accuracy

No aspect of writing is more important than accuracy. Professors often quip, "If your mother says she loves you, check it out." Employees may ridicule an executive who includes inaccurate information in memos. Readers turn away from publications and advertisements where they repeatedly find errors. Students lose faith in textbooks when they uncover wrong data.

The bottom line is trust: If your audience doesn't trust the validity of any part of your message, it will question the accuracy of the entire message. Once it loses trust, the audience will be less willing to believe in future communications from you and may move to other media, never to return.

Research has shown that even one error in a newspaper can cause readers to doubt the rest of the paper and to have less faith in the reporter's abilities. Accuracy, therefore, can build or break your reputation, not just the reputation of the medium that carries the message.

Steps to Ensure Accuracy

• Let your copy cool before checking for accuracy. Take a break for a few minutes so you can approach it with a clear mind. If you read it immediately, questionable material may not stand out.

• Check name spellings. Review your notes. Double-check with the researcher or another writer. Use a telephone book, city directory, or other printed reference. Correct names are essential to avoid confusion—and even legal trouble—when people have the same or similar names. For example, in writing about a nightclub singer named Delsie Harper, a reporter inadvertently left off the D, and the newspaper immediately got a call from a church deacon named Elsie Harper.

• Use reputable sources to confirm information. For example, the city budget director will have more knowledge on changes in the next fiscal year budget than will an anonymous city employee who calls a newspaper to complain.

• Make sure quotes that contain opinion or outrageous claims are attributed, such as this one: "Women get what they deserve," a self-proclaimed antifeminist said today. The quote has some credibility with the attribution but would have more if the antifeminist were named.

• If quotes are libelous—that is, damaging to a person's reputation—either make sure they can be defended or cut them. A person's barroom allegation about his next-door neighbor's drug use is not protected by law and should never be published. You may quote a witness's remark in a trial, however, because what occurs in court proceedings is protected. See more about libel in Appendix A.

• Question statistics. For example, a story reports that the president received positive approval from "more than half" of the nation. The actual statistic was 53 percent. The margin of error, or accuracy of the poll, was plus or minus 3 percent. Adding 3 percent to 53 percent means as many as 56 percent of the country support the president. But subtracting 3 percent from 53 percent also means that as little as 50 percent of the nation approve of him. And 50 percent is not more than half.

• Recalculate percentages. Your boss may tell you that the company CEO will get only a 7.6 percent pay increase. Check it. A raise from $150,000 to $172,500 is a 15 percent pay increase, not 7.6 percent. The inaccuracy would hardly make other employees confident in the public relations department and its message.

• On technical subjects, when there is doubt about an explanation, call an expert source and read your material to that person for comment.

Getting information right is also important because inaccuracies are audience-stoppers. When radio listeners hear statistics that they question, they puzzle over the error and no longer hear what you have to say. The best-constructed message framed in the finest form means nothing if your information is wrong or even confusing.

What if you cannot check a fact? Enlist someone else, such as a reference librarian, to verify what is in question. If you cannot verify information and you are working on a deadline, leave it out. If the information is vital to the message and it can't be checked, the message will have to wait. Never publish information if you have doubts about its accuracy.

Using Clear Language

Editing is hard. It means giving up words. Student writers may have been rewarded for using polysyllabic words found on high school vocabulary lists, or they may have written at length to fill an English requirement for a term paper. Early in life, writers develop a bad habit of writing long. Such writers have a difficult time determining what words to cut to keep prose tight, to the point, and clear.

Consider these questions:

- Is the copy clear and easy to read?
- Are words simple, direct, and easy to understand?
- Are jargon and institutional language eliminated? (Remember the discussion from Chapter 5 on saying it straight.)
- Is redundancy gone?
- Are sentences short and to the point?

This step includes spelling, grammar, and punctuation. In the technological age, many writers use computers that have spelling and grammar checking systems. Few spelling programs adequately check troublesome homonyms, such as affect and effect, red and read, naval and navel, stationary and stationery, trustee and trusty, lead and led, and so on. Appendix C is a guide to how to spell in the computer age.

Just as you have to check spelling, you have to review grammar. Chapter 8 discusses common grammar problems; consult the reference books listed at the end of that chapter for additional help.

Writers must be on the lookout for jargon. Such language should be replaced immediately with clearer terms, so that, for example, "organizational inputs" become "suggestions from parent groups" and "facilitation of new methodologies" becomes "trying a new survey."

In this step of editing, you also need to pay careful attention to word choice. Remember: The right word enhances audience understanding and willingness to pay attention, whether the message is read or heard. "Let your conscious be your guide," may not affect listeners. And some readers might not even notice the confused choice of conscious for conscience. Those who do notice will not be impressed. If necessary, review the discussion of word usage in Chapter 5.

If you need to shorten your article, do so by looking at phrases, groups of words, titles, and word usage for shorter ways to state the same idea. Here is where you can apply what you learned in Chapter 5. For example, the statement, "He decided to take part in the debate," could be rewritten: "He participated in the debate." Or, "The banners that were blue and white fluttered in the breeze" could be changed to "The blue and white banners fluttered in the breeze."

Giving the Piece the Last Once-Over

Read the entire piece again. At this point, no major reworking should be needed. Check, however, for any editing errors that may have crept in during earlier steps. The final reading is the last check to make sure that prior editing has produced a message that is complete, accurate, comprehensible, pertinent, and interesting. This is the time to congratulate yourself.

Now you may send your copy to your editor or to a corporate executive for review, if you are in an organization or business. If you are an advertising copywriter, the message will go to the account executive and then to the client. In print media, the story will go to an editor and in broadcast, to a news director. If you are a high school principal, your memo may be reviewed by the school system's superintendent before it is sent to parents. If you are a student, the article is turned in to a professor or instructor.

But do not think that turning in your piece ends the editing process. The copy may come back for another round of editing and changes before publication.

Watching Style

Part of good editing is ensuring consistency throughout writing. Using a consistent style guarantees that a certain pattern in word usage, titles, punctuation, abbreviations, grammar, and spelling persists. If IBM means International Business Machines in the first sentence of a television broadcast, it will mean the same thing later on. If Dr. means doctor on the first page of the newspaper, it will not mean "Drive" as part of someone's address in the obituary page. Consistent usage builds credibility and reduces chances of audience confusion.

Many media organizations follow a style that guarantees consistency. Most newspapers and public relations firms follow the style found in *The Associated Press Stylebook and Libel Manual*. Others, including *The Washington Post* and *The New York Times,* have their own style manuals. Many universities and publishing houses use *The Chicago Manual of Style* or the style manual of the Modern Language Association.

No one is ever expected to memorize stylebooks, but writers and editors must be familiar with their content. When a question arises, they need to know where to find the answer. Writers will find that certain rules are used so often that they become second nature. For example, most writers become familiar with the capitalization rule for titles: Professional titles are always capitalized before a person's name but never after a name. For example, University President Bill Sandler said classes would end early Tuesday because of the threat of a blizzard. After his name, the title would read: Bill Sandler, university president, said . . . .

Basic Style Rules

The most broadly accepted style rules are those set out by the *Associated Press Stylebook,* which is periodically updated.

TITLES. Long titles should go after an individual's name. William McCorkle's name is not lost if a short title is used before it, such as University President William McCorkle. But his name would be hard to find if his title were University Associate Vice Chancellor for Student Affairs and Services. When an individual has a long title, put the title after the name: William McCorkle, university associate vice chancellor for student affairs and services.

When titles precede names, they are capitalized. After names, they are not.

Most titles are always written out. The only time some are abbreviated is when they precede a name. *The Associated Press Stylebook* indicates which titles can be abbreviated, for example, governor as Gov. Sheila Aycock and lieutenant governor as Lt. Gov. James Ramsey. Titles that are never abbreviated include president, attorney general, professor, and superintendent. Most military titles can be abbreviated.

Stand-alone titles are always written out, and they are never abbreviated or capitalized. The president said he would turn over the files to the Justice Department. The pope will visit the United States in May.

Vice president is not hyphenated.

CAPITALIZATION. The general rule is to capitalize proper nouns that refer to a person, place, or thing. Sacramento is the capital of California. Mayor Harmon Bowles agreed to lead the town's Christmas parade. Easter is usually in late March or early April.

ABBREVIATIONS. Abbreviate only what your style manual permits. Abbreviate states' names when they are used with the name of a town or city; otherwise, write them out. Note that the Associated Press does not use postal abbreviations in text, except when the complete address is used with a zip code, as in 124 E. Main St., Lakeland, FL 33801. In other instances use the following abbreviations: Ala., Ariz., Ark., Calif., Colo., Conn., Del., Fla., Ga., Ill., Ind., Kan., Ky., La., Md., Mass., Mich., Minn., Miss., Mo., Mont., Neb., Nev., N.H., N.J., N.M., N.Y., N.C., N.D., Okla., Ore., Pa., R.I., S.C., S.D., Tenn., Vt., Va., Wash., W.Va., Wis., and Wyo. Eight states' names are never abbreviated: Alaska, Hawaii, Idaho, Iowa, Maine, Ohio, Texas, and Utah. You can abbreviate months when they are used with a specific date: Nov. 12, 1948. Write out November 1948, however. Never abbreviate March, April, May, June, or July.

Don't abbreviate the days of the week or the words *assistant* and *association*.

The Associated Press allows some abbreviations to be used on first reference because people are familiar with them, such as FBI, CIA, UFO, and IBM. But that does not mean to use only the abbreviation. The context of the story may require that the full title be used. On second reference, use the abbreviation or substitute words such as "the bureau," "the agency," "the object," or "the company."

ACRONYMS. Acronyms are abbreviations that can be pronounced as words, such as AIDS for acquired immune deficiency syndrome or UNESCO for United Nations Educational, Scientific and Cultural Organization. See style manuals for the correct first and second references for acronyms, just as with other abbreviations.

NUMBERS. The general rule is to write out numbers zero through nine and use numerals for numbers 10 and higher. Always spell out numbers at the beginning of a sentence, however. In writing numbers above 999,999, write out the words *million* and *billion* rather than using all those zeroes. For example: To clear the site, the construction crew moved 1.2 million cubic yards of dirt. Congressional aides discovered the budget would require an additional $1.4 billion in revenues.

The Associated Press lists two dozen or so exceptions to the rule, but the main ones are these:

Age. Always use a numeral for age. She has a 3-year-old daughter and an 85-year-old mother.

Percent. Always use a numeral. He estimated 9 percent of employees are truly satisfied with their jobs.

Time. Always use a numeral. The guests will arrive at 9 P.M. Classes start as early as 8 A.M.

Dates. Again, use numerals. He was born Jan. 3, 1926.

Temperatures. Use numerals for all temperatures except zero. The weather service predicted the coldest weather in 15 years for the weekend, noting that temperatures would drop to 2 to 3 degrees below zero.

Dimensions. Always write height and weight as numerals. The average height of the team's basketball players is 6 feet 4 inches. The record-breaking carrot weighed 5 pounds.

Money. Write dollars and cents as numerals. The price of an egg is about 7¢. Hemming the dress will cost $7.

Copyediting Symbols

When you send your copy to a higher level for editing, you may get back a printed copy with editing marks on it. Following are some of the common editing symbols.

Paragraph mark	¶ The president met with House leaders about his proposed budget.
Capitalization	Police Sgt. william T. cassidy
Lowercase	The teacher picked 15 Apples.
Delete letter, word	She gave them to the students.
	She gave them to to the students.
Delete punctuation	"Are you going?" she asked.
Transpose letters	She adrdessed 2,345 invitations.

Transpose words	The robber ⌐a had⌐ gun.
Insert punctuation	Marcia˄ her sister, is a pianist.
Insert letters, words	Marian chose chosticks for eating. ᵖ
	chose Marian ˄chopsticks for eating.
Add a space	Four players|are needed for bridge.
Write out	The meeting will be (Tues.) night.
Abbreviate	(Governor) Rex Casey died today.

Copyediting Symbols in Practice

Look at the following sample from a church bulletin to see how it was edited by proper use of copyediting symbols.

At a meeting last month, The Longview Church board
ᵘ
of deacons decided it woᴧld hire an (asst.) director of

special projects.

The ⱡhurch has focus⸝ed much ⌐efforts ⌐of its⌐ on
ₑ
programs for the hom˄less and nee⸝dy, said the Rev. paul
ₐ
Jacobs. The acti⸝ⱡties are more th˄en he can c̶a̶n̶ handle
ⁱ
along ⌐i⸝w⸝th his min˄sterial duties˄ he said.

Applications can be sent to the ⱡhurch before

(September) 1.

Wrap-up

In the age of technology, many writers would like to rely on spelling and grammar checkers, and word and sentence checkers, to polish and refine their writing for them. But no flawless mechanical way to edit exists.

No book on how to improve writing can stress enough the critical role of editing and the acceptance by writers that editing is essential. Remember the words of Doris Betts: We would hardly want to serve spit to our audiences.

The process of editing discussed in this chapter gives writers a more methodical approach to editing and will produce better writing. Ensuring the right structure will improve your ability to reach audiences. Guarding the language will increase audience comprehension and retention. Paying attention to spelling and grammar will reinforce the strength, clarity, and credibility of your writing. Adhering to a set style will give your writing consistency. Being aware of bias discussed in the next chapter will make your writing acceptable. Writers who are serious about their craft and their audiences will take the time to apply the guidelines and to edit, edit, edit.

EXERCISES

• Read the following story. Edit it. Make a list of questions for any missing information that would require more research. Follow Associated Press style, and use proper spelling and grammar. Watch out for redundancies. The audience is readers of the campus newspaper.

> All of the faculty members from the School of Journal-
> ism and Mass Communication will be attending on Thurs-
> day of this week a regional meeting of the Association
> for Education in Journalism and Mass Communication in
> Greensboro.
>
> The meeting will commence at 10 A.M. in the morning
> and conclude at 2 P.M. in the afternoon following a noon
> luncheon.

```
    In the morning, sessions will offer journalism

educators the opportunity to have discussions on

current issues addressing journalism and mass

communication.

    At a luncheon program, professor Walter Blayless

will be speaking on the topic of cigarette advertising

and the effect on the nation's young people of today.

    The meeting sponsored by AEJMC is exemplary of the

several regional meetings the organization holds across

the country each year. The annual meeting is always

held in August each year at different locations around

the country.
```

Compare your editing steps to the following:

First, you learned that the faculty members would be at a meeting on Thursday, the focus of the article.

You considered the lead. You might have wondered, What will happen to classes if all the faculty members are gone on a weekday? More research and interviewing would need to be done. The research might require you to write a new lead geared for the student audience. It would say

```
    Students in the School of Journalism and Mass

Communication will not have class Thursday because

faculty members will attend a professional meeting in

Greensboro.
```

Now, you would check for accuracy. You would check the spelling of Walter Blayless and the organization. You would also double-check to make sure that the meeting is in Greensboro. Then would come the most involved part. The first draft is wordy. Phrases such as 10 A.M. in the morning and 2 P.M. in the afternoon would be shortened to 10 A.M. and 2 P.M. Blayless will be speaking on the topic of cigarette advertising could be tightened to Blayless will speak on cigarette advertising. The final reading would be for overall quality.

Your edited copy might look something like this:

```
Students in the School of Journalism and Mass Communi-
cation will not have class Thursday because faculty
members will attend a professional meeting in Greens-
boro.
     A regional meeting of the Association for Education
in Journalism and Mass Communication will begin at
10 A.M. and end at 2 P.M.
     Educators will discuss issues in journalism and mass
communication during the morning sessions.
     The luncheon speaker, Professor Walter Blayless,
will talk about cigarette advertising and its effect on
youth.
     AEJMC has several regional meetings each year. The
annual meeting is in August in different U.S. cities.
```

• Copyedit the following sentences according to Associated Press style. Also check for any grammar, spelling, or punctuation errors. Use copyediting symbols to save time.

1. Lieutenant Governor Stanley Greene was stripped of his powers by the N.C. Senate.

2. William Williams, Dean of the Graduate School of Journalism, will speak to students about graduation requirements on Wed. afternoon.

3. The students are expected to begin the test at 9:00 A. M. Tuesday.

4. The President lives at 1600 Pennsylvania Avenue, but his mail is delivered to the U.S. Post Office on Twenty-second Street.

5. The state Senate is expected to enact a bill to require polio vaccinations for children under the age of two.

6. The airport in Medford, Oregon was closed yesterday after an Alaskan airlines jet made an emergency landing on their runway.

7. The Atty. Gen. has a B. A. in history from American University.

8. The Soviet block countries sponsored the Friendship Games rather than attend the 1984 olympics in Los Angeles.

9. The city and county used thirteen busses to transport the children to the July Fourth picnic.

10. Water freezes at 0 degrees Centigrade.

11. Three houses on Sims street were destroyed by the fire, which began at 112 Sims Street.

12. Following the Federal Reserve action, three banks announced a one percent increase in the prime rate, putting it at six percent.

13. U.S. Senator Jesse A. Helms (R–North Carolina) used to be city editor of The Raleigh Times.

14. John L. Harris, 48 years old, of 1632 Winding Way Road was charged Tuesday with cocaine possession.

15. The champion wrestler measured six feet six inches tall and won 4/5 of his fights.

16. Army Sergeant Willie York was charged with misappropriating $1,000,000 dollars in construction equipment.

17. Hurricane Diana, blowing from the East, caused millions of dollars in damages to the east coast of the United States.

18. Colonel Max Shaw, who has served as a national guardsman for more than twenty years, is Ed's commanding officer.

19. Ability with a frisbee is not a valid measure of IQ.

20. We heard the kickoff announced over the radio at the Laundromat.

21. The stockings were hanged by the chimney with care, in hopes that Kirs Kringle soon would be there.

22. Travelling the 30 miles, or 60 kilometers, to Kansas City, we got 32 miles per gallon in our new minivan.

23. The five-year-old boy got on the wrong bus and was missing for 2 hours.

24. Sarah sold two hundred and two boxes of Girl Scout cookies to her neighbors on Sweetbriar Pkwy. and Pantego Ave.

REFERENCES

Stuart Hample and Eric Marshall, *Children's Letters to God,* New York: Workman Publishing, 1991.

Norm Goldstein (Ed.), *The Associated Press Stylebook and Libel Manual.* New York: The Associated Press, 1997.

Claire Kehrwald Cook, *Line by Line: How to Improve Your Own Writing,* Boston: Houghton Mifflin, 1985.

Lauren Kessler and Duncan McDonald, *When Words Collide,* Belmont, CA: Wadsworth Publishing, 1992.

William Strunk, Jr., and E. B. White, *The Elements of Style,* 3rd ed. New York: Macmillan Publishing, 1979.

7

Recognizing Bias and Stereotypes

Understanding bias means considering your own background as well as the backgrounds of others. Many people believe they can write about other people without allowing any personal bias to creep into their stories, news spots, or news releases. But few people can step outside personal bias because most people are unaware of how ingrained their beliefs and attitudes can be. Bias is not just overt, as racial prejudice or political beliefs are. It is subtle. And it comes from who you are.

Consider your background. Did you come from a suburban middle-class home where you attended a school with little ethnic diversity? Did you speak a language other than English at home? What is your family's ethnic or racial background? Did you grow up in an urban ethnic neighborhood—Italian, African American, or Laotian?

Did you live in a subsidized housing project, in an inner city, or in a small town of 5,000 people or fewer? Maybe you grew up on a farm or ranch and your nearest neighbor was a half mile away. Did you attend private or public schools?

What is your gender? Do you or does someone in your family have a physical or mental disability? What is your religion? What political party do you claim?

All these aspects of your background and many others built your attitudes and beliefs. As a communicator you must become aware of your attitudes and beliefs to curb the bias that is still evident in many stories produced by the mass media today—and the bias that keeps many stories from appearing.

Bias often surfaces in stereotypes that show up in adjectives or nouns used to describe certain groups. People form stereotypes from their perceptions of individuals' or groups' behavior and from their experiences and those of friends and relatives. Think about the label in the sentence "Jane is a typical college student who wants to have a good time and study as little as possible." As a student you would not want people to ignore your full array of attributes and view you only as a lazy, party-animal student. The generalization is not fair to you or most other students. As a writer you must learn to confront such stereotypes and avoid perpetuating negative overgeneralizations about groups.

In this chapter, we will discuss

- How writers can begin to recognize bias,
- How bias in writing affects specific individuals and groups, and
- Specific tips on how to avoid bias in writing about individuals and groups.

The Bias Habit

Journalists' cultural values can affect their ability to be truly fair. Because of the way the brain processes information, people must categorize and label people and events. Walter Lippmann referred to this phenomenon in 1922:

The real environment is altogether too big, too complex and too fleeting for direct acquaintance. We are not equipped to deal with so much subtlety, so much variety, so many permutations and combinations. And although we have to act in that environment, we have to reconstruct it on a simpler model before we can manage it.

The adaptive process means that people do not see as many perspectives as possible, or they develop a view that does not fit reality. Most important, in this adaptive process, people will select the information that confirms their attitudes and beliefs, according to journalism researchers H. Stocking and P. Gross, who add that people may not even be aware that they process information with a cognitive bias. They do not have to make a conscious effort to be biased; in fact, they may be trying to be unbiased, as journalists do in attempting objectivity.

Bias in Writing

Groups such as journalists construct a shared view of "reality" because of the similarities in the way they view the world. Timothy Crouse in his book, *The Boys on the Bus,* explained the close working relationship among political reporters on the campaign trail:

> *It was just these womblike conditions that gave rise to the notorious phenomenon called "pack journalism" (also known as "herd journalism" and "fuselage journalism"). A group of reporters were assigned to follow a single candidate for weeks or months at a time, like a pack of hounds sicked on a fox. Trapped on the same bus or plane, they ate, drank, gambled, and compared notes with the same bunch of colleagues week after week.*

As early as 1950, one famous study showed how wire editors rely on their own values to select the news. David Manning White reported that "as 'gate-keeper' the newspaper editor sees to it (even though he may never be consciously aware of it) that the community shall hear as a fact only those events which the newsman, as representative of his culture, believes to be true."

It is important to remember that bias surfaces in many arenas. Adjectives and nouns are ascribed to people because of where they live, their political beliefs, their sexual orientation, and their religion. Bias attributes certain characteristics to women, men, people with disabilities, children, older people, and members of ethnic and racial groups. Labels are dangerous. They are offensive and usually imply inferiority. They do not describe individuals, nor do they apply to groups. Writers who do not think perpetuate negative stereotypes and myths.

How Myths Are Perpetuated

Almost half a century after the civil rights movement became a force in the United States, inequities based on race and ethnic background persist. Mass media have both helped and hindered the effort for equal rights in this country. On the one hand, they give voice to various social movements and allow the message of equality to reach a mass audience. On the other hand, they perpetuate misinformation and ignore a myriad of other ethnic groups.

Although the complexion of management is changing, most people who run the mass media are of Western European descent, and a large majority are male. They have little context, therefore, to help them know what it is like to be an African American, Native American, Asian American, Latino, or other person of color in the United States. (Only about 7 percent of journalists nationwide are from these groups.) Too often, stories about those communities are reported with an outsider's perspective, resulting in misinformation or stereotypes. In other cases, the stories may not be reported; the group may be invisible to the journalist.

Consider some of these overt problems of bias in coverage:

• The *Time* magazine cover that shaded football star O. J. Simpson's face so that his complexion was darker, conveying a sinister countenance.

• The rush to believe that Arabs were responsible for the Oklahoma City bombing in 1995.

• The belief that teens with green hair and black leather jackets are drug users.

• The use of black or Hispanic women as the subject of photos about welfare when the majority of welfare recipients are white, not Hispanic.

The California Commission on the Status of African American Males produced in 1997 a 200-page report, "African American Males: The Struggle for Equality." One chapter looked at media portrayals of African American men. One author reported that news media generally equate African American men with aggressiveness, lawlessness, and violence. The entertainment media then builds its portrayals from news accounts. The study pointed out a common stereotype that African American men use drugs in disproportionate numbers. A U.S. Justice Department–sponsored survey showed, however, that 10.6 percent of white respondents said they had used cocaine in their lifetime, whereas only 6 percent of African American respondents said they had used the drug.

Breaking the Bias Habit

Today, writers and reporters are trying, through better awareness, to overcome the cultural bias implanted in the news. But old habits die hard. How can you learn to sift through the information you will be writing about and present the least biased and stereotypical coverage?

Society itself is giving writers some help. Today a multicultural approach is being integrated into numerous aspects of society, from school textbooks to television advertisements. All types of cultures in the United States are gaining a voice. As someone disseminating information, you can learn to tap into these cultures for stories and diverse insights.

Media can have an impact in breaking the bias habit. As newsrooms become more diverse, the types of stories aired or printed will continue to become diverse. Reporters can describe people as individuals, not cast them in broad terms ascribed to a group. Reporters can also become circumspect when using language and learn what terminology individuals and groups prefer.

Many organizations have developed guidelines on language use. The minority professional journalism organizations also have Web sites that may include examples of stereotyping or negative portrayals. For example, the Asian American Journalists Association posted on its Web site in 1997 a letter about the cover of the March 24 issue of *National Review*. The magazine put Asian features that were once stereotypical cartoon features on President Clinton and first lady Hillary Rodham Clinton. The illustration accompanied a story about the Clinton administration's fund-raising. The focus of the story was the legality and ethics of the president's fund-raising practices, not the race of contributors, noted AAJA Media Watch Chairman Aki Soga. The cover illustration perpetuated negative stereotypes.

Students can become more familiar with groups, their goals, their membership, and current issues by accessing Web sites, such as www.latinolink.com for the Hispanic community; www.netnoir.com for African Americans; www.seniornet.org for seniors; www.thirdage.com for adults 50 years of age and older; and www.planetout.com for lesbians and gays. Most sites have links to related organizations.

Considering Specific Groups

John Mitrano, executive director of the National Organization of Italian Students and Educators, noted in a survey

> *While there is usually a grain of truth to stereotypes, over time, these become no longer salient. With the twilight of ethnicity upon us in third and fourth genera-*

tion families, new portrayals must be used to depict groups accurately. Television shows, movies, and advertisements must emphasize the qualities that we see ourselves as having. We must also become vocal and mobilized when we do not like the way we are portrayed.

Many words and images applied to specific groups have historically negative and derogatory connotations. Writers must be aware of them and avoid them.

Racial and Ethnic Groups

Writers must avoid terminology that perpetuates beliefs that all members of any group look alike, talk alike, think alike, or belong to the same political party. Selecting language is the first step.

Some language, although it may seem biased, can be appropriate when used in a historical context or with cultural sensitivity, noted Pale Moon Rose, president of the American Indian Heritage Foundation. Terms such as *redskin* and *brave* are acceptable if used appropriately and in a historical context.

Linda Cook Roberts, who won an International Association of Business Communicators Gold Quill for an affirmative action communication program, developed the following guidelines for writing about racial and ethnic groups:

• Avoid presenting members of racial or ethnic groups as if they are all the same. Too often, for example, African American neighborhoods are presented as "drug-infested." This assigns a negative status to a whole people and their neighborhoods.

• Refrain from using descriptive words that strengthen racial or ethnic stereotypes. Consider this sentence from a *Washington Post* article on less well-known Washington, D.C., monuments.

And he chose an unusual man to help: Benjamin F. Banneker, a free black man who was a math whiz and self-taught in astronomy.

The word *unusual* clouds the sentence with a potential stereotype: the implication that African Americans are not helpful, are not intelligent in math, or are unable to learn astronomy on their own.

• Describe race or ethnic origin only when it is pertinent. In an article about Jessica James becoming the vice president of a local bank, it is not relevant to mention that her great-grandparents were born in slavery.

• Understand the problematic racial and ethnic undertones of some language. For example, the term *minority* is problematic in an international sense because people of color make up the majority of the world's population, and population changes in the United States mean that some ethnic groups are the majority in certain locations. Remember also that *minority* always refers to a group rather than to certain individuals; it is best to use the term *members of minority groups* rather than *minorities.*

• Never use a patronizing focus or treat a member of an ethnic group as a token. Ivan Penn, a reporter for the *Baltimore Sun,* was the first African American to serve as editor-in-chief of the student newspaper, the *Diamondback,* at the University of Maryland. But he describes himself first as a reporter, as a University of Maryland alumnus, and as a former *Diamondback* editor.

• Integrate coverage of ethnic groups into all aspects of articles or broadcasts instead of doing periodic "special" editions.

• Look for a diversity of sources when writing. A Native American might be interviewed about political struggles instead of the meaning of a ceremonial dance.

Sexism

Women have risen to powerful jobs in both the public and the private sectors, but they have not gained enough power to transform their image in the media. Many writers thoughtlessly use language that treats women as inferior or that is demeaning or insulting. They are referred to as girls or mothers and are described by their physical attributes such as "attractive" or "brunette" or "shapely."

For example, Carol Moseley Braun, an African American woman from Illinois, successfully ran for the U.S. Senate in 1992. A *Washington Post* feature referred to her in its lead as "a celebrity with a problem." It then revealed that her problem was having to find pantyhose at a hotel gift shop. A story about a male candidate probably would never focus on his troubles in buying an undershirt.

Years later such writing still appears. Consider media coverage of repeated allegations against President Clinton about his sexual conduct. One of the female protagonists, Linda Tripp, who taped Monica Lewinsky, was described in a *Washington Post* article as "a divorced middle-aged mother who needed to keep the paychecks coming...." The implication by the writer was that Tripp was a woman who would do anything for money. Readers questioned the relevance of labeling her as divorced and middle-aged. The facts would have been better placed in a paragraph devoted to biographical information about Tripp.

At the same time, a *Chicago Tribune* writer described President Clinton's secretary, Bettie Currie, solely as "typically wearing a crisp blazer and pearls, her hair pulled back into a chignon." What is a crisp blazer? Well ironed? And many people wondered what a "chignon" was. The manner in which Currie handled Clinton's appointments proved of more value to readers than a sketchy, imprecise physical description. Writers should use description when it is complete and adds to the understanding of an individual's personality. Feature writers must be especially careful when creating a mood. Often what looks like interesting detail may come across as sexism in disguise. Take, for example, *The Washington Post* lead describing a well-known philanthropist:

—The first thing to know about Betty Knight Scripps is that she's rich. Palm Beach rich. Newspaper magnate rich. Huge-jewelry-that-once-belonged-to-European-royalty rich.

The second thing to understand is that she likes to give away big chunks of her money, often at elaborate balls, dinners, and parties that she spends months planning, with military precision, down to the tiniest detail. This is a woman who will never lack for friends.

But the most important thing to remember about Scripps is that under that perfectly coiffed blond flip and Balmain dress is a woman who just wants to have fun. The recently widowed socialite loves to dance, is just wild about ambassadors ("Isn't everyone?"), and is ready to play in the Takes-Itself-Way-Too-Seriously capital of the world: Washington, D.C.

Writers should guard against describing women in terms of their physical appearance and men in terms of wealth and power.

Beginning writers should also be aware that some other writers and editors are sensitive to the use of gender-specific nouns such as "chairman," "fireman," "stewardess," and "mailman." When possible, use "chairperson," "firefighter," "flight attendant," or "postal service worker" or "letter carrier." Writers should also know their publication's policy about courtesy titles. Many organizations have eliminated courtesy titles such as Mrs., Miss, and Ms. before women's names. The last name is used on second reference.

Sexual Orientation

Writers should also avoid perpetuating negative images based on sexual orientation. Gay and lesbian rights movements since the mid-1960s have worked diligently to recast gay and lesbian portrayals in society. Until the mid-1970s, most news stories that referred to gays and lesbians did so only in the context of police reports. Gay and lesbian issues have been addressed in the schools, in the workplace, and in the military. Despite increased coverage, some editors and reporters still produce stories that present homosexuality as deviant, and negative stereotypes continue.

Writers and broadcasters must be careful not to make value judgments when a source is gay or lesbian or when the subject deals with homosexuality. Saying, for example, that a source "confessed" to being gay communicates negative, secretive feelings about homosexuality that your openly gay source will resent.

A person's gender or sexual orientation should be ignored in a message unless it is relevant. People's sexual orientation may be part of the fabric of the message but should be woven in as part of who they are, not presented as their complete identity. For example, gays and lesbians are well-known actors and leaders in fields such as science, politics, and medicine.

Madeleine Blais of *The Washington Post* wrote a multidimensional profile of Jim Graham, the director of the Whitman-Walker Clinic in Washington for people with AIDS. The article described Graham's life and the clinic's life without making sexual orientation the focus. One paragraph described Graham's coming to grips with his alcoholism and his coming out to his wife. At an Alcoholics Anonymous meeting, Blais reported, "he told her that on the night before their wedding he had sex with a man who kept asking him if he knew what he was doing getting married. He wanted to ask her forgiveness." The reporter's work was done without bias.

Writers should never make assumptions about people's sexual orientation or people's sentiments toward gay and lesbian issues. Some people favor equality for all people. Remember that many people who are not gay or lesbian support gay and lesbian rights, just as many white people support civil rights for people of color.

Disabilities

Unless you or someone in your family has a physical or mental disability, as a writer you may tend to forget people with disabilities exist. Among the derogatory labels applied to disabled people are "crippled," "deformed," and "invalid." The Disabilities Committee of the American Society of Newspaper Editors noted a list of terms to avoid, including "special," which is seen as patronizing; "stricken with or suffers from" instead of "a person who has" a specific disability; "victim of" rather than "a person who has" AIDS or cerebral palsy.

Unlike other groups that receive discrimination because of social norms, people with disabilities face discrimination both from attitudes and from real barriers created by society's architectural and communication barriers. Maybe you have never seen a person who uses a wheelchair in your local grocery store because there is no curb cut in the sidewalk in front of the store or no ramp at the door of the store. Maybe you have had little interaction with a profoundly deaf person because you do not know where to find a Telecommunications Device for the Deaf (TDD), which would allow you to call the person on the phone.

Many people, including writers, forget that people with disabilities constitute a vital, and numerous, part of our society. Government estimates are that 18 percent of the U.S. population, about 48 million people, has some form of disability. Therefore, a significant number of today's audiences either have a disability or know someone who does. Yet, people with disabilities receive only sketchy news coverage or are rarely written about. Writers are missing readable, audience-enticing stories about civil rights violations, new technology, legislation, and changes in business practices. An enterprising reporter could mine such story topics indefinitely.

The late John Clogston, a journalism professor at the Northern Illinois University, said that writers often portray people with disabilities in one of three demeaning ways: They imply that people who have a disability are somehow less human than other people; they present them as medically defective or somehow deviant or different in society; or they go overboard in trying to portray them positively, thus making them superhuman or "supercrips," as Clogston called them.

Writers have a tendency to focus stories on the individual rather than the issues surrounding a disability, and they tend to wrap people with disabilities in pity and sympathy. Joe Shapiro, who covers social policy and disability issues for *U.S. News and World Report,* suggests that "instead of writing the sad story about the 10-year-old boy saving money to buy his mother an electric wheelchair, write the sad story of a health-care system that doesn't provide the funding to get the needed chair for that mother."

Writing about People with Disabilities

Lucille deView, syndicated columnist on aging for Knight-Ridder/*Tribune* and the writing coach for the *Orange County Register* in California, recommends the following tips for writing about people with disabilities:

- Let people with disabilities, not a friend or family member, speak for themselves in your writing.

- Recognize the individuality of all people.

- Look beyond the individual to the issue if possible. If someone who uses a wheelchair is also an athlete, you might ask about the accessibility of local gymnasiums, swimming pools, and outdoor sports facilities.

- Look beyond the person's disability and get a well-rounded view of his or her life. Having a disability is just one small aspect of who a person is. He may collect antique sheet music, or she may have been a police officer during the 1960s.

- Ask about language. Ask which terms they prefer for publication. Do not assume that because they use a term, it is acceptable to all. Someone may refer to himself or herself as a cripple, but this is a derogatory term and should not be used.

- Avoid assigning superhuman traits. People with disabilities participate fully in aspects of life: They have all types of jobs, and they have spouses and families. If they are athletes, it is because they enjoy physical activity. Find out about the societal barriers they may have faced in achieving their goals, just as you do in any interview.

- Mention a disability only if it is pertinent to the message. It is not relevant to mention that a business owner uses a wheelchair unless he or she is talking specifically about access issues or other disability-related issues.

Be careful about writing that someone succeeded "in spite of" a disability—a phrase often viewed by people with disabilities as extremely patronizing. Some writers may contend that a disability implies that individuals are not able, and if they succeed, then the news value of emotional impact and conflict are there to attract readers. Never assume that an accomplishment by a person with a disability is unusual.

In general, people specializing in coverage of disability issues recommend two easy rules in writing about people with disabilities. First, avoid clichés and clichéd constructions. Use value-neutral terms, that is, words that do not stereotype. Avoid saying that someone is confined. The person gets out of the wheelchair to sleep and to bathe. To that individual, the wheelchair is liberating. It is more accurate to say the individual uses a wheelchair. Second, never inject pity or a condescending tone into copy.

Ageism

Older people may also face stigmatization by society, and the mass media play a role in that process. In some instances, older people are labeled as forgetful, senile, rigid, meddlesome, childlike, feeble, fragile, frail, gray, inactive, withered, or doddering. Such adjectives may describe older people at some point in their lives or may be medically appropriate. But if such words are used indiscriminately, they demean older people and perpetuate inaccurate stereotypes. With the repeal of mandatory retirement, older people continue to work into their 70s and even 80s if they choose. They do most things that younger people do.

Consider an example from a *Texas Monthly* profile on then Texas Governor Ann Richards. The story was written because of rumors that she might one day run for president. At the outset, appearance stereotypes were broken: Richards was pictured on the cover in a white leather outfit sitting on a motorcycle.

The article presented the 58-year-old governor, who is also a grandmother, in a multidimensional way—not as an older woman who happens to be governor but as an effective, dynamic governor who happens to be an older woman. Her bouffant white hair is a sign of age and a symbol of her political personality. Her hairstyle, which was popular in the 1950s, successfully contrasts with her liberal feminist beliefs. Her age is relevant only as a part of who she is.

Lucille deView suggests that writers avoid these myths about older people:

- Older people can participate in a variety of activities, so do not adopt a "gee whiz" attitude toward their abilities. Most people over the age of 50 continue the physical activities they enjoyed when younger, whether swimming, hiking, or playing tennis.

- Older people should be seen as individuals, not as members of a senior age group in which people are believed to have the same interests and abilities. Older people's interests are just as varied as those of individuals in other groups.

- Older people are not stereotyped in appearance. They dress in numerous fashions, and not all older people have physical problems or even gray hair.

- Age does not mean loneliness or loss of sexual interest. One study showed that 74 percent of older men and 35 percent of older women live with spouses. Another 23 percent of older women live with relatives or unrelated people, and 7 percent of older men do the same, according to Mary Spencer's *Truth about Aging: Guidelines for Publishers.* Although more people 65 years of age and older are living alone, they often choose that path for more independence.

DeView says that writers should focus on realistic presentations of older people. Some older people have no financial problems, whereas others struggle financially during their later life. Not all older people have ill health or are unable to cope with poor health. Although 45 percent of older people have serious medical conditions, they may not severely limit their participation in society. Only about 5 percent of older people live in nursing homes.

Children also may be portrayed in an unpleasant light. Not all children are immature, naive, whining, sneaky, dishonest, or lazy. Children mature and develop at different paces. Some are responsible, creative, athletically gifted, loving, aggravating, and mean. Each must be considered individually and be allowed to ascribe traits to himself or herself, as did one 5-foot teenager, who described herself as being "vertically challenged."

Overcoming Bias in Writing

Even after a discussion of bias such as the one in this chapter, traces of insensitivity can still creep into writing. You need to be constantly aware of your own background and attitudes to understand when and how bias might surface in writing, to recognize it, and to exorcise it.

Writers, reporters, and broadcasters today must be trained to avoid the flaws of their predecessors in the mass media. They must learn to question their own beliefs and assumptions to understand better the diverse ethnic groups within society.

Today's writers, through better awareness, are trying to overcome cultural bias by sifting through information and presenting the least stereotypical and biased picture possible. Messages—from school textbooks to television advertisements—use a multicultural approach that presents all kinds of people. But despite education, old biases die hard for many, and every time a bias is confirmed by a writer, it is strengthened for readers.

Beginning and even experienced writers sometimes pass along stereotypes, such as the dizzy blonde or dishonest politician, because they think people like and understand such shorthand portrayals, just as they like cartoons. Therein lies the danger. Because mass media professionals present distinctive images of people and groups, they can determine how consumers view people and groups who are not like themselves. Thus, writers must work responsibly in disseminating information rather than misinformation.

Make sure that what you write or broadcast does not perpetuate negative stereotypes. Stereotypes communicate inaccurate information and can undermine the quality of your work. Sensing stereotypes and avoiding them is a critical step on the path to better writing.

EXERCISES

1. Describe yourself culturally and ethnically. List any physical disabilities or other pertinent differences. Make a list of words or phrases, both negative and positive, that you have seen used in reference to your special traits. Compare your list with those of others in your class, and compile a directory of words you should avoid when writing, and why. Explain the connotation of each word. Make a list of acceptable words or phrases.

2. What is the ethnic makeup of your college or university? The town or city where your school is located? Do a five-day content analysis of your local or student newspaper. Count the number of stories each day in the news, sports, and features sections. Count the number that focus on an ethnic group or an issue related to an ethnic group. At the end of the five days, calculate what percentage of the newspaper's stories related to ethnic groups. Do the percentages match the groups' makeup in the university's or town's population? Was coverage positive, negative, or neutral? What types of stories do you believe are missing?

3. Do a similar content analysis of the evening news broadcast, locally and for a national network. Count the total stories and the number concerning ethnic groups. Give your impressions about whether the general coverage was positive, negative, or neutral.

4. You have the opportunity to interview the incoming student government president, a son of two Laotian refugees. List five objective questions you could use to begin the interview, then list two effective questions you could ask to determine his experiences with cultural differences in the United States.

5. Examine your local or student newspaper. Find examples of stories about various ethnic communities or societal groups that do a good job of unbiased writing. Bring examples to class to share and indicate why the stories could be models for writing.

REFERENCES

A. Arluke and J. Levin, "Second Childhood." *Public Communication Review* 1:2, 1992.

"Communities Inc. First to Link Special Internet Audiences Online," CNN Custom News, Dec. 10, 1997. Available at: http://www.cnn.com.

Timothy Crouse. *The Boys on the Bus.* New York: Random House, 1993.

deView, Lucille, "Regardless of Age: Toward communication sensitive to older people and children," in *Without Bias: A Guidebook for Nondiscriminatory Communication.* New York: John Wiley & Sons, 1982.

"Focus on Racism in the Media." *Extra!* July/August, 1992.

M. Johnson and S. Elkins, *Reporting on Disability, Approaches and Issues.* Louisville, KY: Advocado Press, 1989.

Jan Jarbue, "Ann's Plans." *Texas Monthly,* July 1992.

Gretchen Kell, "Media is much to blame for negative stereotypes about African American men, says UC Berkeley journalism professor," Online news release. University of California at Berkeley, June 1997.

Walter Lippmann. *Public Opinion*. New York: Harcourt, Brace and Co., 1922.

Eric Newton, *The Open Newspaper*. A Maynard Institute Workbook. San Francisco, Robert C. Maynard Institute for Journalism Education, 1994.

J. Pickens (Ed.), *Without Bias*. New York: John Wiley and Sons, 1982.

President's Committee on the Employment of People with Disabilities, Statistical Report: The Status of People with Disabilities. Washington, DC: U.S. Department of Labor, 1994.

Reporting and Writing About People with Disabilities, 5th ed. (Brochure). Lawrence, KS: Research and Training Center on Independent Living, University of Kansas, 1996.

Pale Moon Rose and John Mitrano, Comments. *In* Surveys of ethnic and racial groups, by Jan Johnson Elliott, associate professor, University of North Carolina at Chapel Hill, Fall 1993.

H. Stocking and P. Gross. *How Do Journalists Think? A Proposal for the Study of Cognitive Bias in Newsmaking*. Bloomington, *In:* Eric Clearinghouse on Reading and Communication Skills, 1989.

Spencer, Mary, *Truth about Aging: Guidelines for Publishers*. Washington, DC: National Retired Teachers Association and American Association of Retired Persons, 1979.

David Manning White, "The 'gatekeeper,'" *Journalism Quarterly*, Vol. 27, No. 3, Fall 1950, p. 383.

"Women's Lifestyles: A Special Report," *Scripps Howard Editors Newsletter*. Cincinnati, OH: Scripps Howard Newspapers, Spring 1989.

8

Testing Your Grammar

Our world is fast-paced and fast-changing—hardly the kind of place you would expect to need something as tedious as a lesson on grammar. But today's communicator cannot afford to slow down audiences, and faulty grammar does just that.

Consider the reader who encounters *its* where *it's* should be. For a split second, he will pause and wonder about the error, the writer, and the publication. Sometimes the musing reader will stop reading entirely because of the slowdown or because of the reduced credibility or appeal of the flawed message.

People do not have to be grammar experts to stop and wonder about correctness. For example, any unusual use of "whom" or "who" may cause a reader to reflect rather than read on. "Now, what was it we learned about whom?" the reader muses, and the tempo of reading is lost.

Television viewers may cringe when the news announcer says, "The committee will reconvene their meeting tomorrow morning." They know a committee is referred to with an "its," not a "their." They have paused to correct the sentence and lost the remainder of the announcer's message.

Research has shown that when messages are perceived to be error free, they also are thought to be credible and well written. The perception of quality carries over to the writer and to the publication. In other words, publications free of errors are thought to be of high quality, produced by professionals.

If audiences are free from grammatical distractions, they move comfortably through a message. Such comfort and ease are essential for effective communication in the information age, in which distractions are abundant. In today's cluttered communication environment, writers have little control over such audience-stoppers as busy schedules and competing media. But they can control distractions that exist within messages. Editing for common grammar problems will eliminate one important source of audience turnoff.

This chapter will

- Test your knowledge in a diagnostic quiz,
- Discuss five problem areas where grammar problems usually occur, and
- Test your proficiency in each problem area.

But My Grammar Is Good...

Most of us who pursue writing as a career consider ourselves to be language experts, and in general, our grammar and language use are far above average. Even educated people have problems, however. Evidence of grammar problems is found in mistakes made daily by adults in business letters, memos, and reports, as well as in newspapers and on the airways. An ad proclaims, "There's no down payment and no service charge!" To be grammatically correct, it should say, "There are no down payment and no service charge." A newsletter states, "Children will be grouped by age, irregardless of grade in school." There is no such word as "irregardless," which is simply an aberration of "regardless."

Educated, employed people regularly make grammar mistakes that other educated people will recognize. Writers need to learn what their most frequent grammar errors are and how to correct them. A first step in checking your grammar is to know what errors you are most likely to make.

Grammar Problems

Author Katherine C. McAdams, an associate professor at the University of Maryland, has developed "The Grammar Slammer," a workshop on grammar problems. It identifies five areas in which real-life errors are most likely to occur:

- Punctuation, especially commas, semicolons, colons, apostrophes, dashes, and hyphens.
- Subject and verb agreement.
- Correct pronoun choices that provide agreement and that avoid gender bias, such as "Each student has his or her book" rather than the more common and erroneous "Each student has their book."
- Correct sentence structures, especially when sentences use modifiers or require parallel structure.
- Word use—that is, using words (such as regardless) correctly. Often this area involves spelling problems and confusing words that sound alike, such as "affect" and "effect" or "vain" and "vein."

This chapter follows the format of the Grammar Slammer workshop, giving a short lesson on each of the problem areas and following that lesson with some exercises. The approach is designed for writers who are bright, motivated, and capable of learning quickly.

The lessons provide a quick fix rather than an in-depth lesson. The lessons are designed to refresh and renew rather than to reeducate. Going through the grammar lessons will help you to identify your grammar deficiencies. You then can be on guard for your particular problems when writing and editing. You may find that you have many weaknesses in language skills and understanding. If so, you will want to study the books recommended at the end of this chapter or take a grammar course.

Test Yourself

To determine which areas you need to work on, take the following diagnostic quiz. Record your answers on a sheet of paper.

Grammar Slammer Diagnostic Quiz

The following sentences contain errors in grammar and punctuation. No sentence contains more than one error. Read each sentence. Circle the error. In the space provided at the end of each sentence, indicate which part of the sentence has the error by noting the number that follows the error. Sentence 1 is an example.

1. If the regular season is any indication, (1) Maryland should be considered (2) a top challenger (3) for the championship; having downed (4) defending regional champion Kentucky twice in the invitational tournament. _____4_____

2. The list of candidates (1) being considered as successors (2) for the university chancellor have (3) been trimmed (4) to approximately 50 names, including (5) four UMCP officials. _____

3. The computer did not (1) seem to be (2) working today, it kept rejecting (3) the operator's (4) instructions. _____

4. The following afternoon, (1) Wednesday, October 25 a Royal (2) Indian Air Force DC-3 (3) landed in the abandoned dirt strip of Srinagar Airport. (4) _____

5. Traditionally expected to be in control of their surroundings, (1) the insecurity makes freshmen (2) uncomfortable in their new situation. (3) _____

6. Franco's body (1) will lay in state (2) until services are held (3) at the chapel. (4) _____

7. Hopefully, the council will pass (1) a new noise ordinance (2) before the students return (3) to campus in September. (4) _____

8. Among those who attended services for Rein were Dick Crum, head football coach at (1) UNC-CH, (2) Joab Thomas, chancellor at NCSU; John Caldwell, (3) former NCSU chancellor; and (4) Paul Deitzel (5), athletic director at LSU. _____

9. She predicted that (1) neither Howard Baker (2) or George Bush (3) would receive the Republican nomination. (4) _____

10. In its advertising, (1) the Acme Company claims that they are in business (2) only (3) to do good works for the community. (4)

    _____

11. Millie Rosefield, chair (1) of the Rockland Historic District Commission ran (2) fifth in the Nov. 6 race (3) for four council seats. (4) _____

12. One of every five (1) of the state's residents (2) live in the sort of poverty (3) that drove Erskine Caldwell to write. (4) _____

13. Three-fourths of the business district (1) in Long Beach, N. C. was destroyed (2) by Hurricane Hugo, (3) which struck the coast in 1989. (4) _____

14. Many a boy use to believe (1) that he could acquire (2) practically su-perhuman strength (3) just by eating the right cereal. (4) _____

15. Jones said the parade would feature the homecoming queen, (1) the marching band will play, (2) a pep rally, and (3) as many floats as possible. (4) _____

What's wrong with the following sentences? Correct each error.

16. Several people, all of them eager to give their opinions and all of them pressing forward to meet the governor, who was conducting interviews with voters in the area.

17. I like ice cream and cookies, I don't like cakes with icing.

18. Rosalie complained, and she had no heat.

19. Being a weight lifter, his muscles were well developed.

20. The alligator is hunted for their skin.

Several of the following words are misspelled. Circle the misspelled words and write the correct spelling for each in the space provided.

1. principal (of a school) _____

2. sherriff (a law officer) _____

3. marshall (an officer of the law) _____

4. separate (to divide) _____

5. stationery (you write on it) _____

6. recommend (to suggest) _____

7. roommate _____

8. sieze (take control) _____

Answers for the diagnostic quiz are included in Appendix D at the back of the book.

Grammar Problems up Close

Look at the items you missed on the diagnostic quiz. You should have an idea of which grammar problems you need to review. The discussion of each problem is followed by exercises. Test your proficiency and move on. Record your answers on a sheet of paper. To check your work, look at the answers in Appendix D.

Problem 1: Punctuation

Perhaps no problem looms larger than that of punctuation. Few people actually know the rules and regulations of punctuation use. Most of us, much of the time, use the "feel good" school of punctuation, saying, "I just feel like I needed a comma," or "A semicolon just felt right."

Professional communicators must give up their "feel good" philosophy of punctuating. The first rule of punctuating professionally is this: DO NOT PUNCTUATE UNLESS YOU KNOW A RULE. When you even think of adding a mark of punctuation, stop and think about whether or not it is justified by the rules in this chapter. If not, you probably don't need to punctuate at all. This leads us to the second rule of punctuating professionally: WHEN IN DOUBT, LEAVE IT OUT. If you are not sure about where to place a comma, for example, don't put one in a sentence.

One more tip before we move into rules: If you find that you are punctuating excessively—that is, using more than three punctuation marks within any given sentence—it is probably time to rewrite that sentence. Sentences that require many punctuation marks, even if they are all correct, are usually too long and complex to be easily understood by readers. So the third rule of punctuating professionally is that LESS IS MORE. Less punctuation leads to clearer, more readable copy.

Commas

Literally hundreds of comma rules exist. But the nine listed here, distilled by high school English teacher Mary Penny in the 1940s, have been found over the years to take care of most everyday comma problems.

RULE 1. Use commas in compound sentences when clauses are separated by a conjunction such as and, but, for, nor, or yet.

- She managed the restaurant, but he did the cooking.

Note: In such sentences, leaving out the conjunction leads to an error known as a comma splice, whereby a comma is left to do the work of joining two sentences: She managed the restaurant, he did the cooking. Like weak splices in rope, commas are not strong enough for this task. A period or semicolon is needed to make a correct sentence:

- She managed the restaurant. He did the cooking.
- She managed the restaurant; he did the cooking.

RULE 2. Use commas to separate elements in a series. Such elements usually are adjectives, verbs, or nouns. *Note:* Journalism departs from traditional rules of punctuation by leaving the comma out before a conjunction in a series of elements.

English composition version:

- The tall, dark, handsome man hailed, lauded, and applauded Ben, George, Maude, and Rebecca.

Journalism version:

- The tall, dark handsome man hailed, lauded and applauded Ben, George, Maude and Rebecca.

RULE 3. Use commas when attributing from quoted material. Commas set off words of attribution from the words of a one-sentence quotation unless a question mark or exclamation mark is preferred. Use them also in words of saying:

- He said, "Hello." or "Hello," he said.

RULE 4. Commas follow introductory matter.

After an introductory adverbial clause:

- When the team was forced to kick, the coach sent in his best players.

After two or more introductory prepositional phrases:

- In the spring she returned to College Park. (no comma)
- In the spring of 1981, she returned to College Park. (comma)

With a phrase that contains a verbal (that is, a verb form as a modifier):

- Singing as she worked, Mary answered the phone.
- Kicked by a horse, Don was more than stunned.
- To cure hiccups, drink from the far side of a glass.

RULE 5. Commas follow the salutation of a friendly letter and the complimentary close of any letter. Commas follow capitalized elements, such as the complimentary close (e.g., Sincerely, Very truly yours), and a colon follows the salutation of a business letter.

- Dear Reese,
- Dear Dean Cleghorn:

RULE 6. Commas follow all items in a full address or date.

- July 16, 1962, is his date of birth.
- She has lived in Manteo, N.C., all her life.

RULE 7. Commas surround nonessential words or phrases.

- Well, we will just have to walk home.

Commas set off appositives, which are words or phrases that rename a noun. Appositives amplify a subject.

- Betty Brown, his mother-in-law, has been married four times.

Commas set off nonessential modifying clauses and phrases.

- The president-elect, suffering from laryngitis, canceled his speech.

RULE 8. Commas surround words of direct address.

- Betty, please pass the butter.
- I can see, Fred, that you are lazy.

RULE 9. Commas indicate omitted verbs, usually expressed in another part of the sentence.

- Talent often is inherited; genius, never.

Semicolons and Colons

Miss Penny added three more rules to her list to take care of another widespread punctuation problem: the correct use of semicolons and colons. Miss Penny's rules 10 and 11 explain the two uses of the semicolon—the ONLY two uses. Rule 12 explains the use of colons.

RULE 10. Semicolons connect two complete sentences if sentences have a related thought. Use of a semicolon usually creates a sense drama.

- The brown-eyed, dark, and vivacious model, at age 25, seemed destined for quick success; on Dec. 11, 1991, her apparent destiny was altered.

RULE 11. Semicolons are used in a list separating items that require significant internal punctuation.

- He visited Richmond, Va.; Raleigh, N.C.; Greenville, S.C.; Birmingham, Ala.; and Baton Rouge, La.

RULE 12. Colons precede formal lists, illustrations, multisentence quotes, and enumerations.

- The following students received scholarships: Jim Johnson, Juanita Jones, Martha Taylor, Tiffany Eldridge, and Teri Sampson.
- He answered her with a parable: "A man once had six sons. Five of them...."
- Clinton listed the steps in his recovery program: First, to raise interest rates; second, to reduce spending....

Slammer for Commas, Semicolons, and Colons

Now, using Miss Penny's list of twelve rules as your reference, complete the following exercise. REMEMBER: The most important rule is that you DO NOT punctuate unless you know a rule. Defend each mark of punctuation that you use by citing one of the Penny rules in the space provided. Record your answers on a sheet of paper.

Rule or Rules

_____ 1. Although we watched the Super Bowl we don't know who won.

_____ 2. John Blimpo an egocentric man dropped his hat in the fruit salad.

_____ 3. Guitars have six strings basses four.

_____ 4. The tall dark handsome man listed his hobbies as reading fishing painting and writing.

_____ 5. To Whom It May Concern

The spelling and grammar test will be given on March 2 3 and 4 1991 in Room 502 of the Journalism Building.

Grammatically yours

J. School Dean

_____ 6. Dad go ahead and send the money now.

_____ 7. The women's basketball team was down by four points at half-time however they came back to crush their opponents.

_____ 8. Congress passed the bill but the debate took several weeks.

_____ 9. Well just be in by daybreak.

_____ 10. Her blind date was a real disappointment he talked loudly and constantly about his pet snake.

_____ 11. She was elected on Nov. 3 1972 in Baltimore Md. the city of her birth to serve as mayor.

_____ 12. She named her courses for the fall semester journalism English political science history and French.

Check your exercise by looking at the answers in Appendix D. Then go on to tackle some other troublesome marks of punctuation.

Hyphens and Dashes

Remember that hyphens and dashes, although often confused, are different.

The hyphen differs from a dash in both use and appearance. The hyphen is shorter (- as opposed to —), and it comes, without additional spaces, between two words that are combined to express some new concept, such as polka-dot and part-time. Hyphens are useful joiners that bring some creativity to language.

Rather than joining phrases, dashes are useful in separating them—usually where that separation can be heard. Dashes are sometimes used to replace commas to ensure that a pause is audible and even dramatic. Although charming, he was—on the other hand—a thief.

Here is a list of guidelines for using hyphens and dashes correctly:

1. Never use a hyphen after a word ending in "ly."

- The newly elected president stepped to the podium.

2. Use a hyphen to connect two or more related modifying words that do not function independently.

- Todd always ordered the blue-plate special.
- Todd dreaded any face-to-face confrontations.

3. The dash is a punctuation mark that one hears. It is a noticeable pause. Choose a dash instead of a comma so that the audience can "hear" the pause.

4. Dashes work where commas would also work. The only difference is that the dash adds drama—and an audible break in the text. Because dashes may substitute for commas, they are used to set off nonessential material.

- The murderer was—if you can believe it—a priest.

5. Too many dashes in any text may be distracting and even irritating to readers. Limit dashes to only the most dramatic of pauses. In most cases, such as this example, commas will suffice.

- She is—as most of you know—a punctuation expert.
- She is, as most of you know, a punctuation expert.

Other marks of punctuation, especially apostrophes, can be troublesome. Correct use may vary from time to time and publication to publication. Always check your stylebook and keep a current grammar reference book handy.

Problem 2: Subject and Verb Agreement

Few writers make obvious errors in subject and verb agreement, such as "I is interested in cars" or "The class know it's time to go to lunch." But most people struggle with the following subject–verb agreement problems.

1. Collective subjects can be confusing. Some nouns that appear to be plural—such as Girl Scouts, checkers, economics—are treated as singular units.

- The Girl Scouts is a fine organization.
- Checkers is an ancient game.
- Economics is a difficult subject.

Some, however, have Latinate endings and remain plural, although spoken language tends to make them singular, such as media and alumni. In formal writing, these plurals require plural verbs.

- The media have raised the issue of the senator's competency.

2. The pronouns each, either, neither, anyone, everyone, and anybody are always singular, regardless of what follows them in a phrase. Take, for example, this sentence:

- Either of the boys is an excellent choice for president.

The phrase "of the boys" does not change the singular number of the true subject of this sentence: the pronoun "either." Following are some other examples of correct usage.

- Neither has my vote.
- Either is fine with me.
- Each has an excellent option.
- Anyone is capable of helping the homeless.
- Everyone is fond of Jerry.

3. A fraction or percentage of a whole is considered a singular subject.

- Three quarters of the pie is gone.

- Sixty-seven percent of the voters is needed to withhold a veto.

4. Compound subjects, in which two or more nouns function as the subject of a sentence, can lead to agreement problems. To solve such problems, substitute a single pronoun such as "they" or "it" for the sentence's subject or subjects.

For example, transform this problem sentence: The students and the teacher is/are waiting for the bus. By use of substitution, the subject becomes "they": They are waiting for the bus. Some other examples:

- The opening number and the grand finale thrill the audience. (they thrill)
- There are no down payment and no service charge. (they are not there)

5. When subjects are structured with either/or and neither/nor, use the verb that corresponds to the subject closest to it, as in the following cases:

- Either the leader or the scouts pitch the tent.
- Either the scouts or the leader pitches the tent.

Slammer for Subject–Verb Agreement

Check your knowledge of subject–verb agreement by taking the following quiz. On a separate sheet of paper, write the verb that agrees.

1. He did say he would look at the sheet of names, which includes/include the owners of two apartment buildings.
2. Their number and influence appears/appear greatest in West Germany.
3. Experience in the backfield and the line gives/give the coach a good feeling on the eve of any opening game.
4. A first offense for having fewer than 25 cartons of untaxed cigarettes results/result in a $500 fine.
5. Before you make a final judgment on this student's story, consider the time and effort that has/have gone into it.
6. Who does the teaching? Full professors. But so does/do associates, assistants, and instructors.

7. She said they would visit Peaks of Otter, which is/are near Lynchburg, Va.
8. The news media is/are calling for a peace treaty that is fair to everyone.
9. The United Mine Workers exhibit/exhibits solidarity during strikes.
10. There is/are 10 million bricks in this building.
11. The president said that students today are too job-oriented and neglect the broader areas of study that constitutes/constitute a true education.
12. Five fire companies fought the blaze, which the firefighters said was/were the longest this year.
13. Each of the 100 people believes/believe in God.
14. It is/are the boats, not the swimmers, that stir up the dirt in the lake.
15. The editor told the staff there was a shortage of money for the newsroom, a shortage she said she would explain to the board of directors, which decides/decide all matters on the budget.
16. One of my classmates typifies/typify student apathy.
17. Drinking beer and sleeping is/are the most important things in my life.
18. Dillon said he has insurance for everything except the buildings, which is/are owned by Thomas F. Williams.
19. Approximately 51 percent of the U.S. population is/are female.
20. There is/are only one way to beat taxes.
21. Neither the professor nor her two assistants teaches/teach this course in a style students like.
22. Each student is/are responsible for getting the work done on time.
23. All students considers/consider that an imposition.
24. The General Assembly and the governor disagrees/disagree on the solution.

Check your answers against those in Appendix D.

Problem 3: Correct Use of Pronouns

Pronouns are little words—he, she, you, they, I, it—that stand for proper nouns. Look at this sentence:

International Trucking is hiring 20 new drivers because it is expanding in the Southeast.

In this sentence, the word "it" is used to substitute for International Trucking. Pronouns help us avoid needless repetition in language by doing the work of the larger nouns, which are called antecedents. In the example above, "International Trucking" is the antecedent for the pronoun "it."

Pronouns must agree with their antecedents, as in the following examples:

- Marianne said she (Marianne) would never color her (Marianne's) hair.
- Baltimore became a model city after it successfully restored the waterfront.
- Journalism is a popular major, and now it prepares students for many careers.

Following are guidelines to ensure correct pronoun choices.

1. Watch for collective subjects—groups that are treated as single units—and use the correct pronoun.

- The committee gave its report.
- The United Mine Workers gave out a list of its legislative goals.

2. When using singular pronouns, use singular verbs.

- Each of the rose bushes was at its peak.
- Everyone in the audience rose to his or her feet and chanted.

3. Use correct pronouns to handle issues of sexism in language. The generic person is no longer "he."

- Each of the students had his or her book.
- The students had their books.

4. Be attentive to stray phrases or clauses that come between pronouns and antecedents and cause agreement problems.

- He presented the list of candidates being considered for the office and told the committee to choose from it.
- The list of candidates for the position has been trimmed.

5. Use reflexive pronouns only when a subject is doing something to herself/himself or themselves.

- Jan introduced herself to the new chancellor.
- Henry never could forgive himself.
- The relatives had the chalet to themselves.

Slammer for Pronouns

To ensure agreement of pronoun and antecedent, write the appropriate pronoun for each of the following sentences. Use a piece of paper to record your answers.

1. Each student had (his or her/their) assignment completed before class.
2. General Foods plans to change (its/their) approach to marketing baked goods.
3. Larry introduced me and (him/himself) to the governor.
4. The jury took (their/its) deliberations seriously.
5. The board of directors set a date for (their/its) annual retreat.
6. The Redskins (is/are) my favorite team.
7. Neither the Terps nor the Crimson Tide (was/were) having a winning season.
8. Neither of the teams (was/were) victorious.
9. The alumni voted to charge $1 an issue for (their/its) magazine.
10. Any of the three finalists (is/are) an excellent choice.
11. The six-member committee voted to reverse (its/their) decision.
12. The librarian's collection fascinated him, and he asked to borrow from (her/it).
13. The media (is/are) ignoring Perot's speeches.
14. Each of the students could handle the job by (himself or herself/themselves).
15. Everyone in the audience rose to (his or her/their) feet for the ovation.

Check your work against the answers in Appendix D, and prepare to tackle the biggest pronoun problem of all: the WHO/WHOM dilemma.

Who and Whom

The word *whom* has all but disappeared from spoken English, so it is little wonder that few of us know how to use it correctly. Even though usage is changing, writers of published materials still need to know the rules that govern the distinction between who and whom.

1. Who is a substitute for subjects referring to he, we, or she, or the nominative pronoun.

- Who saw the meteor?

The statement, He saw the meteor, as a question becomes, Who saw the meteor? "Who" is substituted for the subject "he." Relative clauses work the same way when "who" is substituted for a subject. In the sentence, He questioned the man who saw the meteor, "who" substitutes for the subject of the clause, He saw the meteor. This is confusing because the entire clause serves as an object of the verb questioned. But the function of the clause does not change the role of a pronoun; in this sentence, the role of "who" is as the subject of the verb "saw."

2. Whom is a substitute for objective pronouns such as him, her, or them.

- Whom did he question for hours?
- He questioned her for hours.

The statement, He questioned her for hours, as a question becomes, Whom did he question for hours? "Whom" is substituted for "her" as the object of the verb questioned. Substitution works the same way in relative clauses. In the sentence, Marcella was the one whom he questioned for hours, "whom" substitutes for the object "her" in the clause, He questioned her for hours. Again, it is the role of the pronoun within its subject–verb structure that determines whether it is subject or object and therefore *who* or *whom*.

That and Which

Another fine distinction between pronouns is the difference between "that" and "which." Again, the spoken language no longer follows strict rules regarding these subordinate conjunctions, but careful writers need to observe the following guidelines:

1. "That" is a restrictive pronoun, indicating that the information it precedes is essential for correct understanding of the sentence.

- Dogs prefer bones that improve their dental health.

The use of "that" tells us that dogs prefer only this specific kind of bone.

2. "Which" precedes nonessential material; therefore, it typically appears with commas (the ones used to set off nonessential information).

- Dogs prefer bones, which improve their dental health.

The use of "which" tells us that all bones improve dogs' teeth.

3. "That" and "which" are not interchangeable. As you can see in the example sentences, the meaning of the sentence is affected when the comma is added in the second sentence and "that" becomes "which." In the first sentence, dogs like only bones that are good for them; in the second, dogs like bones better than other things, and bones just happen to be good for dental health. The second sentence is far more logical.

Slammer for Who/Whom and That/Which

On a sheet of paper, write the appropriate pronoun in the sentences below.

1. Alvin, (who/whom) everyone adored, absconded with the family fortune.
2. Betty, (who/whom) was the apple of his eye, followed him to Mexico.
3. The FBI agents (who/whom) Alvin had avoided for several months finally arrested him.

4. Veronica, Alvin's sister, (who/whom) needed the money desperately, refused to post bond.
5. Alvin, (who's/whose) health was delicate, wasted away in prison.

Select the appropriate pronoun, then note the proper punctuation as needed in the following sentences.

1. Betty bought a gun (that/which) was on sale and set out to free Alvin.
2. She headed north from Mexico in a car (that/which) had more than 130,000 miles showing on its odometer.
3. The car (that/which) had New Jersey license plates was quickly spotted by police in Texas.
4. The Texans (that/which/who/whom) spoke in a slow drawl told her she was wanted in New Jersey for conspiring with Alvin.
5. She pulled out the gun (that/which) she had in her glove compartment and started shooting.
6. The policeman (that/which/who/whom) was standing closest to her car died after he was struck by a bullet.
7. Other officers took Betty's gun (that/which) now was empty of bullets.
8. They also arrested Betty and placed her in a jail (that/which) overlooked the Rio Grande.

Check your answers against those in Appendix D and move on to the next grammar problem: modifier placement.

Problem 4: Sentence Structure

Aside from fragments and run-on sentences, two other categories cause most adult problems with sentence structure: faulty parallelism and modifier placement.

Journalists often struggle with giving sentences parallel structure, that is, making sure that series or lists of phrases are parallel in form. Rather than, "He enjoys reading and to go skiing," use the parallel form, saying, "He enjoys reading and skiing." Writers must always remember to check lists within sentences as well as bulleted lists to see that phrases are stated in parallel form, as shown in these examples:

- Marvelene listed steps in planning a successful party: sending invitation early, greeting guests personally, and supplying abundant food and drink.

- A successful hosts always is sure

  To send invitations early,
  To greet guests personally, and
  To supply abundant food and drink.

Other sentence errors may occur when modifiers are placed incorrectly and give readers an inaccurate, sometimes humorous, picture, as for example, in these sentences:

Wrong: Swinging from an overhead wire, we saw a kite.

Better: We saw a kite swinging from an overhead wire.

Wrong: When wheeled into the operating room, the nurse placed a mask over my face.

Better: The nurse placed a mask over my face after I was wheeled into the operating room.

Wrong: We saw a herd of sheep on the way to our hotel.

Better: On the way to our hotel, we saw a herd of sheep.

To solve modifier placement problems, place modifying clauses and phrases closest to what they modify.

Slammer for Modifiers

Modifiers are placed with what they modify. Rewrite the sentences below on a piece of paper, and correct misplaced modifiers. Some sentences are correct as written.

1. The waiter served ice cream in glass bowls which started melting immediately.
2. The Simpsons gave a toy robot with flashing eyes to one of their sons.
3. We saw a herd of sheep on the way to our hotel.

4. Most people have strawberry shortcake topped with mounds of whipped cream.

5. The house is one of the oldest in Rockville, where Mrs. Rooks taught ballet.

6. Flying at an altitude of several thousand feet, the paratroopers could see for miles.

7. I could not convince the child to stop running into the street without yelling.

8. After the first act of the play, Brooke's performance improves, the critic said.

9. While watching the ball game, Sue's horse ran away.

10. The museum director showed me a spider with the orange diamond on its belly.

11. The bank approves loans to reliable individuals of any size.

12. After being wheeled into the operating room, the nurse placed a mask over my face.

13. Riding in a glass-bottom boat, we saw thousands of colorful fish.

14. Aunt Helen asked us before we left to call on her.

15. Do it yourself: Make up a sentence suffering from modifier malady. Then correct it.

Check your work against the answers in Appendix D, and prepare for the final grammar problem: word usage.

Problem 5: Correct Word Usage

English is a language enriched by words borrowed from other languages, resulting in a rich vocabulary—but also, in many cases, in unorthodox spelling and idiosyncratic usage. It makes little sense to have both "affect" and "effect" in the same language, functioning so similarly but not identically. And why do we distinguish between "pore" and "pour," or "flair" and "flare"? Who cares?

Careful writers have to care because subtle usage errors can cause big misunderstandings. In addition, correct usage leads to credibility; readers have confidence in error-free reading.

The number of troublesome words in daily use is so great that no attempt is made to list them all here. Instead, we have included as Appendix B Professor Thom Lieb's Abused Word List, a catalogue of usage problems that most often plague writers. Get acquainted with the Abused Words List by working on the following exercise.

Slammer for Abused Words

Use Appendix B to help identify correct usage for each of the following troublesome words.

Hopefully

Affect *versus* effect

Less *versus* fewer

It's *versus* its

Lie *versus* lay

Sit *versus* set

Comprise *versus* compose

SUGGESTED READINGS

Theodore M. Bernstein, *Dos, Don'ts and Maybes of the English Language.* New York: The Times Book Co., 1977.

John Bremner, *Words on Words.* New York: Columbia University Press, 1980.

E. L. Callihan, *Grammar for Journalists,* 3rd ed. Radnor, PA: Chilton Co., 1979.

Lauren Kessler and Duncan McDonald, *When Words Collide.* Belmont, CA: Wadsworth Publishing, 1992.

Katherine C. McAdams, *The Grammar Slammer.* College of Journalism, University of Maryland, 1991.

Mary Penny, Class handouts, Needham Broughton High School, Raleigh, NC, 1974.

9

Research and Observation

Writing begins with an idea. During a trip to the ocean, a writer is fascinated with the porpoises that periodically surface and roll as they travel offshore. She wants to write about porpoises. But she needs more information than just her observations to write a factual, accurate, complete, and entertaining article. She must learn more.

Gathering information is like detective work. As a sleuth you start with a clue. Step by step you add pieces until you have enough information to reconstruct events and solve the case. As a writer you add to your knowledge until you can create an accurate and complete summary of the topic.

Writers, like detectives, gather information from research, interviews, and observations. Research allows writers to study what others have already found out. That information may be in books, magazines, statistical abstracts, encyclopedias, data banks, or any number of other sources. In today's information age, writers can access thousands of documents that have been stored online and in computer databases.

Armed with facts retrieved in research, writers can interview expert and relevant sources to add personal comment on the topic. Personal reflections add context and interest to facts. Interviewing, quotes, and attribution are discussed in Chapter 10.

Writers also note their own observations. Student writers are sometimes reluctant to include their impressions for fear they will appear too subjective and not objective. They must overcome that fear. In the porpoise story, the writer would be remiss not to describe the rolling action as the sleek, gray mammals break water a hundred yards off the beach. Audiences want to know what the animals look like and how thrilled the author is at seeing a school of several hundred porpoises dotting the waves as they surface for air.

In this chapter you will learn

- How to think about topics and questions,
- How to develop search strategies that will mine libraries, databases, and online resources,
- About the wealth of information in government documents,
- How to be wary of factual errors endemic to print and electronic sources, and
- How observation is a part of gathering information.

Getting Started in Research

Writers start out as generalists; they know a little about a lot of subjects. Some develop specialties or subject areas they prefer, whether they are newspaper or electronic media reporters, public relations practitioners, or advertising copywriters. They may cover general assignment topics or report on special beats such as business, medicine, sports, the environment, children's issues, government, religion, or the media.

Whether they are generalists or specialists, writers need to do research. A medical writer may know medical terminology, but if he wants to write about holistic treatment of cancer, he must become knowledgeable about the topic. A network's government reporter must learn about the newly elected members of Congress before she goes to the opening session.

Writers need to find information that is accurate, relevant, and up-to-date. Time is their greatest enemy. Most writers have deadlines and have limited time to devote to research, particularly if they write for daily publications. So they need to find information quickly and efficiently.

Barbara Semonche, a former newspaper librarian, is the librarian at the School of Journalism and Mass Communication at the University of North Carolina at Chapel Hill. She has developed a dozen guides for students in the quest to find information. She notes

You can be certain of two things: either you will find useful information efficiently or you will not. You will find too much information or too little. Your success will

depend, to a certain extent, upon the quality of your search strategies. The other part is finding the best reference sources.

Developing a Strategy

To be successful in research, you need a strategy to find information. Once you have defined your topics, you must make a list of questions, identify obvious sources, conduct searches for additional sources, review those sources for additional leads, refine their questions, and then interview.

You are a medical reporter and want to write a story on childhood immunizations. You first list information you need to know, such as the following questions:

Initial Question List for Story on Childhood Immunizations

Who has to be immunized?

What are the state laws?

What shots do children have to have?

At what ages do children get which shots?

Are there any reactions to the shots?

How much do the shots cost at a doctor's office?

Can children get shots at public health clinics? How much do they cost?

Where are the clinics here? What are the hours for immunizations?

How many children register for school and aren't immunized?

Is this a problem locally?

Have any other diseases surfaced locally?

Why don't parents get their children immunized?

Additional Questions after Research

What are the risks to children who aren't immunized?

Do children ever die from immunizations?

What are the reactions parents can expect?

How many children in the state aren't immunized properly when they
   start school?

How many immunizations are given each year in the state? In our county?

What childhood diseases are appearing again?

How much of the cost of immunizations does the government pay?

Do we consider some diseases eradicated?

Thirty years ago children suffered from mumps, measles, and even polio. Now children can be protected against even chicken pox. Are we too complacent about a resurgence of diseases?

Are there any diseases left that children need to be protected from?

If a certain number of children are immunized, does that protect other children, as in the herd effect?

What factors prevent parents from having children immunized at the proper time?

The obvious sources would be newspaper and journal indexes, articles and information in databases, pediatricians, and local health department and school officials. As you do research you uncover articles that name experts in the field, identify agencies that oversee immunizations, and show a reappearance of some childhood diseases.

Eventually your source list grows to include state health officials, state statutes that stipulate which immunizations children must have to enter school, officials at the Centers for Disease Control, legislators who allocate funds for immunizations, parents, and even children. You refine your list of questions for each source and prepare to interview your sources.

Your search strategy is similar if you are writing a story for the alumni magazine on a graduate whose first novel has been published. She is an assistant professor at a college in another state. Before the interview, you need to find information on the author. The first part of the strategy is to start close to home: the university's alumni files and the yearbooks for the time the author was on campus. Perhaps her publisher's Web site contains biographical information on authors.

You then might consult general biographical reference books. Your alumna might be notable enough to be included in *Who's Who*. But you discover she's not. If you can find no accessible biographical history, you will have to rely on a strategy that includes interviewing former professors, roommates, colleagues, friends, and family members. You may have to call the

English department where she teaches and have someone send her curriculum vitae via facsimile. You may have to consult newspaper indexes in her home state to find specific articles about her. If one source indicates an organization to which she belongs, you may need to look for references on that organization. Articles about the organization may include material about your up-and-coming author.

Basic Reference Sources

A multitude of references exist. Many are in libraries, and many are online—and some appear in both places. Traditional texts such as *The Canterbury Tales* or *Bartlett's Familiar Quotations* exist as searchable Web sites. Whatever the form, writers always need general reference books such as encyclopedias or the *World Almanac,* which is updated annually. Some reference books furnish interesting or unusual data, such as an *Acronyms, Initialisms and Abbreviations Dictionary,* which can clarify the meaning of the acronym M.A.S.H. Or you may check quotes in publications such as *Familiar Quotations* or the words of a presidential speech on the White House Web site. *Standard and Poor's Register* lists officers of major corporations and their addresses and telephone numbers, which can lead to expert sources.

The best place to launch your research is the online catalogue of your college or university library. The online catalogues permit searching by keywords as do Web browsers that link users to relevant sites. Keyword searches greatly increase the ease and speed of getting useful results.

Today's researchers and writers use hundreds of sources and always must be sure sources are credible and updated. Listed here are some types of publications that writers traditionally have relied on for information.

BIOGRAPHICAL SOURCES. Such sources list information about well-known people. Some are specific, such as *Who's Who in American Politics* or *Who's Who in the United Nations and Related Agencies.* The information will include birthdate, parents' names, education, career, awards and achievements, and family data. Among other biographical sources are *Who's Who, Contemporary Newsmakers, Current Biography, Contemporary Authors,* and *Who's Who among Hispanic Americans.* More than 100 biographical dictionaries exist, each focusing on a special group or profession.

STATISTICAL INFORMATION. *Statistical Abstracts of the United States* is one of the most widely used reference books. It provides information from the number of police officers in Albuquerque to the number of houses with indoor plumbing in Lincoln, Nebraska. Data are based on information collected by the federal government and other sources. *Census of Population of the United States* is published every ten years after the U.S. Census is conducted. Census information also is available on CD-ROM and on the Internet. *Editor and Publisher Market Guide* contains data on cities, such as the number of shopping malls a city has and whether its water is fluoridated. Most states compile statistical books, particularly those dealing with vital statistics: births, deaths, marriages, and divorces. Writers can find information on states, counties, cities, and even sections within cities that is especially helpful if they are looking for the local angle on a story. For international information, writers can consult the *United Nations Demographic Yearbook.*

A word of caution: Many statistical books do not come out quickly, so online information, if it is available, is preferable. For example, a state's 1999 statistical data may not be published until May 2000 because of delays in reporting year-end figures and in producing the copies.

POLITICAL AND GOVERNMENT INFORMATION. The *U.S. Government Manual* contains information on departments and agencies in the executive branch. *Congressional Quarterly* publishes a weekly report that catalogues the voting records of Congress and major political speeches. States annually publish manuals that contain information about branches of government and legislatures, summaries of the state history, the state constitution, and biographies of major state officials. Information on foreign governments and leaders can be found in reference books such as *Statesman's Yearbook* and *Current World Leaders.*

GEOGRAPHIC DATA. Writers may need to locate cities, towns, and countries. They can refer to the *Times Atlas of the World* and *Rand-McNally Commercial Atlas.* A gazetteer, such as the *Chambers World Gazetteer,* will describe an area and its location, population, and history.

BUSINESS INFORMATION. Writers may need data on a company or an industry, and students may need information on a potential employer. Today's competitive companies usually have extensive and interactive Web sites.

Research on companies may also be found in annual reports, which are on file in many libraries. Comparative data on companies may be found in resources such as *Dun and Bradstreet Reference Book of Corporate Managements, Standard and Poor's Register,* and Moody's *Manuals.*

Writers should always remember basic sources such as telephone books, city directories, and maps. They should rely on assistance from reference librarians to direct them to current and complete indexes and other references. Many beginning writers waste time trying to find information on their own when they could do research much faster if they would ask for direction. Librarians can help writers with search strategies and key words that will expand their source list.

Pitfalls in Research

The hunt for information may be complex. Librarian Barbara Semonche warns that not all information is in a compact, convenient form. At the start of a search, students may discover people with the same name, such as William Perry. William Perry was a football player also known as "the Refrigerator." Another William Perry was secretary of defense under President Clinton.

Information may be dated. Some biographical reference material is not cumulative, and you may have to look in earlier editions. Students and other researchers must remember that not every reference includes every individual, and those that do may not have all the facts about an individual. Researchers must look at many sources to find complete information. Searching for information is rarely one-stop shopping. But using many sources helps uncover discrepancies and inconsistencies about information and also helps ensure that information is as accurate as possible.

Writers should look continually for other sources. The research game is a detective hunt. Names or sources mentioned in an article or in references can lead to nuggets of information elsewhere. The only constraints will be time and deadline pressure.

Government Sources

Local, state, and federal governments produce millions of pages of documents every year. Documents range from official findings, such as federal Food and Drug Administration studies, to county tax records and the disposition of local traffic cases. Most government documents are open and accessible to the public. Many are free by mail on request, and others are available at the city hall, at the county courthouse, at a regional federal repository, on the World Wide Web or at the Library of Congress. They provide a wealth of information for writers and curious citizens.

Writers should find out where federal depository libraries are located in their states. More than 1,400 exist across the country and contain thousands of federal documents. The 52 regional depositories house all federal documents available to be deposited but not necessarily all federal documents that are produced. A writer can ask a librarian in a federal depository to obtain material from a regional depository via interlibrary loan.

Public Records

When government documents are produced in the course of business, the documents are considered to be public. The documents have been created by government, which is supported by taxpayers' money. Researchers, writers, and anyone who wants the documents can request to see them or to have copies made. All states have laws that pertain to what is and what is not a public record. The general rule most journalists follow is that any document is considered to be a public record unless the agency or individual who has the document can cite the section of state statute that prevents its disclosure. If the agency cannot, it must relinquish the information.

Media writers should know what the open records laws are for their particular state. State press associations can provide the law and its exceptions. Publications such as *The News Media and the Law,* published by the Reporters Committee for Freedom of the Press, can be consulted. The Electronic Frontier Foundation is a valuable resource and can be accessed via Internet.

Agencies can charge a reasonable fee for photocopying documents. Most states have regulations pertaining to computer storage of public documents and reasonable charges for making copies or providing access to computerized information. Some news organizations have the computer capability to tap directly into state databases, such as drivers' license records.

Freedom of Information Act

In 1966 the U.S. Congress passed the federal Freedom of Information Act (FOIA). The act became law in 1967 and has been amended three times.

The law is much like state laws regarding public records. Anyone is allowed to make a written request for information from any federal agency, but not all information is available. The act provides broad exemptions, such as information relating to national defense or foreign policy, internal personnel rules and practices of an agency, personnel and medical files that would constitute an invasion of privacy, information compiled for law enforcement purposes, and geophysical information such as that related to well locations.

The media have worked continually to reduce the number of exemptions. Michael Gartner, former president of the American Society of Newspaper Editors, once lamented in a speech on national Freedom of Information Day that the name "Freedom of Information" implies that government is holding information hostage. He objected to many of the restrictions, particularly those that prevent publication of what the United States broadcasts to developing countries over the Voice of America.

The act sets out the procedure for requesting information, the time required for an agency to respond, appeals procedures, and fees. Individuals must pay the cost of photocopying the information but can request waiver of that cost if the release of the information is in the public interest.

Writers or individuals seeking information under the act may be frustrated. Delays can occur even when procedures are followed. The request must be specific and must be sent to the proper agency. When the information is uncovered, a reporter may receive sections or entire pages inked out to protect exempted information. The reporter pays the cost of photocopying all pages—even the blackened ones.

FOIA searches can be time-consuming and costly, but many journalists and researchers have used them to find information for fact-filled articles. For example, graduate student and former journalist Elizabeth Witherspoon used the FOIA in 1997 to obtain copies of documents in a U.S. Air Force pilot's impending court martial. First Lieutenant Kelly Flinn had been charged with adultery, conduct unbecoming an officer, failure to obey a lawful regulation (fraternization), failure to obey a lawful order, and making a false statement. Flinn was a graduate of the Air Force Academy and the first female B-52 bomber pilot in Air Force history.

The charges were in connection with an affair she had with the husband of an enlisted woman and sexual relations she had with another enlisted man at the Minot Air Force Base in North Dakota. If found guilty, Flinn faced up to nine years in prison.

When Flinn's case became public, a national media frenzy developed around her allegations of sexism and a double standard by the Air Force in prosecuting adultery cases. The television magazine show *60 Minutes* aired an exclusive interview with Flinn. U.S. Senator Slade Gordon came out in her support, and her family enlisted the help of a public relations firm and even established an Internet Web site to tell her story and raise funds for her legal defense.

To avoid a possible criminal conviction and prison term, Flinn petitioned Secretary of the Air Force Sheila Widnall, also the first female in her post, for an honorable discharge immediately before the start of her court martial proceedings. In May 1997, Secretary Widnall granted Flinn a general discharge, making her ineligible for service as a pilot in the Air Force Reserves, and ordered her to repay part of the cost of her education at the Air Force Academy.

Graduate student Witherspoon wanted copies of Air Force documents so she could compare them with what the media had reported about the case. Witherspoon and others had noted many distortions and misrepresentations of the facts. She also wanted to look at how Flinn had used the media and public relations tactics to advance her innocence.

In June 1997, Witherspoon first requested these documents by telephone both to the staff judge advocate (attorney) and the public affairs officer of Minot AFB. When she did not receive a complete set of documents, she made a formal Freedom of Information Act request in writing to the staff judge advocate. Her husband, who had served as an attorney with the U.S. Navy, guided her in the procedure. She had to identify the specific documents and explain the academic or research basis of her request to qualify for a waiver of fees.

Officials at Minot AFB first responded that they were not sure what documents they could release and later that her request had been forwarded to their superiors in Langley, Virginia. In August, a letter from headquarters command stated that they could not meet the FOIA time limits because they were still reviewing records for possible release. Finally, in a package dated October 22, 1997, Witherspoon received most of the documents she had requested. Certain personal information about Flinn was removed, and in some of the documents, the names of other parties in the case were deleted.

Nevertheless, she did receive details of the charges, copies of handwritten testimony by Flinn and her former lover, a transcript of oral testimony obtained at the military's equivalent of a grand jury proceeding, and copies of love letters. Witherspoon noted

> *"Like any journalist, I wanted to compare actual documents — the facts — with what people were saying about the case in the media. This was a very emotional issue for many. The FOIA process took four months, which is a long time in the world of journalism. However, it is very reassuring to see that the process does work and that we can exercise this freedom of requesting and obtaining government documents in this country."*

Online Research

Technology has changed the way writers collect, transmit, and share information. Telephone lines, most of which are multifaceted fiberoptic cable, transmit data bits. Distance is irrelevant. A public relations practitioner in Detroit can write a statement and send it via fascimile to a company official at a conference in Switzerland. A reporter can write a story on a laptop computer during a meeting and transmit it in a matter of seconds to the city desk 30 miles away. Photographs, maps, and other visuals in color, as well as text, may be sent as computer files over fiberoptic cable in a matter of seconds.

The major change in recent years has been the way information is stored. People who began writing careers in the mid-1980s and earlier have seen a phenomenal change in the way they seek information. In the "old days" before 1985, most searches for information centered on treks to libraries—newspaper, city or county, university—or wherever resource books were housed. People handled paper to get information.

Writers today still use paper sources, particularly if they are doing historical research and need to read an individual's correspondence. But more and more they can call up information in a matter of seconds while sitting at computers in the office, at home, or in the library. Newspapers, books, magazines, library holdings, and even job banks are online for writers who have Internet access. People can find bibliographical citations and information on individuals or agencies. They can access local computer databases, broader networked systems that combine other databases, or the Internet. So today's searches most often begin in the newsroom as the reporter clicks away at a computer.

Computers have allowed anyone who produces information to store it so that others can access it. This public storehouse of information within the Internet is commonly called the World Wide Web. As the Internet has developed, many databases have been made public on the World Wide Web. The lines are blurring between traditional databases, once accessed through library or university services, and what is stored on the Web. The number of databases available online grow daily in number, diversity, and ease of access. A count in 1998 of more than 8,000 online databases could easily be double that number (or more) today. The *Gale Directory of Databases* has two volumes of databases listed.

Government has taken advantage of the computer information age. Writers can access government files, such as population statistics, via Web sites, such as in Figure 9.1 on page 234. Information-seekers can access THOMAS, a congressional online system; *Congressional Record;* congressional legislation digests; and directories of congressional members' e-mail. Federal, state, and local government agencies have Web sites that provide history, facts about elected officials, and other relevant information. Even the White House has its own Web site featuring news releases of the day, speech transcripts, and e-mail access to the president, first lady, and White House staff.

A group of advertising researchers reports that more than 20 million host computers serve data onto the World Wide Web. Who reads all this material? Nielsen Surveys also reports that more than 50 million adults worldwide are online, about half of them in the United States. And the numbers are growing.

Getting Online

Individuals can get online by subscribing to commercial services that allow them to access online services or to set up e-mail accounts. Subscribers pay a fee to secure logons and passwords to enter the systems. They also pay for the service, generally a flat rate per month. Some commercial services are owned by the media such as America Online, a database service owned by Simon & Schuster publishing company. Telephone companies and private firms are providing Internet access.

Many people have Internet access through workplaces, libraries, or schools as online communication becomes essential. At many universities, students' registration, scheduling, and billing are completed online, just as are tax forms and bank statements. Getting online still remains difficult for many individuals because they cannot afford the cost of a home computer

United States Department of Agriculture

News & Information	What's New
About USDA	Agencies
Opportunities	Search and Help

[News/Information] [What's New] [About USDA] [Agencies] [Opportunities] [Search/Help]

Send comments and suggestions about content of USDA's Home Page to **vic. powell@usda.gov**

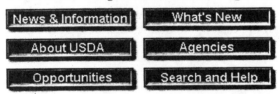 **News and Information**

News...

USDA News Releases
Speeches '97 or '98
Agency Reports/Schedule
Special Events

● **Publications**

Information...

Ag Calendars
Disaster Assistance
Domestic Assistance
Farmers Markets
Gleaning/Food Recovery
Home Gardening
Weather

Fed. Gov't Status [DC]
1998 Budget Summary
1996 Farm Bill
Civil Rights
How To Get Information
Privacy/Security Notice

●**FOIA Information**

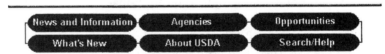

News and Information	Agencies	Opportunities
What's New	About USDA	Search/Help

FIGURE 9.1   *The USDA home page has links to sites within the agency.*

and subscriber fees for a commercial service. Students can log onto the Internet through universities that have Internet access.

Once online, researchers can do the following: search for information, download data or text to their computers, send e-mail, or chat, that is, send and receive messages while online in "real" time. They can also look at home pages for organizations, individuals, government agencies, and others. To find a specific home page, a researcher uses software referred to as a "search engine" and types in key words to find information on any topic. Web site addresses are displayed everywhere—in brochures, advertisements, publications, and even on cereal boxes.

What Students Need to Know

Most students entering college today are comfortable with computers and are eager to experiment. Developing a familiarity with one system eases the transition to other programs. Technology changes fairly quickly. College students today have computer skills unknown to those who graduated five or even three years ago. Faculty members now assign and review work via e-mail. Students submit assignments to class Web sites.

For many students, e-mail is the first step in getting online. Information is available through e-mail. For example, e-mail discussion groups exist. Discussion groups are organized by topic, such as journalism, and information is sent to all subscribers on the mail list. Usually an editor or moderator controls what goes out in the group.

Apart from discussion groups, students can get information via e-mail about other sources, such as government. By sending an e-mail message to a specific address, students and writers can be added to lists and receive continual updates. As with any source, however, information should be double-checked whenever it is to be used. The pitfalls of online research covered later in this chapter apply to information obtained through e-mail.

Schools of journalism and mass communication have recognized that students need skills in using online sources, and many have begun specific courses on electronic information retrieval. Most universities offer workshops and peer training in online search and communication skills.

Using Databases

Databases provide information in two basic ways: citation format or full text. A citation format summarizes the information: title, author, publication, date of publication, and a 25-word summary. A citation database contains references from newspaper and magazine indexes. Citation format allows writers to screen quickly dozens of articles, then select the ones that are most relevant. A writer then would find the full text of the desired articles. The writer could read the entire article on the screen using a database service such as Nexis/Lexis, which has complete articles from publications, including newspapers and magazines. The writer could store noteworthy articles in a computer folder.

Obviously, scanning and reading articles via databases is much faster than searching indexes for individual publications and then searching for the publication and the desired article. Writers who use databases do not have to handle microfilm or old print copies as they once did to find information.

Anyone who uses databases needs to stay current on developments and regulations. With the proliferation of available information, more and more discussion will ensue on issues surrounding privacy, legal uses, copyright, and ethics. A little enterprise will put students in touch with the experts or books on how to use databases. One helpful publication for students is Nora Paul's *Computer Assisted Research: A Guide to Tapping Online Information,* published by the Poynter Institute for Media Studies in St. Petersburg, Fla. Updates are available online.

Pitfalls of Online Research

Newcomers to databases may be so overwhelmed with the ease and efficiency of retrieving information that they overlook the drawbacks. Anyone using a database or retrieving information from the Internet must remember

• Online research requires investment in a powerful computer and one or more telephone lines.

• Online databases may not be complete. Many government documents and historical information are not stored in databases.

• Databases, home pages, and other Internet sources may not be up to date. Although information may be accessed quickly, it may not be as current as a researcher would like. Lag times exist for adding new information to databases. Check for dates when information was last updated.

• Information in a database or on the Internet is not necessarily accurate. It is difficult to tell if information is credible. Writers must double-check the accuracy of what they find in databases.

• Information may be costly. Signing onto a service may require a service fee. Users may pay as little as $30 a month or as much as several hundred dollars per hour to access information, depending on which service they are using and whether they have a discount.

• High demand may make it difficult to sign on. Writers may be frustrated if they repeatedly hear busy signals or are told all access lines are in use when they try to log on.

• Users may have to wade through a lot of junk to find what they want. Computer publications are so accessible that people are pushing information out without regard to the quality of writing or the content.

Most important, researchers—whether freelance writers or student journalists—must remember that the online research is not the final choice. It is just a first step in the research process and only one tool for finding information.

Beyond Documents and Online Sources

You may remember from Chapter 2 the two stories on the North Carolina Appeals Court's decision regarding an indecent exposure case. The stories used different sources, the Associated Press account relying on judges' opinions. Look at the two stories again, and compare how many more sources *The News & Observer* used to develop its story. Reporters should consider documents—whether paper or online—as a start to writing but add interviews for interest and context. Interviews provided context and a clue as to the future of the case in question. Interviewing is discussed in Chapter 10.

> RALEIGH—Baring one's bottom in public may be offensive and indecent, but it doesn't meet the legal standard to be prosecuted for indecent exposure, the state Court of Appeals ruled in a divided decision.
>
> The court ruled 2–1 Tuesday in a 1995 Mecklenburg County case. Judge William H. Helms refused to dismiss the indecent exposure charge against Mark Edward Fly. He was convicted of a misdemeanor after a jury decided Fly dropped his shorts and flashed a woman walking up a staircase to her condominium.

The appeals court ruled that state law prohibits the baring of "private parts" but that doesn't include a person's buttocks.

"We recognize that the conduct engaged in by the defendant in this case is indecent as that term is generally defined," Judge K. Edward Greene wrote for the majority in a divided three-judge court panel. "It is not within the province of this court, however, to vary from the natural and ordinary meaning of words used by our legislature to define the criminal offense.

"In this case there is no evidence that the defendant exposed his genital organs and the trial court therefore erred in denying the defendant's motion to dismiss."

In a dissenting opinion, Judge Ralph A. Walker said the court should including mooning as a violation of the indecent exposure law.

"The buttocks are a part of the human body which morality and decency require to be covered in the presence of others. Thus, our statute should be reasonably interpreted to include buttocks within the meaning of 'private parts' and to protect citizens from the exposure experienced by the witness on this occasion," Walker wrote.

The *News & Observer* printed this account on its front page:

Moonstruck? Well, there's no redress. Not right now in North Carolina, anyway. In language not the least bit cheeky, the state Court of Appeals ruled Tuesday that baring one's behind in public may be bad manners, but it's not indecent exposure because state law doesn't consider the buttocks among a person's "private parts."

The buttocks in question belong to Mark Edward Fly, who revealed them to Barbara Glover on the steps to Glover's Mecklenburg County condominium in 1995 before riding off on a bicycle. Fly was convicted of a misdemeanor and appealed.

The appeals court ruled 2–1 that "private parts" means the reproductive organs only, and that because there was no evidence that Fly showed his, the case should have been dismissed.

Judge Ralph Walker, dissenting, had a more expansive definition of "private parts."

"I really don't know what message the decision sends," said Karen Eady, Fly's public defender. "It says on the one hand we have a free-for-all and we can go around mooning anyone in North Carolina that we want to. On the other hand, I don't think the average Joe Blow would base his actions on the decision like that."

Even if he did, Judge K. Edward Greene points out in a dictum to the decision, the conduct still may be considered a disturbance of the peace.

And even with this case, the end may not be in sight. With a split decision, the state attorney general can appeal the ruling to the state Supreme Court.

William Hart, an assistant attorney general, said his office is considering whether it will do just that.

Observation

Observation is an old method of research that still is a key tool in gathering information. At the same time writers note what speakers are saying, they should be noticing how speakers deliver their remarks, how they move their bodies, what they are wearing, and how the crowd reacts to their comments. Such details are part of the reporting process.

Many students and inexperienced writers, however, are reluctant to include too many details. They fear that audiences will doubt their descriptions. They believe that using description borders on being subjective when, in fact, leaving out description may distort an event. For example, a story may reveal a speaker's eloquence and pointed remarks on world peace, but the reporter may not include that only 22 people were seated in an auditorium that holds 550 people. Although the speaker may have been eloquent, the speech's title failed to attract a sizable audience.

Seeing Isn't Enough

Many people notice their surroundings or the events happening around them in one dimension. They see. Rarely do people consciously smell, taste, hear, or touch their environment. Even using only sight, most people miss much of what goes on. So do writers. They have not trained themselves to observe events that happen simultaneously. At the state fair, a writer may notice the lines in front of concessions but not see the child wailing for more cotton candy, the youth loaded with three bright green teddy bears, the overflowing garbage at a nearby trash can, and the cigarette hanging from the hawker's lips. The unobservant writer does not smell the odor of fried dough, taste the grease in the air near the ferris wheel, hear the ping-ping from the shooting gallery, or feel the slap of heat from the barbecue cookers.

To be skillful observers, writers must hone all their senses. To be complete and successful writers, they must describe scenes to absent audiences. Even when viewers see events on television, they still need the reporter's or news anchor's observations. When television covered the funeral of Diana, Princess of Wales, correspondents identified each location along the route of the cortege. Without that information, viewers would not have known what they were seeing.

General Observation

Many people exist on autopilot. They drive the same route to work, live in the same house or apartment for years, and work in the same office. They become less and less observant. What about you?

Any person or writer can hone observation skills. Try this experiment: Take a piece of paper. Describe what your roommate or friend wore to school or work today. Note colors and types of fabric, if possible. What did you eat for breakfast? Can you remember the smell as well as the taste? What about the color or feel? What sounds do you hear in this room? Can you name more than three?

Keep a notebook in your car, backpack, or pocket. Start recording what you see and hear in multidimensional ways. Although most people can note different sounds, it is harder to catch and record events happening simultaneously. The oft-told adage is that two people on a street corner would give two different accounts of an accident witnessed by both.

Think of ways to compare what you see with events or items that are common knowledge. When author Barbara Victor met Iraqi leader Saddam Hussein, she noted to a group of college students, "He looked like [singer] Tom Jones in an Yves St. Laurent jumpsuit." She could have said that he looked like a pop singer in a one-piece outfit, but the image would not have been the same.

How Observation Changes the Action

Often you need to take notes unobtrusively, especially when the act of notetaking may change the behavior of an individual you are observing. Did the person across the aisle on the bus sit up straighter when she noticed you writing? Did your friend start picking up his clutter when you started taking notes about the room? Your presence can change the way events unfold.

When reporters cover a meeting, a rally, or a store opening, their presence affects how people behave. The town council members sit up straighter and look busy when the public access television channel is airing the meeting. Rally organizers look efficient and engaged when reporters approach. Store officials beam smiles of success on the first day of business.

The trick to accurate observing is to observe over time. Most people can maintain a facade for some time, but they cannot keep it up forever. You may have to observe for more than a few minutes. Despite the television cameras, the losing team's cheerleaders are hardly as media conscious at the end of a game as they were at the outset. Two hours into a meeting, the mayor may forget the unobtrusive camera and rail against the accusations of an unhappy citizen.

Participant Observation

Social scientists have long used observation by participants as a means of getting information about groups. They join a group as participants to observe individual behavior within a group and the individuals' interactions. Journalists also have adopted the practice, gaining admission and recording the interactions of the group. Such intrusion by journalists affects the way people interact. Over time, however, reporters become accepted, and other members may forget their role.

Because their presence does affect how members relate, some journalists have opted to become members of groups and not to identify themselves as reporters. In the 1890s reporter Nellie Bly pretended to be a mental patient to get a true picture of how the insane were treated at Blackwells Island, New York's asylum for the mentally ill. Some have joined cults, followed the Hell's Angels, or gotten jobs in nursing homes. One reporter in her mid-20s enrolled in a Philadelphia high school to observe it firsthand—and was invited to the senior prom. Before resorting to undercover work, reporters and their editors must determine that a change of identity is the only way to get the story.

In either case, problems can arise when it is time to write. Reporters may feel a kinship to the group and have difficulty setting themselves apart. Journalists who become group members put their impartiality at risk in writing a story. Writers may become too emotional or too attached to sources and not be able to distance themselves. They also run the risk of not knowing completely whether their presence altered the group in any way. They can double-check their reactions and observations, however, by interviewing a balanced mix of sources. Reporters may also suffer complaints from group members who may feel betrayed when the article appears.

Nonverbal Communication

Although writers get the bulk of their information from sources and from interviewing, they can add details from nonverbal communication. Such cues come from the way people move or act when they say something. A politician may raise his eyebrows at a constituent's question. A child may shift his hands behind his back when leaving the kitchen. A teacher may frown while correcting student essays. Each action implies a thought or behavior to the observer. The politician may be surprised. The child may be guilty of swiping a cookie. The teacher may be unhappy about a good student's low grade.

When recording nonverbal cues, reporters must be careful. The same cue may carry different meanings for different observers. Furrowed eyebrows may indicate puzzlement or anger. Waving hands can mean agitation or enthusiasm. A smile may be sincere or forced. Generally one action alone is not sufficient to indicate how an individual is feeling. The gestures must be catalogued in addition to words and other body movements. A reporter may have to go so far as to ask an individual what a particular posture meant. For example, pacing during an interview may not be a result of nervousness; the interviewee may suffer from restless legs syndrome, but no reporter could tell that simply by observing.

In addition, nonverbal actions may have different meanings across cultures. In some cultures or ethnic groups, individuals do not have eye contact while speaking. An ignorant or inexperienced reporter might be suspicious of such behavior, thereby including a cultural bias. When business leaders from the United States engage in negotiations with Japanese officials, they have to learn etiquette and protocol. For example, the Japanese consider it offensive to write on a business card, while in the United States, executives and others make notations or add home telephone numbers to business cards. The good reporter learns about cultural differences or asks questions to clarify behavior. Such sensitivity and awareness is essential to accurate reporting.

Dangers in Observation

John Salvi was charged with murdering two people and injuring five others in shootings at two abortion clinics in Boston. When Salvi was arraigned on weapons charges in conjunction with the shootings, Gary Tuchman of CNN gave a live report and description for audiences who were not in the courtroom. Tuchman described Salvi as wearing a blue blazer, white shirt, white socks, loafers, and nice pants. The description implied that Salvi had dressed conservatively and neatly. A print news account reported that Salvi was wearing "an ill-fitting blazer." The implication here contradicted the neat appearance of Tuchman's report. Which account was right? Audiences who heard and read the two accounts may have noticed the discrepancy and been puzzled. Or maybe it just added to their belief that you cannot trust the media to be right.

Tuchman also took his reported observation one step further. He noted to viewers that if they had a stereotype of someone who would be charged with committing murder, Salvi did not look like that stereotype—that is, Salvi did not look like someone who would commit murder. Viewers may have wondered: "What does the stereotypical murderer look like? Why didn't Tuchman give us a description of that stereotype?"

Observation plays a major role in writing, but we must be circumspect about the descriptions we use. As was discussed in Chapter 7 on bias, we as writers carry our prejudices and biases with us as we collect information and write. We must be careful. Think about Tuchman's reference to a stereotypical murderer. Can you describe one? Of course not. If murderers were readily identifiable, people who have been killed would have had some warning. But murderers vary in shape, size, age, gender, skin tone, hair color, and clothing preference. They do not all have greasy hair and shifty beady eyes and act furtively or in a suspicious manner.

The Importance of Accuracy

As we noted in the account just discussed, Tuchman's observations may have been distorted by his experiences. He may have a stereotypical idea of what a murderer looks like. Writers can bring biases to observation, just as they can to any aspect of reporting. Chapter 7 discusses bias in reporting.

Just as you double-check facts, you should be circumspect about your observations. Take emotions into account. If you covered an antiabortion rally, you may have found your emotions surging if you are pro-choice. Despite your role as a journalist, your feelings may not be neutral. Your feelings may influence your description. Be aware.

To ensure accuracy, you should record impressions in your notebook at the scene or as soon as possible afterward. The longer you wait, the fewer details you will remember accurately. Memory fades over time.

Like other kinds of research, observation leads to a more complete message. Description that is simple, clear, and complete also will aid accuracy. Writers should lay out description alongside other facts and allow audiences to judge for themselves. Audiences invariably will apply their own biases to the description and form their own opinions, but the writers' choice of words should not be the deciding factor.

EXERCISES

1. Gene Roberts, former *New York Times* managing editor and *Philadelphia Inquirer* editor, is coming to campus to give a lecture. Before the lecture, he will have a news conference, and you will attend for the campus newspaper. First, you need to find out more information. Using three biographical sources, answer the following questions. Cite the reference used. One reference should be online.
   a. When and where was Roberts born?
   b. Where did he go to college?
   c. What newspapers did he work for other than the *Times* and the *Inquirer?*
   d. Has he written any books? If so, list the titles.
   e. Has he won any awards? If so, list them.

2. Identify a reporter in your college community or in your hometown by reading bylines and articles in the respective paper. Call the reporter and ask what sources he or she uses in researching stories. Note whether the reporter uses online sources to retrieve information. Find out how the reporter ensures accuracy in using sources. Share the information with your class.

3. You are the state desk researcher for the local newspaper. The state editor wants to do a story on parents who are charged with killing their children. In making the assignment to a reporter, the editor asks you to do an online search of national newspapers and magazines to find accounts of such crimes. Your task is to prepare a memo to the state editor that lists six references to substantial articles on parents who are charged with killing their children. The references need to be annotated, that is, they

should be accompanied by explanatory notes as well as enough information to enable the reporter to find the articles.

4. Select a commercial online service. Contact the company and get information about the cost to become a subscriber, how to access it, services, and whether it positions itself as a leader or unique among computer services offering databases and why. Write a synopsis and share it with the class.

5. Attend a campus or town government meeting as an observer along with another student. Use your senses to take notes on what transpires outside the actions of the officials. Write a description of the meeting, using aspects such as the room, the mood, the speakers' attitudes, the officials' attitudes, the tone of the meeting, and how many people attended. Then compare your account with the other student's account. See what each of you chose to include and chose to ignore. Compare the ways you described aspects of the meeting. Then discuss what made your observations different.

REFERENCES

Freedom of Information Act, 5 U.S.C. 552, 1966. Amended in 1974, 1986, 1996.

Michael Gartner, Speech in honor of national Freedom of Information Day. Washington, DC, National Press Club, March 1989.

Global Commerce Link Web site. Available at: http://www.commerce.com.

Bruce D. Itule and Douglas A. Anderson, *News Writing and Reporting for Today's Media*, 3rd ed. New York: McGraw-Hill Inc., 1994.

Margaret Jackson, *Selected Resources for Journalists*. Chapel Hill, NC: Business Administration/Social Sciences Department, Davis Library, University of North Carolina at Chapel Hill, 1989.

Lauren Kessler and Duncan McDonald, *Mastering the Message: Media Writing with Substance and Style*. Belmont, CA: Wadsworth, 1992.

Mary McGuire, Linda Stilborne, Melinda McAdams, and Laurel Hyatt, *The Internet Handbook for Writers, Researchers, and Journalists*. New York, NY: The Guilford Press, 1997.

Network of Australia and New Zealand Web site for advertisers. Available at: http://www.admedia.aust.com.

Nora Paul, *Computer Assisted Research: A Guide to Tapping Online Information*, 2nd ed. St. Petersburg, FL.: The Poynter Institute for Media Studies, 1994.

Randy Reddick and Elliot King, *The Online Journalist: Using the Internet and Other Electronic Resources.* Orlando, FL: Harcourt Brace College Publishers, 1995.

Chip Rowe, "A Journalist's Guide to the Internet." *American Journalism Review,* January 1995.

Barbara Semonche, Personal interview. Chapel Hill, N.C., School of Journalism and Mass Communication, University of North Carolina at Chapel Hill, 1995.

U.S. Department of Agriculture Web site. Available at: http://www.usda.gov.

U.S. Department of the Treasury Web site. Available at: http://www.irs.gov.

Elizabeth Witherspoon, Personal interview. Chapel Hill, N.C., School of Journalism and Mass Communication, University of North Carolina at Chapel Hill, 1998.

10

Interviewing, Quotations, and Attribution

Asking questions and collecting answers—interviewing—is an essential skill for all media writers. Becoming a skilled interviewer takes practice; it is not something someone does naturally.

Most of us interview in a casual way when we are introduced to someone new. We ask questions: Where are you from? Are you a student? What year are you in school? What is your major? We hope to get responses that help us learn more about the person.

But if you are going to write about that individual, your questions have to be much more specific. You hardly have enough for a story to know that Mark Monroe is a junior from Lake Geneva, New York majoring in computer science. You need more detailed information, perhaps his career objective and how he sees the role of computers in information retrieval.

So good interviewing is more than just carrying on a casual conversation. It takes skill, and it takes practice. This chapter will start you on the road to becoming a good interviewer. In this chapter you will learn

- How to prepare for an interview,
- How to conduct an interview,
- How to handle off-the-record information,

- How to use quotations, and
- The importance of accuracy, attribution, and punctuation in quotations.

Interviewing as a Challenge

Writers do interviews in different ways. The medium they work for, deadline pressures, the accessibility of sources, and people's willingness to talk affect how well a writer can plan and do interviews. Writers face challenges as they work diligently to reach as many sources as possible before a deadline. They become detectives as they figure out just whom they should interview and how. Like anyone else, writers feel nervous and even excited when they have the chance to interview a well-known newsmaker or celebrity. And they feel great satisfaction and accomplishment when a source answers their questions and gives them something extra.

Martin Merzer and Phil Long of the *Miami Herald* combined their talents to write a story about a murder suspect who took two children as hostages and held off police for almost three days. The story relied on dozens of interviews with police, neighbors, the suspect's family, and others to create a factual account that read almost like a short story. As Merzer described

> *This is the kind of writing you don't do frequently and only under special circumstances. The story broke early in the day, so by the time we first covered it, the story was 24 hours old. We knew the basic facts, but we wanted to do a story that would embellish what people already knew and at the same time add details that people didn't know.*

Merzer went to Orlando, Fla., to cover the story the first day, then returned to his office to write from there. Phil Long from the *Herald*'s Vero Beach bureau stayed in Orlando to interview "and to get inside people's heads," Merzer noted. His reports plus Merzer's background produced the story that follows. A first paragraph used next to a photograph that accompanied the story described: "At 5:06 A.M. Friday, after three days and nights of sleepless tension, police rescued two youngsters held hostage by career criminal John Armstrong. The kids emerged unharmed. Police shot the gunman dead through the heart. Here is how it happened."

"I have never prayed so hard in my life"

BY PHIL LONG AND MARTIN MERZER

Herald Staff Writers

ORLANDO, Fla.—Two hours before dawn. The 68-hour mark. Thick fog and light rain muffle 626 18th Street. Three people remain inside the house—murder suspect John Edward Armstrong and his two hostages, Malcolm Phillips, 4, and Tedi Priest, 2.

Armstrong has a gun. He threatens to use it. He also promises to surrender. Three days now.

The police eavesdrop on the house with a button-size microphone snaked through the Venetian blinds and dropped to the floor. They spy on the place with a tiny TV camera hidden next door. They wait, and they wait, and they wait.

One of them, Scott Perkins, 32, has a son nearly the same age as Malcolm. Soon, after a burst of improvised valor and a cascade of bullets, Scott Perkins will be called a hero.

Now, the police perk up. Something new. Armstrong finally—*finally*—slips into a deep sleep. They hear his snores on that microphone.

The cops look at each other. Now, they whisper. Now.

They've been waiting for their chance. Only a few hours ago, though profoundly deprived of sleep by police and sinking out of a crack and heroin binge, Armstrong again refused to surrender.

"I told you, stop bothering me," are among his last words. "I'm not coming out until I'm ready."

Arrested 17 times since 1980, nearly always released early from prison, he faces a murder charge in nearby Winter Park. He crashed into the home Tuesday morning with police in pursuit. He evicted the toddlers' mothers. He shielded himself with the kids.

Now, Police Chief William Kennedy fears that sleep will freshen Armstrong's resolve.

Kennedy also knows that young Tedi is developing a cough and possibly a bronchial infection. He gives the order.

Go in now. Get those kids out of there.

Dressed in black flack vests and other armor, Perkins and six other SWAT officers creep through the fog toward the house. They slip through the kitchen door. The lock had been picked, stealthily and skillfully, 48 hours earlier so it seems locked from the inside but opens from the outside.

They pause. They listen.

A block away, their commander, Frank Fink, and two deputy police chiefs gather outside the command post. They form a circle. They lock hands. They bow their heads.

With the others, Fink prays intensely. He has three sons of his own.

Now inside the house, the commandos tip-toe to the bedroom door. They pause again. They look at each other.

One. Two. Three.

Boom. They kick it open.

And confront an ominous scene: Armstrong is in the middle of the bed. The two kids, in their pajamas, are asleep on either side.

He has a gun in his hand. He has his finger on the trigger.

Now, chaos.

Perkins, a six-year veteran, leaps atop Armstong so he can't point the gun at the kids.

A shot resounds.

A bullet tears through Perkins' left hand, ripping his fingertips, Still, the 5-foot-6, 165-pound officer scoops up the youngsters, one under each arm.

Then, it's over in seconds. At least one bullet penetrates Armstrong's heart.

Clutching the kids, Perkins hustles across the yard. They are met by two burly SWAT officers in combat fatigues and steel helmets. Each holds a teddy bear in Christmas colors, green sweater, red hat.

Malcolm and Tedi, reunited with their mothers and relatives, bear no physical scars of their experience aside from a scratch on Tedi's knee.

"I am so relieved," says Margaret Vickson, Tedi's grandmother.

Tedi's uncle, Alphonso Wright: "I had faith they were going to come out OK."

Armstrong's relatives are outraged. Dorothea Owens, his sister, repeatedly begged him to surrender, repeatedly implored police to remain patient.

"He didn't have to die," she says over and over.

The shooting is being investigated by the Florida Department of Law Enforcement and so police refused to discuss details late Friday.

But they praised Perkins, the nimble saviour of those children.

"He actually dove on the suspect so he couldn't possibly point his weapon at the children," said SWAT Lt. Bob Gregory. "In my opinion, he is a hero."

Said Fink, the SWAT commander: "He was willing to sacrifice himself as a shield."

And they did say that Armstrong gave them little choice but to act.

"We were concerned," said Kennedy, the police chief. "He had nothing to gain by giving up. He knew what charges were facing him.

"We gave Mr. Armstrong every opportunity to come out peacefully. He did not."

They said they had to rescue those kids, which they did. Malcom and Tedi are with their relatives today. It is over.

"I have never prayed so hard in my life. You don't have a heart in your body if you didn't cry when we gave those kids back to their moms," Fink said.

"We were all crying."

(Reprinted with permission of the *Miami Herald*.)

The reporters restructured the dramatic rescue in the present tense so readers could experience the events as they unfolded. The writers used their knowledge of what police were thinking based on extensive interviews and the facts of the hostage-taking and rescue. Note the good writing techniques: simple but active language, subject–verb–object sentence order, short sentences, sentence variety, strong quotes. Long and Merzer maintained the time sequence with phrases "now" this, "now" that. A fifth-grader could read and understand the compellingly written story, and the story is one that would pull most readers from beginning to end. Read the story again and count how many obvious interviews Long and Merzer conducted to produce the single story. The report is an example of what newspapers can provide that audiences would not find in many other media.

Research before Interviewing

The first step in interviewing, of course, is to know your topic. The second is to do research. Before any interview, you should have knowledge of your topic and the people you will interview. The general rule is not to go into an interview cold. You will have more success if your source quickly sees that you are prepared. Preparation shows that you are serious about the interview, and it flatters the source.

With deadline pressure, however, some journalists may find that they do not have time to do research before they have to be on site to cover an event. On some occasions you may go into an interview unprepared. Experienced writers or reporters will tell you that such an experience is uncomfortable and often embarrassing. No one wants to walk up to the newest Nobel Prize winner for medicine and ask, "Now just what was your work that caused you to win?" With the advantages of communication today, a reporter can be on his or her way to an interview while a researcher searches files for background information. The reporter can get data by computer from the researcher and arrive somewhat prepared.

Writers—whether print or broadcast reporters, freelancers, public relations practitioners, or advertising copywriters—look in their own files first for information, then move to the company's or community's library. They may find other articles or broadcasts about their topic, or they may consult research materials such as statistical abstracts. Some may access the Library of Congress or other information databases via the Internet. Specific tips on research can be found in Chapter 9.

Remember that research goes further than printed sources or computer databases, however. In many cases, other people are the best sources of information. When evangelist Billy Graham announced a six-day crusade in Raleigh, N.C., a reporter secured an interview with him in Black Mountain, N.C. She scoured clippings files and other written materials about Graham and his career. The day before the scheduled interview she and a photographer spent the day in Black Mountain. She interviewed the local golf pro, the pharmacist, and even a local minister who on occasion preached to Graham out in the pews. She secured anecdotes and personal recollections that gave her a more complete picture of Graham the man and the evangelist. The information proved valuable for her stories and also let Graham know that she was well prepared for the interview.

Getting the Interview

Once you have sufficient knowledge, you must determine who it is you want to interview. In a story on a local bank president, he would be the primary interview. But for a story on credit card fraud, you must talk to experts in the financial services industry, consumers, and whoever is knowledgeable about the subject. Some names may appear during research, and some may come as referrals in other interviews.

Setting Up the Interview

When you know who it is that you want to interview, you need to determine the best method of interviewing and make an appointment, whether the interview is by telephone or in person. Some interviews can be conducted by e-mail. Online questions and answers are fast and convenient, but remember that they have serious limitations. The writer who interviews only online loses the candid spontaneity that comes with live interviews, as well as any sense of the source's surroundings and personal characteristics. A low chuckle or a timely grin are impossible to detect online.

In setting up any interview, you may have to go through a secretary or a public relations person who maintains the source's schedule, or you may be able to call the person directly.

Make sure that the source is the best for the topic and has firsthand information. If you are working on a story that requires expert opinion, for example, be sure that the source is the appropriate one. The primary surgeon for a lung transplant is a much better source than a hospital public information officer or a physician who assisted during the operation. People who have never been involved in a child abuse case and are just giving you secondhand or hearsay information are not good sources for a story on that subject. A few filter questions up front can eliminate unnecessary interviews: "I am looking for people who tried to break into the country–western music market. Did you ever sing professionally? Or perhaps prepare a demonstration tape for an agent?"

In setting up the interview, be sure to specify the amount of time you will need. Don't underestimate, or you will lack time to ask all your questions. Some people may be willing to be interviewed on the spot, so be ready with your questions. Others will want to set a specific time at a later date. Ask for more time than you will need.

Select a comfortable place for the interview. The source's terrain is best, as he or she is usually more relaxed in a familiar environment. The reporter also has the opportunity to observe personal items, such as family photographs or collected memorabilia, that can add to the story.

Avoid doing interviews during meals. People have difficulty talking while eating, and a discussion over who should pay for food—source or writer—can be uncomfortable. If the individual is from out of town and staying at the local hotel, you may choose to do the interview over coffee—a fairly inexpensive way of meeting and talking.

Dress appropriately for the interview. If you are interviewing the chief executive officer of a Fortune 500 company, wear a suit. If you are meeting a cotton grower in his fields, shuck the high heels. And, if you are meeting with teenagers at the local hangout, blue jeans are okay.

What to Work out in Advance

Do not agree to pay for an interview. Only in very rare situations should you consider paying for information. The news organization may agree to pay because the source's information is newsworthy. Any payment should be worked out ahead of time and be consistent with company policy. If you are a freelancer, you should not agree to pay for information; publications may not buy your work if sources were lured by profit.

Before you start on your list of questions, work out arrangements if you plan to use a tape recorder. A tape recorder is advisable if you are planning an interview that is long or one that might contain controversial or important information. You might want a tape as a backup if you suspect the source might question your quotes in the printed article. Some people may feel uncomfortable with a tape recorder present, and they may need reassurance before you show up. One good way to have a source agree to be taped is to stress your need for accuracy in getting quotes right. Few people will argue.

If you are doing the interview by e-mail, establish a time period for questions and answers so that you will get responses by your deadline. You also might want to agree on a code word that the source will include at the end of responses so that you know the source answered the questions and not someone who had access—whether legally or illegally—to the e-mail account.

Some people will want to see a list of questions before they respond. Such a request can be honored if sources need to collect specific information, such as statistics. People who are not used to being interviewed may want some time to formulate responses. Or if you are getting an actuality to use in a radio broadcast, a source may want a few minutes to write a few sentences. In many cases your deadline will determine whether you have the luxury of submiting questions and waiting for responses. In any case, don't give up the right to ask a question that is not on the list.

Some sources will ask if they can see the article before it is printed or listen to the tape before it is aired. Of course, if you are a public relations practitioner or an ad copy writer, your source—who may be your client—will have final approval. But in the news business, the answer is no. Deadline pressure generally precludes spending the time for a source to review the message. Sources can become editors, wanting to change more than what applies to them.

If a source insists on previewing the piece, check it out with an editor or producer. You may want to find someone else to interview. Be clear if the answer is no. One inexperienced reporter caused herself and her newspaper some unpleasantness because a source thought he would have the right to edit before a story citing him was printed. The reporter did not flatly say no, and the source misunderstood, believing he could review the story in advance. When the story appeared, the source felt deceived.

Writing the Questions

Interviewers, no matter how skilled or practiced, should write a list of questions before an interview. The list can be typed and printed or scribbled on an envelope. The questions ensure that all important aspects are covered during the interview. A reporter can review the list before ending the interview to make sure all points were asked. Questions also serve to keep the interview on track. A minister may divert the interview to a discussion of the writer's religious beliefs. The writer can refer to the list and remind the minister that she is there to interview him. The list can also fill in lags in the conversation.

Covering the Basics

Obviously, when you are planning questions, you want to ask the basics: who, what, when, where, how, and why. But you need to ask other questions to get more information and to make the message complete. One formula for interviewing is called GOSS, an acronym for Goals-Obstacles-Solutions-Start, devised by Professor LaRue Gilleland of the University of Nevada. It can be applied to many interviews and is based on the assumption that people have goals, that obstacles loom before goals, and that solutions can be found to obstacles. Talking about goals, obstacles, and solutions gives the source plenty to talk about. During the interview, you may discover that you need to "start"—to go back to the beginning of an event or topic to get a more complete understanding.

For example, you may interview a chemist who does research on polymers. Using GOSS, you would ask what are the goals of his research, the obstacles to discovering new uses, and the solutions to overcome the obstacles. "Start" would lead you to ask about the whole field of polymer research and what is happening in this particular laboratory compared with others.

Ken Metzler, author of *Creative Interviewing,* has suggested two more letters to Gilleland's GOSS: E for evaluation and Y for why. Evaluation suggests a need for an overall assessment of the situation—seeking meaning beyond the facts. To get such information, the writer asks for the source's interpretation: What does all this (polymers and research) mean to you? The Y is a reminder not to forget to ask why a situation has occurred.

Think about quantitative questions. How many times has the baseball star struck out? How many ounces of marijuana were in the 20-ton haul, and what is the street value? How many tons of concrete are needed for the runway, and is that equal to filling the high school football stadium to the top row?

When formulating questions, think of the unusual aspects. Don't hesitate to include questions you would like answered. Your audiences might as well. You might even ask friends or colleagues what questions they would include if given the chance.

The Interview Itself

Always be punctual for an interview. Making a source wait is rude and may cost you the interview. Call to let the individual know if you will be late.

If you are interviewing a celebrity or high-ranking official, avoid having the air of a fan or worshiper and avoid appearing nervous or excited. Few people would be calm the first time they interviewed singer Whitney Houston or Speaker of the House of Representatives Newt Gingrich. Butterflies are to be expected, but you should show respect rather than adulation.

Getting Started

After you introduce yourself, start the interview with some questions that will set a relaxed mood. For example, if you are in the person's home, comment about trophies, collections, or decor. Show you are interested. Don't ask weighty questions right away.

If you are using a tape recorder, put it in an inconspicuous place. A source who is uncomfortable with the tape recorder may spend more time looking at it than at you. Make sure to use a tape that will cover the length of the interview. You don't want to waste time every 15 minutes checking to see whether the tape has run out.

Most states require that you notify people if they are being taped. If you are doing a telephone interview and plan to tape it, you must ask the individual's permission before you turn the recorder on. Rarely, if ever, will you need to hide a tape recorder in your briefcase or under your clothing.

Avoid starting an interview by asking people what they do. They will know that you haven't done your homework, and they could be insulted. Try to avoid having to ask routine information about a person. You may need to verify your information, however. A student who interviewed author Barbara Victor discovered in a biographical source that she was born in 1944. A question revealed that Victor actually was born a year later, in 1945.

Asking the Questions

Be straightforward and specific in questioning. Don't beat around the bush. "So, Mr. Rich, you have investments and your construction business. And you have inherited money from your uncle and aunt. And I imagine there are lots of people out there who are wondering how much you are worth." Of course, you can preface a question with a statement, but don't talk around a question—ask it. "Mr. Rich, you have investments and inheritance that have many people asking the question: Just how much you are worth?"

Maintain control. Don't let the person lead you. Keeping the interview on track may be difficult for a student writer or inexperienced reporter. Someone who is accustomed to being interviewed may have an agenda or may have what seem to be the usual canned responses. A politician, for example, may ignore a question about changes in tax laws and answer instead about his plan for economic development. If the person digresses, wait until there is a suitable pause, then steer the interview back to the subject. Use your list of questions as a reference. If you interrupt, you could be cutting off some valuable comments.

Avoid becoming interviewed. Try to keep yourself out of the interview. Often a person will throw questions at the interviewer. Be polite and firm and remember that you are there to do the interview, not to be interviewed.

Watch your body language. Avoid any behavior, such as nodding your head, that may subtly indicate you agree with comments. If the source believes you are sympathetic and empathetic, he or she may expect a positive story.

Maintain a professional distance. Do not become the source's friend. Writers who get too chummy with their sources can create tension when the article is published. The source may believe that the writer betrayed confidences.

Leave all preconceptions and misconceptions at home. You may be a single working journalist with no children, and your interview is with a stay-at-home mother with five children. Mask any feelings of envy of her domestic life or notions that her job is not as fulfilling as yours. Do not be antagonistic if you disagree with a person's philosophy. Some people will open up if they sense that you do not agree with them, however.

Listen to the source. Be aware of inconsistencies. Be willing to divert the conversation from the prescribed list of questions if you hear a tidbit that should be developed through another line of questioning. If you do not understand a response, ask for clarification. Remember: If you aren't clear about information, you'll never convey it clearly to audiences.

The Tough Questions

Save all embarrassing and controversial questions for the end of the interview, such as those dealing with a person's gambling debts or reports that a director has bipolar disorder. Of course, if a suitable occasion to ask such a question occurs during the interview, ask it. Be aware that you run the risk of having the interview terminated if you ask a particularly sensitive question. When asking these questions, be straightforward. If you act embarrassed, you will transmit that feeling and possibly not get a response.

Many times writers must interview people who have suffered trauma or witnessed a traumatic event. Such events vary. An individual may have endured years of repeated physical abuse, survived a plane crash, been a hostage in a domestic dispute, or been wounded. A person may have witnessed a friend's drowning, seen a fiery truck crash, or found a house full of diseased and starving animals.

Writers must understand that people who have suffered trauma or an atrocity recover from those events in different ways and at different times, depending on the particular trauma and their personalities. Judith Lewis Herman notes in her book, *Trauma and Recovery,* that part of the healing process is remembering and telling the event. People seeking quotes and information may find individuals who are quite willing to talk and others who refuse to be interviewed. Herman writes:

> *People who have survived atrocities often tell their stories in a highly emotional, contradictory, and fragmented manner which undermines their credibility. . . . It is difficult for an observer to remain clearheaded and calm, to see more than a few fragments of the picture at one time, to retain all the pieces, and to fit them together. It is even more difficult to find a language that conveys fully and persuasively what one has seen. Those who attempt to describe the atrocities that they have witnessed also risk their own credibility.*

Reporters must be aware of the psychological state of people who have just experienced a tragedy or atrocity. They should ask the questions but understand when they do not get complete or even accurate responses. Interviewing more than one source may be required to get a full picture of what actually happened. Reporters may have to come back later for follow-up interviews well after a traumatic event occurs.

Just as it is difficult to approach victims and witnesses, it is hard to interview victims' families. Again, reporters must try to ask the questions, but they must respect a person's right not to answer.

The media, particularly the electronic media, have drawn criticism for asking family members of victims "How do you feel?" only minutes or hours after a relative's death. Although some may view such questioning as aggressive, others regard it as heartless. In some instances, reporters might find that a family member is willing to talk and is helped by remembering the individual. Again, reporters must use judgment and good taste in what they include in their writing and how far they should go in trying to get information.

The fact that the person does not answer a tough question is often noteworthy in a story. A former foreign service diplomat who settled in a small town was arrested on charges of shoplifting. When he refused to answer reporters' questions after his trial, the reporter noted his refusal in the story. His silence supported statements that he was close-mouthed about his current life. But don't fail to ask a question in the expectation that a person might not answer it. You may be surprised and get a response.

Off-the-Record Information

In the middle of an interview, a public official says, "The following information needs to be off-the-record." Stop the official. Don't let him talk any longer. Off-the-record means you cannot use the information. As a writer you don't want information you cannot use. Politely refuse the information. Then you can proceed to clarify what the official means. People have different definitions of what off-the-record means: Don't use the information at all; use it but don't attribute it to me; use it to ask questions of others, but I never said it.

As an interviewer you must remember that many people who have information want to share it but may not want to take responsibility for making it public. They will let you as the writer do it anonymously, or let you, the writer, find someone else to confirm it and become the public source. Be careful. Audiences do not necessarily believe information that is attributed to "a source close to the president" or "a high-level State Department official."

Refusing to accept the information from a source may just get it for you. People who have juicy information usually feel important and want to show they know something you don't. Think about it. Has a friend told you some gossip about someone else and sworn you to secrecy? Within 24 hours had you shared it with someone else, despite your promise? Few secrets exist that are known only by one person. If you refuse off-the-record information that you cannot use, the source may open up.

Think about the Consequences

A final warning: Make sure you and the source are clear on how the information can be used before you accept it. If you agree to use the information but not the individual's name, you must comply. If you agree the tidbit is confidential, you must not publish it. You may want that person as a source again. If you act unethically and violate the agreement, you can write that person off your source list, and you may attract unflattering attention to yourself and your employer.

Consider the problems *The New York Times* encountered with off-the-record information. A *Times* reporter, Marian Burros, was one of five reporters invited to lunch at the White House with first lady Hillary Clinton. Mrs. Clinton set up the luncheon to discuss her image problems with media representatives. The first lady's comments during the two-and-a-half hour luncheon moved from on-the-record to off-the-record. A *Times* article on the luncheon included Mrs. Clinton's statement that she was politically "naive and dumb" in her health care proposals during her husband's first term. The White House, and even other reporters present at the lunch, claimed those particular comments were among the off-the-record statements. The *Times* defended its reporter.

Confusion would have been avoided if the entire conversation had been either on- or off-the-record, rather than jumping around. The publication of off-the-record comments, such as Mrs. Clinton's, whether in good faith or in error, creates problems between sources and reporters. Sources may be more skeptical and guarded if they have to fear that comments shared in confidence will be attributed to them. Reporters may not have access to necessary background or off-the-record information because sources do not trust the media.

The Clinton snafu occurred on the heels of another much-publicized reporter-source incident. Most people felt that Kathleen Gingrich's comments were private when she confided to then CBS anchorwoman Connie Chung the name her son, House Speaker Newt Gingrich, had used in describing first lady Hillary Clinton. Just before Mrs. Gingrich shared the word, Chung had assured her that the confidence would be just between the two of them. Television cameras, on hand to tape the interview, kept rolling while Mrs. Gingrich confessed. The segment was aired, Mrs. Gingrich felt betrayed, and Ms. Chung and her ethics—as well as those of CBS—were blasted by citizens, politicians, and the press.

Note-taking Tips

Most people talk faster than an interviewer can write. If you have trouble keeping up, politely stop the source and ask for a moment to catch up on notes. You could preface it by saying, "I want to make sure I record this correctly, so I need a moment to complete your last comment." Few sources would respond, "I don't care if you get it right. I want to keep talking."

Be sure when you are writing comments that you get them completely rather than in bits and pieces that may not fit together when you write the article. Complete notes help you avoid taking quotations out of context or misinterpreting quotations later.

If you have a quote that is complete, put it within quotation marks in your notebook. Then you will know you have the speaker's exact words when you review your notes and are ready to write.

You may find it handy to flag your notes as you take them. Put a word or two in the margin to indicate where certain information occurs. For example, you may have a wide-ranging interview with the incoming Republican speaker of the state legislature. "Welfare," "tax cuts," "power," and "education" would remind you where each topic was discussed.

At the end of the interview, take a few moments to review notes and questions to ensure that you have asked all your questions. Most sources won't mind waiting while you double-check. If a quote is not clear, ask the source to repeat it. "You said during the interview, Mr. Speaker, that changing the rules will help the House pass legislation faster. Could you clarify the parliamentary procedure a little more?" You also might want to ask if you can telephone if any clarification is needed when you are producing the story.

After the Interview

Take time after you leave the interview to review your notes. Fill in any blanks that might appear confusing later. Note your feelings, the qualities of the source, any additional description, and other details while they are fresh in your mind. You may wish to transcribe your notes immediately to retain important details or impressions. If you store your notes on your computer hard drive, you can call them up easily when it is time to create the piece.

After the interview, you may want to write the person a thank-you note.

Selecting and Using Quotations

You have pages of notes from your interview. How do you determine which quotations to use? The same rules for using quotations from interviews apply to selecting quotations from speeches, presentations, or even published works. You want to select quotations that are vivid, show opinion, reflect the speaker's personality, support the speaker's thesis, and unify a piece of writing.

When to Use Quotations

In organizing material, writers have to decide whether to quote an individual, then whether to use that information in an indirect or direct quote.

Direct quotes give the exact words of the speaker. In some cases, writers will clean up grammar, and they may eliminate profanity. But the quotation marks signify to readers "here's exactly what was said." Direct quotes are used for colorful statements, opinion, and emotions. Direct quotes can convey an individual's personality and manner of speaking. Here's one rule to follow: Use a direct quote if it is better than any paraphrase.

Direct quotes can be either complete quotes or partial quotes. Here is a complete direct quote:

> "We are not selective about whom we arrest," said police chief Martin Bray.

Or

> "The federal government spent millions of dollars to enact the 1986 Truth in Mileage Act, and now it has pulled $600,000 in funding to enforce it," said Charles Bradley, president of the National Odometer and Title Fraud Enforcement Association in Nashville, Tenn.

A partial direct quote would be written as

Company President William Olsen said he would not discuss the reasoning behind the 3 percent pay increase for employees, noting only that "we have to consider many factors in our operating costs and employees' salaries and benefits are part of those factors."

Or even shorter, as in

The coach said the player was "furious at the lack of compassion" exhibited by the fans when he made the error in the third inning.

Or

The senator vowed "to use every last little bit" of his influence to block the bill increasing military spending.

In mixing indirect and direct quotes, be careful not to switch person, for example, switching from third person ("the senator") to the first person ("my influence") as in the following sentence, a flawed rewrite of the one above:

The senator vowed to "use every last little bit of my influence" to block the bill increasing military spending.

A grammatical sentence would use the words "his influence," but then the quote would be inaccurate. In such cases, rewrite, quoting only the phrase "to use every last little bit" as in the first example above.

As a note, most writers avoid using what are called orphan quotes, that is, quotation marks used for emphasis on a single word. For example, "The special envoy said the cease-fire represented a monumental effort." Why use quotations? "Monumental" is hardly an inflammatory phrase or an unusual adjective.

To Paraphrase or Not

Indirect quotes are used to summarize or paraphrase what individuals say, particularly if they have rambled about an issue or topic. They do not use a speaker's exact words and are not set off with quotation marks. Writers use indirect quotes to keep quotes relevant and precise.

Many writers find indirect quotes particularly valuable when speakers have digressed from the main topic or when they inject jokes or anecdotal material that cannot be used.

Here is an excerpt from a speech by Dan Quayle to the National Press Club on Freedom of Information Day during his tenure as U.S. vice president. As with many speeches, these comments are ideal for condensing.

> *I'm particularly pleased to be here on SDX Freedom of Information Day. As I told the national religious broadcasters convention in my first major address as vice president, I come from a First Amendment family, and I'm convinced that a strong, vigorous, and skeptical press is vital to the health and well-being of American democracy, even though some might say that it hasn't always contributed to the health of my own political career. But just as I am convinced that freedom of the press is crucial, I think that all of us recognize that a powerful press poses certain risks as well.*

The result is a single indirect quote.

Quayle said a strong, vigorous, and skeptical press is vital to the health and well-being of American democracy, but a powerful press poses certain risks.

Indirect quotes are valuable in providing a source's information. They are effective in balancing direct quotes within copy.

Correcting Speakers' Grammar and Other Slips

Reporters who covered a high-level state official quickly learned that the man was not a good speaker. He had a vernacular accent for that region of the state, used incorrect grammar, and stated goals that seemed out of reach. How to quote him?

Early in the official's tenure, most newspaper and print journalists chose to paraphrase his remarks so they could clean up the grammar errors. Even in some of the direct quotes, the official sounded well schooled. But a few print journalists soon discovered that cleaning up the official's language was not good practice. Audiences who also watched local television broadcasts saw and heard the official as he really was. The image they read in the newspaper did not match.

Journalists are faced continually with deciding how to use quotations. If a speaker uses improper subject–verb agreement, should the writer correct it in a direct quote? How far should writers go in cleaning up quotes? In the case of the state official, print journalists figured out they had to be true to the quotes or else paraphrase. They could not dramatically clean up the quotes, put them in direct quotations, and tell audiences, "Here's exactly what the man said." He didn't.

The Associated Press Stylebook advises writers:

> *Never alter quotations even to correct minor grammatical errors or word usage. Casual minor tongue slips may be removed by using ellipses but even that should be done with extreme caution. If there is a question about a quote, either don't use it or ask the speaker to clarify.*

Are Profanities and Obscenities Acceptable?

The Associated Press Stylebook also advises writers not to use profanity, obscenities, or vulgarities unless they are part of direct quotations and there is a compelling reason for them. Writers are cautioned to warn editors of writing that contains such language. The language should be confined to a single paragraph so that it can be easily deleted. Writers should not modify profanity such as changing damn to darn. Editors may change the word to d— to indicate that profanity was used by the speaker but no compelling reason exists to spell it out in the story.

Writers need to check with their publications and news organizations to determine their particular rules on profanity, obscenities, and vulgarities. Some specialized publications and television shows include such language. Audiences who subscribe to or buy such publications or who view programs are familiar with such language and either do not find it offensive or overlook it.

Some General Rules about Quotations

- Never make up a quote. Quotes must be accurate.

- Don't take a question that is answered "yes" or "no" and turn it into a direct quote. For example, if an interviewer asks a high school basketball coach if he believed many students bet on the outcome of games, and the coach answered, "No," the quotation in the newspaper should not read

> Coach Lyman Jones said, "I don't think many students bet on the outcome of our basketball games."

All you can really say is this: When asked whether he thought many students bet on the outcomes of games, Coach Lyman Jones replied, "No."

• Watch out for redundancies when setting up quotations. Use the direct quotes to expand.

> *Avoid:* She said she was surprised at being chosen the school's outstanding senior. "I was so surprised when they called my name," Melissa said.
>
> *Rather:* Melissa said she was surprised when the principal called her name. "I couldn't move or react," she added. "I felt glued to my chair in shock."

• Set up situations before using the quotation so that readers will have a context for quotes, as in the following Associated Press story:

> —An exercise program supported by the federal government and the trucking industry is aimed at eliminating spare tires on the truckers.
>
> The goal is to make interstate drivers slimmer, healthier—and safer.
>
> The Rolling Strong Gym has opened at a truck stop in North Little Rock, Ark., and others are planned elsewhere along Interstate 40. The president of the Richardson, Texas, health club company, as well as government and industry officials, are watching to see if the truckers will work out.
>
> "It's been long overdue," said Paul Todorovich of Myrtle Beach, S.C., an independent driver. "I'm hoping it catches on and they flourish."
>
> Transportation Department officials also hope so. "Research shows that drivers who are physically fit are safe drivers and that exercise is key to getting people into healthier lifestyles," said Transportation Secretary Rodney E. Slater in a statement endorsing the concept.

• Use "according to" only with printed or factual information. Do not use it as an attribution to a person.

> *Avoid:* The state's prison system is 3,456 inmates above the legally allowed level, according to the secretary of correction.

Rather: The state's prison system is 3,456 inmates above the legally allowed level, said the secretary of correction. According to prison documents, the level has been too high for the past seven years.

• Use attribution in the middle of a sentence only if it occurs at a natural break. Otherwise, put it at the beginning or the end so that you don't interrupt the flow of the person's statement.

Avoid: "We can always," he said, "commission a new statue for the college commons."

Rather: "We can always commission a new statue for the college commons," he said.

Acceptable: "The marine sciences lab is vital to the state's economy," he said, "and we must persuade the legislature to allocate more funds this year."

• Always use attribution for statements that use "hope," "feel," or "believes." You as a writer are not inside another person's head; you know how he or she feels, thinks, or believes because you were told.

Write: The district attorney said he believes the verdict fell short of what he expected the jury to do. He said he believes the community will be angered that Ammons was not found guilty of first-degree murder.

More on Attribution

Quotes, whether direct or indirect, must be attributed completely and adequately. Readers or listeners must know who is talking, who is making each statement. They need to know the proper sources of information. The general rule is that attribution should go at the beginning of each new quotation or at the end of the first sentence, whether the quotation is one sentence or more than one sentence.

If the quotation goes on for several paragraphs, attribution usually is placed at least once in every paragraph, and most writers follow the rule of attribution somewhere in the first sentence. Some writers will omit attribution in a middle paragraph if they have several short paragraphs of quotations by the same speaker. The key is to ensure that readers know who is talking.

If paragraphs contain strong statements of opinion, however, the writer must use attribution for every sentence.

For many writers, particularly news writers, "said" is the attribution word of choice. "Said" carries no underlying connotation as to a speaker's emphasis or meaning; it is neutral. "Added" and "told" are also fairly neutral. Attribution words that contain subtle meanings include "emphasized," "stressed," "declared," "demanded," "ordered," "stated," "criticized," and "contended." Writers avoid many of these words.

Do not use words such as "smiled," "laughed," "grimaced," "chuckled," and so on as attribution words. They are descriptive words that tell how a person said something. Rather than writing "'Hello,' he smiled," use "he said with a smile." Prefer phrases such as "she said, and frowned," "he said, and grimaced," and "she said, then laughed."

When using attribution that includes a person's title, do not place the title between the person's name and the attribution verb.

> *Avoid:* The University will accept 3,475 freshmen for the 2003 class, Polly Wilson, director of undergraduate admissions, said.

> *Rather:* The University will accept 3,475 freshmen for the 2003 class, said Polly Wilson, director of undergraduate admissions.

Punctuating Quotes

In Chapter 8, "Testing Your Grammar," are general punctuation rules. Here are the basic rules for punctuating quotations.

• Attribution at the end of a quote—whether direct or indirect—must be set off with punctuation. In most cases, the punctuation will be a comma.

Fifteen barrels of sardines will be delivered Wednesday, he said.

"Fifteen stinking, dripping barrels of sardines will be delivered Wednesday," he said.

"Will you deliver the barrels of sardines before noon?" he asked.

• Attribution at the beginning of an indirect quote is not set off with punctuation.

He said 15 barrels of sardines will be delivered Wednesday.

• Attribution at the beginning of a direct quote requires punctuation. If the quote is only one sentence long, use a comma. If the quote is two or more sentences long, use a colon.

Correct: Johnson said, "We have spent three days examining the department's books, and we have found no evidence of impropriety."

Correct: Johnson said: "We have spent three days examining the department's books, and we have found no evidence of impropriety. We will recommend that no further action be taken."

• Quotations within a direct quote are set off with single quotation marks.

"He said, 'Go ahead and throw it away, just like you have done every game,' and he walked out and slammed the door," Smithers said.

"I think 'Scream' was a frightening movie," she said.

• Commas and periods go inside quotation marks in direct quotes.

"Fifteen stinking, dripping barrels of sardines will be delivered Wednesday," he said.

Matthews said, "This race should be the test of every man's and every woman's physical and mental stamina."

• When placing the attribution at the end of the first sentence in a direct quote, the attribution is closed with a period. It marks the end of a sentence.

Wrong: "The new gymnasium is fantastic and humungous," said basketball player Brad Jones, "We're proud to play there. We really feel important playing our games now."

Right: "The new gymnasium is fantastic and humungous," said basketball player Brad Jones. "We're proud to play there. We really feel important playing our games now."

- Question marks go inside or outside quotation marks depending on whether they are part of the quotation.

Mark said, "Are you asking me whether I cheated on the exam?"

One of Dionne Warwick's popular renditions included "Do You Know the Way to San Jose?"

- Consider what may be slightly confusing but correct punctuation here:

Sara asked Kate, "Have you ever seen the movie 'Gone With the Wind'?"

Here the writer has a movie title that must be set off with quotation marks within a direct quote plus a question mark that is not part of the title.

- If the attribution breaks up a direct quote, it must be set off with commas and the quotation marks continued.

"Go ahead and throw it away," said Smithers, "just like you have done every game."

- If a speaker is quoted for several continuing paragraphs, the quotation marks are closed only at the final paragraph. Each paragraph must open with quotation marks to indicate the person is still speaking.

Resident John Loftis of Hollowell Road said, "We have been waiting two years for the southeast area to be annexed, and we are getting annoyed that the town council has further delayed a decision.

"I have written and my neighbors have written all the council members to say we want town services and are willing to pay for them.

"We just don't understand what the holdup is," Loftis said. "If a decision doesn't come after the next public hearing, I plan to picket city hall."

Not closing the quotation marks at the end of the first and second paragraphs tells the reader that Loftis has not finished talking. The quotation marks at the beginning of graphs two and three reopen the continuous quote from Loftis.

Covering Speeches

Covering speeches presents a challenge to note taking and organization. Taking notes during a speech is much more difficult than during an interview, discussed earlier in this chapter. In an interview, you can ask an interviewee to wait a few seconds while you fill in your notes. During a speech, you cannot stop the speaker; you have to keep up with what he or she is saying.

Taking notes during a speech, however, is somewhat like taking notes for a professor's lecture: You want to have as much material to study as possible, and you may have the opportunity to ask a clarifying question after the lecture is over. You may find that developing a shorthand is the easiest and fastest way to get complete notes.

Use times when the speaker is telling a joke or an anecdote to review your notes and to complete sentences. Put quotation marks around remarks that you know you can use as direct quotes. That helps when writing the stories.

Good note taking means listening carefully to what speakers say. Ears can deceive. Consider the following errors made when writers did not listen carefully and then did not think when writing the story.

"Bureaucrats are never seizing in their efforts to keep information from the public," he said.

The speaker actually said "ceasing" not "seizing."

"Having a big hearth has nothing to do with how big your wallet is," said Mrs. Bush.

She actually said "heart" not "hearth."

"The creation of new toxic dumb sites has all but been eliminated," Browner said.

She really said "dump" not "dumb" sites.

She saluted American industry, small business, schools, and American citizens for banning together to solve the country's environmental problems.

The speaker said "banding" not "banning."

People in countries have "the need to create extinct, stable governments," he said.

What the speaker said was "distinct," not "extinct."

Canada stepped outside its democratic laws to get the treaty written, she said.

The speaker actually said "diplomatic" not "democratic."

Sometimes writers hear the right word but misspell it. That damages their credibility and can be embarrassing. For example, one writer called a school's lecture series the "Wheel" lecture when it is named the Weil lecture. Another referred to a river as the Noose River when it is spelled Neuse. Consider these:

Investigators found millions of land mines sewn into the earth, Williams said.

The writer should have written "sown."

"Our commitment cannot waiver," she said.

She said "waver."

"Congress is trying to role back the progress of 25 years of environmental legislation."

It's "roll" not "role."

"America should be neither a claste nor a classified society."

The speaker said "classed" not "claste."

Some specific tips for writing about speeches:

• When you start to write the story, always look for a theme. It may be in the speech title, or the speaker may deviate and pick out a pet subject on which to elaborate. The theme will be a clue to the lead for your story. Generally, in the lead, a summary of what the speaker said will go first, and then attribution will end the first sentence. An exception is made for a prominent speaker, such as the president or a local government official. Then the name goes first.

• Do write a lead that states what the speaker said. Use attribution verbs such as *said* or *told*.

• Do not write a label lead that just identifies the topic of the speech. That means *do not* use attribution words such as *discussed, talked about, spoke about, expressed concern about.*

See the difference:

Label lead: Three members of the Broadcasting Board of Governors held a panel discussion on the future of international broadasting in Howell Hall on the University campus last Wednesday.

Summary lead: U.S. government broadcasts to regions all over the world can explain democratic values to people living in countries that have repressive governments, according to a panel of experienced broadcasters and journalists who spoke at the University last Wednesday.

• Do have a second graph that follows the lead.

• Do not have a second graph that burdens readers with background on the speakers.

See the difference:

Graph 2: The panelists were David Burke, chairman of the Broadcasting Board; Evelyn Lieberman, director of Voice of America; and Kevin Klose, director of the International Broadcasting Bureau, which oversees Voice of America, Radio and TV Marti, and Worldnet Television.

Better second graph to follow the summary lead: "By providing news and public affairs broadcasting, we can help them establish stable democracies," said Kevin Klose, a panelist and director of the International Broadcasting Bureau, which oversees Voice of America, Radio and TV Marti, and Worldnet Television.

The third graph would note the other two panelists and the qualifications that speak to their credibility. You do not have to include a complete vitae. If the panel had a discussion title, it would be included in graph 3. Writers would also summarize here the topics covered such as

The panelists primarily focused on the role of U.S. broadcasts since the fall of the Berlin Wall, but they also discussed new technology and how to bring their organizations into the twenty-first century.

- Have a balance of direct and indirect quotes.

- Look for a direct quote as a good way to end a story. Or end the story with more background about the speaker.

- Make sure your story has adequate attribution, even if you cover only one speaker.

A Parting Shot

Whether you are using quotes from an interview or a speech, remember the following:

- Be circumspect in your use of quotations. Just because you have a quote doesn't mean you have to use it.

- Look for variety in quotes when you are writing, and use a mix of indirect and direct quotes.

- Remember *The Associated Press Stylebook* rule about correcting quotations.

- If you are not sure about a quote, follow this rule: When in doubt, leave it out. Don't try to reconstruct it as a direct quote. And be sure you have the gist of the remarks if you convert the comments to an indirect quote.

- Develop tape recorder skills so that you can use one to assist in long or complicated interviews.

EXERCISES

1. Interview a friend or classmate about social life on your campus. Take careful notes. Then list five quotes, with correct attribution, that you might use in a finished story about social life at your school. Focus on correct attribution and use of both indirect and direct quotes.

2. Look at the following transcript of a speech by Supreme Court Justice Sandra Day O'Connor. Highlight those quotations that you would keep as direct quotes. Explain why. Indicate which quotations could be better paraphrased.

Surviving Cancer

A Private Person's Public Tale

Supreme Court Justice Sandra Day O'Connor addressed the National Coalition for Cancer Survivorship and for the first time publicly talked about her own battle with breast cancer. Following are excerpts from her speech.

I don't have a magic wand to wave. I'm here this morning really to chat very informally with you about this business of being a cancer survivor.

It's been six years since I underwent surgery for breast cancer. The impact of the diagnosis of cancer that I received is one which has not been far from my thoughts at any time during these six years. But . . . this is the first time that I have spoken publicly about my experience. And I'm not sure that my experience is any different than anyone else's. In fact, I'm quite sure it isn't. So what I have to say this morning for those of you who are here as survivors or friends or relations of survivors is going to sound hauntingly familiar, I suspect. . . .

We begin with the anxiety of going through the testing, something that's seen in a mammogram or an

X-ray or there's some little spot on your back—whatever it is. . . . And the initial impact for me was one of general disbelief. I felt fine, just fine, but I was told you better go have these tests and find out.

And then . . . I was told that I had a potentially fatal disease. Now that gets your attention. The Big C. The word cancer, it overwhelms the psyche, just the word. I couldn't believe it. I was unprepared for the enormous emotional jolt that I received from the diagnosis.

I can remember, all of a sudden my face and hands, my whole body tingled, I couldn't believe I was hearing this. It couldn't be true. I'm too busy. I feel fine. You can't be serious!

Well, the next thing was reality sets in. . . . But I was quite unprepared for the suddenness and the urgency of the rapid treatment decisions to be made. I had planned to go through a couple more rounds of oral argument in court and I said, well maybe in December we can work this out. I was told that was not an option. So I was simply totally lacking in appreciation for the fact that everything had to stop and I had to focus on this and I had to start educating myself about what it was I had and what the treatment options were. This was a very tough time.

I discovered I needed other ears than my own because I was so emotionally involved in this situation that I wasn't sure I was hearing everything. . . . I brought my husband along [to meet with doctors] because I thought he could listen with greater objectivity than I could and we both tried to take a few notes so we got everything down. I mean this was a world that was new to us. We didn't know the medical terms, we didn't have any experience with this and I wasn't sure I was even equipped to absorb the information I was hearing. . . .

Added to the stress was that I had to make so many decisions about the course of my treatment. That never occurred to me either. I mean I thought if I got sick, I went to my doctor, the doctor said what ought to be done and that was the end of it. Right? Wrong! With this disease it isn't always that way. . . . You run into this whole business of what do you do, a lumpectomy, a mastectomy or a radiation approach, do you have chemotherapy, do you not, if you have surgery what kind, how extensive. I just was quite unprepared to . . . make so many choices.

It helped to have close friends to talk to, people who had gone through the same experience. That meant a lot. . . . It was amazing how many people would send me a letter or come up to me and say, I've had that too, I've had that, my mother had that, oh my aunt had that. This was good because I then could start to come to grips with the fact that it isn't the end of the line and you are going to have a life that's going to go on. . . .

Now it is clear that the decisions about what to do, what treat-ments . . . had to be made promptly. And you just have to sweep in every bit of information you can possibly absorb, just become a real student, like cramming for an exam in college when you let slip all during the semester and you've got to get it all at once.... And then I did what I do at the court. When I'm at the court faced with a case I try to find everything out about that case that I can. I do as much research as I possibly can do and then I make my decision and I don't look back....

Now for me the decision was to have a mastectomy, and the postoperative period was depressing. I felt weak, I felt very emotional, I was hearing things I didn't want to hear, I was in some discomfort. It was really a tough time.... It was so intense that I called that friend of mine at home and I said, Could you come down to the hospital by any chance, do you have time, could you come down and see me? And she did. She dropped everything and came down and we shed a tear or two together and we talked everything over and somehow that helped....

I was told, you're going to have to have chemotherapy and this is going to take several months....

Somebody suggested that I see a particular hairdresser and it turned out this was one of the kindest, most learned men I have ever met. And he was totally sympathetic and he had lots of women who'd lost their hair and he found a wig or two for me and he just was terrific. And that really did help me.... You do feel lousy and look lousy, so if you can im-

prove that little bit it does help your attitude.

I was tired...and I'm not used to being tired. I had a lot of energy in my life and I couldn't believe that I needed all that sleep. I'm a person that didn't sleep much. Well, I could hardly get up, and in the afternoon I felt like I needed a nap. And this was frightening.

It wasn't just me.... My condition was causing distress to my family.... My husband was affected by it, my children were.... So you feel grateful that I had my work to do....

And it also helped me to resume physical exercise as soon as I could. I'm someone who just loves to have an exercise class...or...to play tennis or golf or ski or do something.... And it was hard because I lost the strength in my arm and it hurt. I was told, Well, for at least six weeks you can't do X, Y, and Z. But even long before the six weeks, I went back to my exercise class and there was a lot I couldn't do. But I did a little, I did what I could. My legs were okay so I used those, and I still had a fat stomach so I could work on that. That helped.... Soon...I could chip and putt on the golf course.... And eventually my nice friends were patient and hit a few soft tennis balls to me. So I worked back in.

Now what was the worst? The worst was my public visibility, frankly. There was constant media coverage. How does she look? When is she going to step down and give the president another vacancy on the court?

She looks pale to me, I don't give her six months. This was awful. There were people in the press box with telescopes looking at me in the courtroom to see just what my condition was. I didn't like that. Press would call my office and say they'd heard all these dire rumors and I better tell them exactly what was what or they were going to publish them all. It was really difficult. . . .

Let me tell you my dream of what I would like to have had in my situation which probably is very much like many of you:

I think it would be helpful to have all those tests done, the biopsies and the X-rays and whatever it is they are going to do, get all that information and then have a consultation with all the experts available at the same time, who've already looked at these things, they've looked at everything and they're all in the same [place] and they are there to help you reach a decision. The surgeon, the radiologist, the oncologist, the plastic surgeon, the nurse, a psychologist and so on—everybody there to help you

through the process of what to do. I think that would be terrific. . . . I thought moving from doctor to doctor with separate appointments and separate approaches and one doctor not hearing what the other said increased the uncertainty and increased the trauma.

[And] we need knowledge. Now how do I deal with the fear of death, where do I find the best and latest research on cancer treatment, what's reliable and what isn't and where is it and what about these state-of-the-art treatments, how do I find that, will my insurance cover the costs, do I need a counselor to help me through this, do my children need help?. . .

Is there an up side to all of this? Yes, there is. Having this disease made me more aware than ever before of the transitory nature of life here on Earth, of my own life. And it made me value each and every day of life more than ever before. . . .

3. Identify a campus leader who has been in the news recently. Select a specific topic related to the leader's expertise. Set up an interview and prepare questions as outlined in the chapter. Take a tape recorder to record the interview. When the interview is over, transcribe the tape and create a question-and-answer format story of the interview.

4. Using your transcribed interview from Exercise 3, write a story that focuses on the campus leader's view. Use a mix of direct and indirect quotes.

5. You are a reporter for the campus newspaper. Your editor has asked you to come up with a story based on money, specific to the campus. Ideas might be the cost of tuition or books, lack of enough financial aid, lack of funds to maintain classrooms, cost of getting settled in a job after graduation, increased student fees. Think of a story that would interest your audience: students. Stick to the campus for interviews. You must use more than one source. If the story relates to campus funding, you will need to talk to an administrator. You would also want to talk with a student who is affected. Be sure to have balanced sources. After the interviews, write a story showing both sides of the issue.

6. Many publications reveal how average citizens feel about or react to an event. Editors will select a current topic and assign a reporter to get public reactions. Scan today's daily newspaper and select a current topic, such as an ongoing international conflict, national legislation, a campus issue, or another major event that students and staff would have read or heard about. Interview ten people. Ask each one the same question. If you have to ask a question that is answered yes or no, you will need a follow-up "Why?" or your responses will be skimpy. Get each individual's name (check the spelling) and two other identifying labels: year in school, academic major, hometown, age, residence. Your attribution would look like this: Jane Smith, a senior chemistry major, or Alex Jones, 19, of Whiteville. Write the story. The first paragraph should have a summary lead, giving the results of your informal poll: Five of ten university students interviewed Thursday at the student union said they believed the presidency is a tough job that receives little credit, and not one student would want the job. The second paragraph gives the question: The students were asked, "What is your assessment of the job of president, and would you want the job?" Then you can proceed with each person's response.

REFERENCES

John Brady, *The Craft of Interviewing.* Cincinnati: Writer's Digest, 1976.
Rene J. Cappon, *The Word: An Associated Press Guide to Good News Writing.* New York: Associated Press, 1991.

Norm Goldstein (Ed.). *The Associated Press Stylebook and Libel Manual*. New York: Associated Press, 1997.

Judith Lewis Herman, *Trauma and Recovery*. New York: Basic Books, 1992.

Ken Metzler, *Creative Interviewing*, 2nd ed. Englewood Cliffs, NJ: Prentice-Hall, 1989.

Justice Sandra Day O'Connor, speech to the National Coalition of Cancer Survivorship, Washington, DC, November 1994.

Dan Quayle, speech to the National Press Club on Freedom of Information Day, Washington, DC, April 1989.

11

Electronic Media

WHEN YOU WRITE FOR ELECTRONIC
MEDIA, YOUR COPY WILL LOOK LIKE
THIS: A SCRIPT FORMAT. BUT THE
CONTENT WILL REMAIN ACCURATE,
CONCISE, AND COMPLETE, JUST AS IN
ANY WRITING YOU DO.

Writing for the electronic media—radio and television—requires the basic writing skills discussed in earlier chapters. Broadcast messages must be concise, clear, and simple so that audiences can understand the information.

Even though electronic messages are written before they are aired, broadcast writing differs in some respects from writing for print. Audiences tuning in to radio, for example, have to rely on their ears to get the message. Writing must be clear and specific. Writers have only one chance to catch audiences, who cannot go back and reread the lead.

In broadcast messages, writers and reporters must look past the written word for audio and visuals that enhance the message. A radio reporter can use an actuality or sound bite, such as a recorded interview or the sounds of traffic. But the actuality must attract audience attention and fit the report. Television reporters must combine writing with audiotapes, videotapes, and even live shots from the scene of an event. The writing must match the visuals and make the report come alive, appealing to the audience's senses.

In this chapter you will learn

- The similarities and differences between print and electronic media writing,
- The essential qualities of electronic media writing,
- How to write a script for radio and for television, and
- One reporter's view on writing for radio and television.

Writing for Print versus Electronic Media Writing

Similarities exist between good writing for print and electronic media. The media themselves—primarily radio and television—dictate some differences in format and approach for their particular audiences. All reporters, regardless of medium, adhere to standards of accuracy, good taste, ethical reporting, and legal requirements. The code for the Radio Television News Directors Association follows.

Radio-Television News Directors Association Code of Ethics

The responsibility of radio and television journalists is to gather and report information of importance and interest to the public accurately, honestly and impartially.

The members of the Radio-Television News Directors Association accept these standards and will:

1. Strive to present the source or nature of broadcast news material in a way that is balanced, accurate and fair.
   A. They will evaluate information solely on its merits as news, rejecting sensationalism or misleading emphasis in any form.
   B. They will guard against using audio or video material in a way that deceives the audience.
   C. They will not mislead the public by presenting as spontaneous news any material which is staged or rehearsed.
   D. They will identify people by race, creed, nationality or prior status only when it is relevant.
   E. They will clearly label opinion and commentary.
   F. They will promptly acknowledge and correct errors.

2. Strive to conduct themselves in a manner that protects them from conflicts of interest, real or perceived. They will decline gifts or favors which would influence or appear to influence their judgments.
3. Respect the dignity, privacy and well-being of people with whom they deal.
4. Recognize the need to protect confidential sources. They will promise confidentiality only with the intention of keeping that promise.
5. Respect everyone's right to a fair trial.
6. Broadcast the private transmissions of other broadcasters only with permission.
7. Actively encourage observance of this Code by all journalists, whether members of the Radio-Television News Directors Association or not.

(Copyright by Radio-Television News Directors Association. Reproduced here with permission of RTNDA.)

RTNDA's Web site at http://www.rtnda.org has helpful links for any electronic media journalist to its publications and Internet resources for journalists. Through its survival guide, reporters and students can find additional links to organizations in areas such as politics, education, sports, and other topics.

Similarities

THE WRITING PROCESS. The skills learned in the writing process discussed in Chapter 1 apply to electronic media. Broadcast reporters start with an idea, do research and interviews, then produce copy that is well written and relevant to their audiences. The writing process stage of outlining is critical for electronic media writers, who must plan a story before they leave the scene of an event. They must have an outline so they can get necessary audiotape, such as a quote from a county commissioner, or videotape, perhaps a shot of fire trucks, that will be needed to produce the final story package. Once in the editing lab, they may not have time to go back and shoot a visual for the 6 P.M. news.

NEWS VALUES. All mass communication writing has to have some news values from among those discussed in Chapter 3: prominence, timeliness, proximity, impact, magnitude, conflict, oddity, and emotional impact. Electronic media writing is no exception. Timeliness is the most critical news element for electronic media. Radio and television, because of their ability to broadcast live, can get information out to audiences as news events occur. Immediacy is the key. For a news clip to last throughout a 24-hour cycle, the event must be compelling. In radio and television, news that happened in the morning may be old in the afternoon, whereas newspapers can and do print yesterday's news. Conflict is another key news value for electronic journalism. Viewing conflict firsthand on television can make an audience remember a story for a lifetime.

CLEAR, CONCISE WRITING. The rules of using short sentences and short words, avoiding jargon and technical language, cutting wordiness, and getting to the point quickly are particularly critical in broadcast writing. Broadcast stories are generally shorter than those in print. Whereas a print news story may use 120 words to tell an event, a broadcast report may have to condense the account to 15 seconds. Newscasters read about 10 words in four seconds; a 15-second broadcast is about 35 words long. Every word counts, therefore, and language must be clear and precise. Few listeners will understand jargon or complicated language.

RESEARCH. Like print reporters, electronic reporters develop sources and do research and interviews. Research can be more difficult. Print reporters can access stories in library files or on computer databases fairly quickly. Electronic media reporters must review tapes to learn what the station may have covered before—a time-consuming process. Most electronic reporters do not accumulate clips and files they can readily consult. Television stations, for example, have file footage, but those archives are not as extensive as are newspaper libraries or morgues.

At some stations electronic media reporters must be generalists and cover a variety of topics, even within a single day. Many reporters are assigned to several beats. They may attend the governor's news conference in the morning and a fire the same afternoon. Radio reporters rarely have the opportunity to specialize in a particular area or beat, such as medicine, business, or local government. More and more television reporters, however, are assigned to specific areas such as politics, health, education, and others.

Differences

DEADLINES. Reporters for electronic media often work under tighter deadlines. Print reporters may have a 7 P.M. deadline for a morning newspaper, whereas a television reporter must have a story on the air at 5 P.M. The television reporter also may be producing several stories for that evening broadcast, perhaps two news briefs and one package that includes a standup, or appearance, by the reporter.

WRITING STRUCTURE. Because radio and television reports are shorter than print versions, they must be written to be understood the first time. And they must make it through clutter. Most radio and television audiences are doing other things: driving the car, listening to children's voices, cooking dinner.

Electronic media reporters start a story with a headline to grab listener or viewer attention. Then they give a lead to the story, which generally sets up the context for the story. Next comes explanation. The wrap-up usually focuses on the possible effects. For television, the entire story may run an average 30 seconds; for radio, the report may be only 20 seconds.

In addition to writing the story for television and even radio, the reporter will have to write several advance headlines or teasers that anchors can use to promote an upcoming newscast. In a teaser, reporters give only enough information about a story to make viewers watch it later. For example, a story may need a teaser or lead-in during an afternoon newsbreak, plus another teaser or a lead-in just before the 6 P.M. news. Then a reporter must write a lead-in for anchors before being introduced. Finally, a reporter will give her own lead on the story. All are different and gradually add information but without revealing the entire story.

FORMAT. Because electronic media require audio and visuals, the format for producing or typing stories differs from print format. Electronic and print journalists follow some of the same guidelines, such as double-spaced copy with one-inch margins, but electronic reports must add cues for audio and visual elements. Radio reports are typed across the page, just as print journalism stories are, but notes on what prerecorded elements will be inserted must appear between blocks of copy that will be read aloud.

In television reports, copy fills the right-hand side of the page; cues for audiotape, videotape, and who is speaking appear in the left-hand column. Abbreviations, such as VO for voice-over when the announcer or reporter is speaking, are indicated in the left-hand column.

Some broadcast journalists type their copy in all caps, but others prefer upper- and lower-case. Paragraphs are not split between pages, and each story is typed on a separate page. Specific style rules on how to use abbreviations, numbers, and attribution are explained later in the chapter.

COST. One point to remember is that electronic production—whether for an hour-long documentary or a 20-second news spot—is expensive and requires a team effort. Movies cost millions to produce; budgets for staff and equipment in television newsrooms are costly.

For example, print journalists can get by with collecting information in an 89¢ notebook with a 25¢ pencil. A television reporter's field unit—camera, battery pack, and lighting—costs $20,000 to $50,000. A news production van costs at minimum $100,000. Add satellite or microwave equipment, and the price tags start at $250,000. If the van is a top-of-the-line model, the cost can reach $500,000. Print journalists need computers and printing presses. Television reporters require editing equipment, studios, and satellite dishes. Radio reporters are on the economical end of electronic media production, requiring less in-house equipment to air their broadcasts.

The Differences in Practice

A radio reporter and a print journalist are rewriting wire service copy for their respective media. How would their leads look, based on the differences between broadcast and print writing? Let's see.

The print journalist writes:

ALBANY, N.Y.—New York Gov. George Pataki may fulfill a campaign promise today and sign legislation to create a death penalty.

The broadcast writer develops this lead:

NEW YORK'S GOVERNOR IS EXPECTED TO SIGN A DEATH PENALTY LAW TODAY.

The broadcast writer does not use a dateline, uses the present tense, avoids a complicated proper name, and establishes a context of death penalty legislation that can be explained later.

Consider two other examples:

A survey reports that all women have similar concerns.

Women are most concerned about balancing home and job, health insurance, and stress, according to a survey released today.

Which is the broadcast lead? The first one is. It is short and uses attribution at the beginning to establish the source immediately. It also establishes a context for the story to follow.

Electronic Media Writing

Writing for electronic media means writing for the ear: using short sentences, having speech that is more conversational, following a subject–verb–object sentence order, having copy that is clear and understandable, and putting smooth, clear transitions between thoughts. Let's look at producing broadcast copy, following these guidelines.

Broadcast Leads

The lead for a broadcast story is short and gives basic information. As noted earlier, the lead generally establishes a context for the story. Specific information will follow. The lead may be catchy and even entertaining. It causes the audience to stop and listen to the story:

THIRTEEN PEOPLE GOT RICH IN INDIANA LAST NIGHT.

THE MAYOR WILL ANNOUNCE TOMORROW THAT NEW JOBS ARE COMING TO THE AREA.

The context is clear in each example. The first story will be about Powerball lottery winners. The second lead sets up audiences for a story on economics with information about how many and what kinds of jobs and the name of the company. In both instances, the leads are much shorter than in print.

Broadcast writers who cover continuing or recurring stories try to find leads that will pique audience attention and interest in just a few words.

UNION WORKERS PICKET AT BALTIMORE HARBOR TODAY.

A SURPRISE WITNESS MAY TESTIFY TODAY IN THE MARVIN ALBERT TRIAL.

WHAT'S UP IN THE STOCK MARKET TODAY?

Broadcast Structure in the Message

Again, the structure of any electronic message must consider the audience's ear. The message must be clear and direct. Sentences are short and are written primarily in subject–verb–object order. Language must be simple. The writer develops the story using the three-part format: context, explanation, and effect. The lead sets out the context or the reason why the story is being written. The lead may focus on one news value or latest information, that is, timeliness. The second part is explanation, whereby listeners or viewers get more information, whether it is background, a historical perspective, or more details of the current situation. Then the writer wraps up with the effect, generally a look to the future or the impact of the event.

Look at this story:

IN ESPANOLA STUDENTS WILL RETURN TO FAIRVIEW ELEMENTARY SCHOOL TOMORROW AFTER ALMOST TWO WEEKS OF NO SCHOOL.

THE SCHOOL CLOSED MONDAY OF LAST WEEK AFTER A PLUMBER DOING ROUTINE MAINTENANCE WORK DISCOVERED A GAS LEAK. THE SCHOOL WAS BUILT IN 1966, AND ADMINISTRATORS SAY EXTENSIVE REPAIRS WERE NEEDED.

SCHOOL OFFICIALS PRICED THE REPAIRS AT MORE THAN 20 THOUSAND DOLLARS. THEY SAY THE SYSTEM'S OTHER SCHOOLS WILL BE CHECKED FOR LEAKS, TOO.

The message clearly lets parents in the audience know that children will go back to school, and it gives other general-interest members an update on a story that has been in the news. The writer follows the lead with context by giving background on why the school was closed. The next sentence says why the school was closed for so long. Listeners then learn that the repairs were expensive. The effect or impact is an investigation of other schools' plumbing.

As for language, all words are simple. According to the readability formula discussed in Chapter 5, this story is easy for viewers to understand. The most complicated words are "maintenance" and "extensive."

Writing Guidelines

Basic writing principles apply for broadcast stories. Because timeliness is crucial to electronic media, writers should use the present tense if possible. Even if they have to shift to past tense later in the story, they find present tense preferable in the lead.

Avoid: A convicted rapist was executed today after months of appeals failed.

Rather: A convicted rapist died today after months of appeals.

Avoid: Sixteen winners were declared in the long-awaited state lottery.

Rather: Sixteen people are winners in the long-awaited state lottery.

Some other writing rules to follow:

• Avoid strange names or those of little-known people. Describe people in terms of employment or life's work, then name them in the second sentence. Use names only with prominent people.

A ROCKLAND SECOND-GRADE TEACHER IS THE NATION'S TEACHER OF THE YEAR.
    RONNIE MILLER, ...

Or

ROCKLAND MAYOR JOAN TILLIS IS IN GOOD CONDITION AFTER BACK SURGERY.

• Avoid tongue-twisters that can cause problems when reports are read on air. Always read copy aloud before it is aired or broadcast. "The clandestine clan committed continual crimes" or "the player's black plastic pants" may look clever on paper, but it may be difficult for an announcer to enunciate.

• Use action verbs. Remember that verbs can paint pictures, an especially important aspect of radio reports. "Race car driver Kyle Petty roared to victory" has more life than "Race car driver Kyle Petty won."

• Use quotations sparingly. Paraphrased statements are more easily understood. If a quote is particularly good, use it live from the source. Make sure that the writing does not imply the statement is from the reporter or newscaster. Direct quotes that use "I" or "we" can cause such confusion. Consider this quote: Chamber of commerce president David Fall says, "I have doubts about the town's development practices." Listeners who miss the attribution may infer the reporter is doubtful. Instead, write

Chamber of Commerce President David Fall says he has doubts about the town's development practices.

• Put attribution at the beginning of a quotation: Medical experts say the new treatment may cause cancer cells to die. If you must use a direct quote, try "Johnson said in his own words, and I quote, . . ."

• Avoid writing that uses a lot of punctuation. Punctuation—even a question mark—cannot be heard. Listeners may miss the inflection.

• Avoid long introductory clauses with participles, like this one: "While doing a routine maintenance check at the school, a plumber found . . ." The story example used earlier puts that information at the end of the sentence.

• Avoid separating subjects and verbs, particularly with phrases in apposition. "Marian Johnson, a director for the Rockland Little Theater, will leave her job in two weeks" becomes "Rockland's Little Theater director will leave her job within two weeks. Marian Johnson . . ." Don't leave verbs at the end of the sentence. Follow subject–verb–object order as much as possible.

• Break up lengthy series of modifiers and adjectives, "Police described the suspect as a blond, long-haired, blue-eyed, five-feet, two-inch man."

Rather, write: "Police say the suspect has long blond hair and blue eyes. They also say he is about five feet, two inches tall."

• Avoid negatives. A listener may miss the negative words "no" and "not" in a broadcast and thereby be misinformed. Use alternatives:

"Police could find no motive for the shootings"

can be translated

"Police say the motive for the shootings is unknown."

• If your report runs long, say more than 30 seconds, look for ways to unify the story. Repetition of key words is one way to help listeners and viewers follow along.

Style in Copy

In Chapter 6 on editing, we looked at copyediting style for print. Electronic media have style rules for preparing copy.

• If a name is difficult, spell out in parentheses following the name how to pronounce it. Anchors and reporters can stumble in stating people's names. Sound it out. For example, names with "ei" or "ie" can be confusing, such as Janice Weinberger. Write out (WINE BURGER) so the announcer will use a long "i" pronunciation. For Iraqi leader Saddam Hussein, the pronunciation is (WHO SAYN).

• Put titles before names and keep them short. Use Texas Governor George W. Bush rather than George W. Bush, the governor of Texas. A person who is a university vice chancellor for institutional research services becomes a university administrator. You can use a descriptive title if audiences easily identify a person that way, for example, evangelist Billy Graham or publisher Katharine Graham.

• Use people's names the way they are commonly cited. President Clinton is known as Bill Clinton, not William Clinton. Former vice president Dan Quayle was rarely called Daniel T. Quayle.

• Write out most numbers between zero and 999. You can combine numerals and words as long as they can be read clearly. For example, write 10 thousand two hundred and 22 billion.

• Round off numbers. Say more than 10 thousand rather than 10 thousand two hundred and thirty-two subscribers.

• Write out amounts for dollars and cents, percent, and fractions:

Gasoline prices are three to four cents a gallon higher.

Three-fourths of town residents say they are pleased with the mayor's performance.

About fifty-five percent of what you read, you remember.

• Keep statistics to a minimum. Put them in a format people will understand. If a poll says 67 percent of the state's residents support NASA's plan for a lunar space station, report that two out of three state residents say they favor NASA's plan for a lunar station.

• Write out Roman numerals. Write out Harry Holland the third rather than Harry Holland III, or Queen Elizabeth the second, not Queen Elizabeth II.

• Avoid acronyms. Use the full name, such as Department of Housing and Urban Development, not HUD, and Environmental Protection Agency, not EPA. Some acronyms can be used on second reference, such as FBI after Federal Bureau of Investigation has been the first reference. For local or state law enforcement, it is better just to say police or law officials on subsequent references.

Broadcast Formats

A major difference between print and electronic media is the format for the final message, as noted earlier. Broadcast media use a script format that indicates the text along with the sound bites or visuals. Time is critical in broadcast writing. Scripts indicate how long the total story runs plus the length of specific segments within the story. Radio reports are typed across the page, much like a print story, with audio cues. Following is an example of a radio news script.

7/30/97 MK Road Construction

SPEEDING ALONG HIGHWAY 86 IN NORTH CHAPEL HILL COULD COST YOU AS MUCH AS 165 DOLLARS. THAT'S THE WARNING FROM THE CHAPEL HILL POLICE TRAFFIC UNIT. OFFICER CHUCK QUINLAN SAYS A CONSTRUCTION WORK ZONE WILL STRETCH FROM ASHLEY FOREST TO INTERSTATE 40 FOR THE NEXT YEAR-AND-A HALF. QUIN-LAN SAYS THE WORK ZONE WILL HAVE A UNIFORM 35-MILE-PER-HOUR SPEED LIMIT WITHIN WEEKS. THAT MEANS DRIVERS NEED TO PAY ATTENTION.

#145 QUINLAN:21 A:....ROAD, ETC.

QUINLAN SAYS HE AND HIS COLLEAGUES HAVE BEEN DEALING WITH REAR END COLLISIONS IN THE WORK AREA. AND HE SAYS THE SITUATION COULD GET WORSE, AS CREWS CONTINUE MOVING DIRT NEAR THE ROAD-WAY.
(Reprinted with permission from WCHL radio, Chapel Hill, NC, July 1997)

In television reports, the cues on the left-hand side of the page give such information as the title or slug of the story, what newscast it will appear on, the tape number, the length of the story, the name of the anchor, and any graphics to be used. After the story text begins, cues will tell whether the story has a voice-over, that is, a reporter who is not seen reading text to go along with the visuals. Cues also indicate who is speaking, for example, a source who is interviewed for the story, the reporter, or the anchor. The following example shows cues.

Cues	**Explanation**
REALESTATE PG.8	Story slug and page of newscast script.
NEWSCAST=6PM	Tells computer in which newscast to find script.
TAPE#=95-1001	Edited stories are put on numbered tapes for the computer reference system.

ANCHOR=TERESA	Cue for the computer system to connect directly to the TelePrompTer when the anchor is speaking.
CK=TWO SHOT A7N 6	Tells the director and graphics operator what to put in the Chroma-key. TWO SHOT A7N 6 means the camera operators are to frame both anchors in the shot. The Chroma-key or label is to appear between them on the screen and read "Action 7 News Live at Six."
LIVE IN DROPKEY	A computer-generated box somewhat like the Chroma-key but in which a reporter appears as he or she waits to deliver a live report.
TAKE LIVE	Tells the director and technical director to put in the live shot.
ROLLCUE="TO THE OFFER"	Tells the director and the person rolling the tape when to start the videotape to play the story.
RUNS=1:30	Tells the computer how long the package is so it can take the introduction and the tag line and estimate the total run time of the piece.
OUTCUE	Cues the director to return to the anchor desk or to a live shot.

When the story text is typed, all capital letters are used. That helps clarify writing where a lowercase "l" might resemble a capital "I" and create problems for announcers. Capital letters are also easier to read from a distance.

When students study electronic journalism, they learn the codes and copy preparation style early on. The complete radio story may seem to be longer than a story typed for print because cues take up space on the left-hand side of the page. The goal is to make the copy legible for the anchor and the reporter who read from the copy.

Television News Script

DOTOFFICE PG.3
NEWSCAST=6PM
TAPE #=98–1056
ANCHOR=DAVE
CK=JOHNSON

<<(D) SOME CONSUMERS ARE CALLING FOR THE STATE TO ABOLISH THE STATE BOARD OF TRANSPORTATION. THE MOVE CAME IN THE WAKE OF A DEPART-MENT OF TRANSPORTATION HEARING TODAY. BUT AS MARGA-RET STEELE REPORTS, POLITICS MAY MAKE THAT DIFFICULT.

CVTR SOT FULL (******PKG*****)

SUPER=14-Secretary's office/
Raleigh; at:03

SUPER=21-Norris Tolson
Transportation secretary; at :15

SUPER=@SSMR-Raleigh; at :46

RUNS=1:06
OUTCUE="... Action 3 News."

P-DOTOFFICE PG.3P   TWENTY-FOUR STATES DO NOT HAVE TRANSPORTATION BOARDS MADE UP OF POLITICAL APPOINTEES. THOSE CALLING FOR THE CHANGE WANT STATE OFFICIALS TO INVESTIGATE OTHER OPTIONS.

Radio and Television Careers

Reporting staffs in electronic media are generally small, particularly for radio stations and even in large television markets. Some radio stations have given up having reporters who actually go out and cover events. They rely on wire service copy and some taped telephone interviews to compile their news reports.

Newspaper and even radio reporters are independent compared with television reporters, who always work as part of a team. The team may include a news director, an assignment editor, editors for the story and the visuals, a producer for each newscast, a photographer, a director for technical equipment, a reporter who puts names below visuals, and perhaps a graphics editor.

So dozens of careers exist for students within electronic communication. The key is to get experience while in school and in the first few years after graduation. Real-world experience will help students clarify what type of work interests them most and will help them define their next career moves.

Students may start out as reporters for the local radio station and eventually be promoted to news directors. They may become production assistants for television stations. They may stick with news or move into the station's public affairs department. After years of experience, they may become freelance writers and produce documentaries.

Within the electronic communication field, most professionals have traditionally tended to stay with the medium they started with: radio or television. But more are making the switch from radio to television, and some print people have even moved into electronic fields such as television. One well-known example is Michael Gartner, former president of the American Society of Newspaper Editors. He moved from publisher of the *Courier-Journal* in Louisville, Kentucky, to president of ABC News, then to the Ames, Iowa, newspaper as editor. ABC's Cokie Roberts worked for National Public Radio.

From Radio to Television—and Beyond

Sabrina Smith was a reporter for KOAT-TV in Albuquerque, New Mexico, the ABC affiliate. Smith began her career as a radio reporter, then made the transition from radio to television. She found the transition fairly easy, although she admits that some people in television had doubts about the move.

In both jobs, she notes, reporters must write clearly, concisely, and conversationally.

> *You have to be able to write. In radio, all audiences have is your voice and what they hear. As a reporter, you have to write the story colorfully and to visualize for audiences what they only can hear. If you can do that, you are ahead of the game. In television, good writing is also essential. So many people in television write in a boring way because they rely on visuals. Do this test: To see if the video matches, turn down the volume and just watch the video to see if you know what the story is about. As a viewer, you should have some idea. If you can write well and integrate visuals well, then you will do well.*

The biggest difference Smith found in moving from radio to television was the added element of video. Students who want careers in television have to know how to shoot videotape. As the reporter in the Los Alamos bureau, Smith shot her own videotape, then wrote the text.

In television, reporters have to have the pictures that match the words they are saying. They have to consider what visuals they will need when they are out in the field and to know what film footage might be available back at the office. Visuals reinforce the message. If audiences don't get the message, then the visuals probably didn't match.

> *One day I wrote a short story about city services. I went out and shot lots of video then went back to the office to edit. When I wrote the story, I had two words: fire protection and road maintenance. But I had no photos of fire trucks and road crews to put in the story. So I had to go back out and shoot again.*

Television reporters have to do standups. A standup shows the reporter who is covering the story standing in a location important to the story. A standup may show the reporter at the beginning of a segment as the anchor makes a transition from the set to the reporter's package, or it may be the closing shot. It is the chance for the audience to see the reporter, and audiences should learn something from it. A standup should be specific, not vague. The standup can be a challenge to the television reporter because it must fit in with the rest of the story and be coherent.

Sabrina Smith made another job switch after leaving KOAT and working for a television station in North Carolina. She joined a nonprofit group that is working to get classrooms in North Carolina wired and outfitted with computers. The writing and people skills she gained during her years as an electronic reporter have proved invaluable in making presentations for fundraising. And she notes that in a nonprofit organization where much is expected of a few staff members, being able to change gears quickly—just as she did as a television reporter—comes in handy.

Wrap-up

Just as jobs change and expand within electronic media, so does technology. One piece of equipment is Web television, which the conventional television set with World Wide Web access. Users cannot create, publish, or print, but they can visit Web sites and get information. The cost is about the cost of a television set.

As this book goes to press, the television industry is in the midst of a massive transition to a new technology: digital television (DTV). The Federal Communications Commission adopted in December 1996 a new standard for transmitting television signals, called DTV. Under that standard, television signals will be transmitted in digital rather than the existing analog format.

The highest form of DTV is called high-definition television or HDTV. It can transmit more than six times the information of the old analog system, which means higher quality pictures and sound. HDTV screens are one-third wider than existing television screens; the picture is much crisper and more detailed, giving viewers the feeling of seeing images in a three-dimensional form. With HDTV, the television picture is studio quality, whether the viewer's television set is 6 miles or 60 miles from the broadcast station's antenna, points out John Greene, station manager for WRAL-TV in Raleigh, North Carolina.

WRAL has established WRAL-DH, the first HDTV station in the country. It began limited programming in fall 1997. The major networks are to begin some prime time programming in fall 1998, and consumers will see more programming in 1999. The FCC has required that the top four network stations in the nation's ten largest markets begin digital delivery by May 1, 1999. The top network affiliates in the top thirty markets must begin delivering a digital signal by November 1, 1999.

What do the changes mean for viewers? Eventually, new television sets, videocassette recorders, and camcorders. None will pick up the new digital signals, although HDTV sets will pick up older analog station signals. The first HDTV sets—as with any newly introduced technology—are expensive, averaging $3,500 to $7,000. But prices are expected to drop as manufacturers compete for customers. A set-top converter box will allow viewers to pick up digital stations on their analog TV sets, but pictures will be smaller and not as crisp as with HDTV equipment.

The FCC has set 2006 as the date finally to turn off all analog television sets, but some industry analysts expect Congress to extend that date until more people—at least 85 percent—have access to digital television signals.

What do the changes mean for professionals? Although writing styles will remain the same, pictures will change dramatically, Greene notes. Because the pictures will be wider and show detail greater, news videographers—those people who take the pictures—will have to adapt to the new wide-screen format and improved clarity.

Although much of the discussion here has focused on electronic media and news, student journalists are not limited solely to radio and television news. They may opt to go into film or into writing scripts for situation comedies or drama. They may produce documentaries on the plight of endangered animals or women in mass media jobs. They may be public relations professionals who have to produce public service announcements.

Whatever field students choose and whatever job they ultimately hold, they must be good writers. Experienced electronic media professionals deplore what they see as a decline in writing skills, in small and large market stations, and stress that clear, accurate, concise copy that addresses audiences is critical. Television is competing now with other information-age technology, and broadcast reporting will have to be compelling to keep audiences tuned in.

EXERCISES

1. Write a broadcast lead for each of the following stories:

   ```
   Sam Snyder, president of the Rockland Chamber of Com-
   merce, has been elected to the board of directors of the
   National Chamber of Commerce.
   ```

The Federal Reserve Board raised interest rates one-quarter percent, which means consumers will be paying higher rates on their adjustable-rate home mortgages and if they are seeking mortgages.

David Parkinson of Waverly County won first place at the county fair yesterday for the largest squash. It weighed 6 and ½ pounds. David is 6 years old.

Competition begins Thursday for the National Collegiate Athletic Association title. The tough competition has been dubbed March madness.

2. Using the formula that a 60-space typed line equals 4 seconds of air time, write a 20-second radio script for the following information:

A masked man robbed the university dining hall of $3,000 and escaped after locking the dining hall manager in a closet.

Tony Jones, the manager, escaped unharmed. Police are looking for a heavy-set white man about 5-feet, 5 inches, and weighing about 175 pounds. He has a round face and broad shoulders. Jones could give no description of the man's facial features because he had a stocking pulled over his face.

Jones was preparing the payroll when he heard a noise in the kitchen. When he went to investigate, he said, the man came charging at him. The man ordered him to open the safe and put money in a blue sack. Jones complied, and the robber locked him in a closet before leaving.

3. Write a 20-second radio script for the following information and indicate an audio you could use to illustrate the spot.

The legal age for minors to buy cigarettes in most states is 18. Studies show that underage youth or minors still buy up to 500 million packs of cigarettes a year, despite the states' laws. About 25 states have agreed there should be stricter laws on tobacco products, and even tobacco industry officials claim their advertising is not geared to teenagers.

4. Write a 30-second television script for the following information. Type the copy in the right-hand column and indicate what visuals you would use.

A coalition of child-care advocates marched on the state legislature today. They distributed flyers encouraging legislators to approve monies during the current session that would subsidize the cost of day care for families earning below $16,000 a year. They claim that day-care costs in the state have skyrocketed, and even working families are finding it hard to pay for quality day care out of their salaries. The coalition estimated 15 percent of the state's population fell below the federal poverty level guidelines last year. The coalition officials said that last year it had to turn away almost 400 families who needed financial assistance, because funds just were not available.

5. Watch the local evening news. Do a tally that covers the number of stories, story topics, whether they were local or based on a national event, the length of each, and numbers and types of sources used. Write several paragraphs on whether you felt adequately informed about news items from the television account.

6. Based on the information collected in Exercise 5, look at the local or regional newspaper the following day. See how many stories from your evening television newscast were covered in the newspaper. Look at the length of those stories and what new information you learned.

REFERENCES

Seth Finn, *Broadcast Writing as a Liberal Art.* Englewood Cliffs, NJ: Prentice-Hall, 1991.

John Greene, Personal interview, written communication, Raleigh, NC, December 1997.

Floyd McKay, "Writing for Broadcast," Course Packet for Journalism 201. College Park, MD, University of Maryland, Spring 1990.

Radio-Television News Directors Association Web site. Available at: http://www.rtnda.org.

Sabrina Smith, Personal interview, written communication, Raleigh, NC, January 1998.

Mitchell Stephens, *Broadcast News,* 2nd ed. New York: Holt, Rinehart and Winston, 1986.

J. Clark Weaver, *Broadcast Newswriting as a Process.* New York: Longman, 1984.

12

Public Relations Writing

A student in an introductory writing course told her classmates that she wanted to pursue public relations (PR) as a career. Why? "Because I want to talk to people about the organization I work for," she said.

Her professor quipped, "You won't do much talking; you'll be much too busy writing."

Writing is the single most important skill in public relations, all experts agree. Good writing is at the heart of every successful and effective public relations campaign and event, regardless of who does the talking.

Public relations practitioners must be able to communicate information about their organizations to targeted audiences. People will call an organization only when they know that it exists and what it does. The public relations practitioner must send the news release on company earnings before reporters will call. The mother must read the brochure on a community's child-care offerings before calling for more details. The college student must peruse the company's home page to learn about its internship program.

Being a successful public relations practitioner takes more than talking and a ready smile. Public relations practitioners must identify audiences to determine the best methods to communicate with audiences, conduct research, plan and carry out communication strategy, and evaluate plans. Writing is crucial at each stage, but particularly in communicating messages to important publics.

This chapter looks at the importance of

- Good public relations writing,
- Audiences that public relations professionals call *publics,*
- Communications tools used by public relations practitioners,
- The media as a major public, and
- Methods of reaching audiences.

What Is Public Relations?

Professor James Grunig at the University of Maryland defines public relations as the management of communication between an organization and its publics, or audiences: employees, clients, customers, investors, or alumni. Grunig emphasizes the importance of strategy and thinking in approaching those relationships.

Successful public relations builds and maintains good relationships between an organization and its publics through balanced, open communication. Public relations may be as simple as an announcement by the local literacy council about its success rate for the past year. Or it may be a complicated integrated marketing program that incorporates public relations with advertising, investor relations, and market research.

Diverse organizations use public relations: local, state, and national nonprofit organizations such as the American Heart Association; schools and universities; small companies; multinational corporations; and local, state, and federal government, including the president and the armed services. Public relations practitioners share information with the public to help the organization achieve its objectives. The objective of public relations efforts may be to announce new products or to show how a company works as a good corporate citizen or as a leader in its field. The objective may be public service, as in a broadcast message to reduce teenage pregnancy or to warn smokers about the risks of heart attacks.

Some people erroneously think of public relations as free publicity, believing that there is no cost. But real public relations—ongoing programs of communication with various publics—is expensive. Organizations must pay salaries and production costs, buy supplies and equipment, and cover additional overhead expenses such as office space, computer support, and utilities. Most are hidden costs that the public does not see or consider.

Public Relations Tools

Public relations practitioners often use the terms *public relations tools* or *communications tools* to describe the techniques or methods they use to reach audiences. All require solid writing skills. Among the more common communications tools are these:

- *News releases.* Articles that describe newsworthy events and are sent to media outlets. They are written in a style ready to be used.

- *Feature releases.* More in-depth, less timely articles about organization employees, projects, or services. These generally are targeted to a specific publication.

- *Media kits.* Folders that contain relevant information on the organization or company or a special event. Included are fact sheets, backgrounders, photographs, reprints, biographies, and other material.

- *Direct mail letters.* Letters written to targeted publics, generally to solicit support for a project or event.

- *Brochures.* Booklets or folders that include general information or targeted information about an organization or a special project. These are designed to be easily mailed or distributed at events or in racks.

- *Web sites.* Full-service Web sites that give information about an organization and invite the public to interact via e-mail and links to other sites.

- *Face-to-face contact.* Speeches or appearances at meetings, conventions, or other programs.

- *Audiovisual presentations.* Slide shows and multimedia shows that supplement information in speeches and visually depict an organization or its services.

- *Specialized publications.* Newsletters, annual reports, and magazines produced for internal audiences such as employees or for external audiences such as customers and the general public. In some corporate settings, annual reports are produced by the investor relations department; the public relations practitioner may help with some writing. Many specialized publications are online and linked to Web sites.

- *Video news releases.* Actual film footage with or without sound, especially voice-over, to give television stations ready-to-use material.

- *Public service announcements (PSAs).* Short announcements, generally sent ready-to-read to radio stations or posted on Web sites. May be produced in video form.

- *Image advertising.* Attempts by an organization to improve an audience's perception of it. Often done in conjunction with marketing departments.

Communications tools are incorporated into plans that serve as guides for public relations activities or campaigns. Corporate communications departments, for example, begin work in the fall on the next year's plan to support goals, specific actions, and target dates. Communications plans are discussed later in the chapter.

Of course, not all public relations is planned. A reporter may call the corporate communications department about a story idea, and the public relations practitioner will respond or arrange for a company executive to reply. The practitioner may send the reporter a media kit that contains a mix of communications tools, often called *collateral materials,* such as a news release, a fact sheet, and a brochure.

Public Relations Stages

In the late 1960s Scott Cutlip and Allen Center identified four stages of a public relations campaign: research, planning, communication, and evaluation. Public relations practitioners still follow those stages today.

For example, a bank plans to change its checking service in three months. The public relations department is charged with informing the bank's publics of the change. Look at how the public relations practitioner would use each stage.

- *Research.* Research is essential to enable the bank to state public relations goals, identify relevant publics, describe the service, and identify its strengths and weaknesses. For example, the bank's reputation would be a strength; competition from other banks' services would be a weakness. Research could use focus groups, as discussed in Chapter 2, to determine what the bank's customers would like in a checking account.

• *Planning.* In planning, the practitioner devises a communications plan or strategy. The practitioner determines what communications tools will be used during the next three months and sets deadlines for each one. For example, dates for news releases to trade publications differ from those for statewide media. Magazines usually need copy two months before publication dates; daily newspapers can print information within 24 hours of receiving it.

• *Communication.* In the communication stage, the practitioner carries out the plan. Information is written and distributed via the communications tools: news releases, brochures, fact sheets, annual reports and other publications, and speeches, just to name a few. Although writing is important in developing the plan, good skills are critical in the communication stage.

• *Evaluation.* In evaluation, the practitioner uses qualitative and quantitative ways to evaluate the success of the communications plan and strategy. For example, the bank can use focus groups of customers to determine how well they understood communication about the service. After the news release is distributed, the public relations staff can count the number of newspaper clippings to determine how many times the news release information appeared in newspapers.

Public Relations Jobs

As a public relations professional, you could be at the forefront in affecting public opinion about nuclear energy, at the podium conducting a news conference for the State Department, or on the campaign trail for a popular county commissioner who is running for the United States Senate. Practitioners do much more than write news releases and answer the telephone.

If you work for the corporate communications department of a large company, your job description will be specific. You may be the media relations manager for statewide media, coordinating news releases and answering inquiries. Or you may edit all in-house publications from bulletin board announcements to the quarterly company magazine, or you may update the company's home page. More and more companies are advertising for people with skills to create and maintain Web sites, another way to reach audiences. See the example in Figure 12.1 on page 308.

In the nonprofit or independent sector, you may do many jobs under one title. Many nonprofit organizations cannot afford to hire large public relations

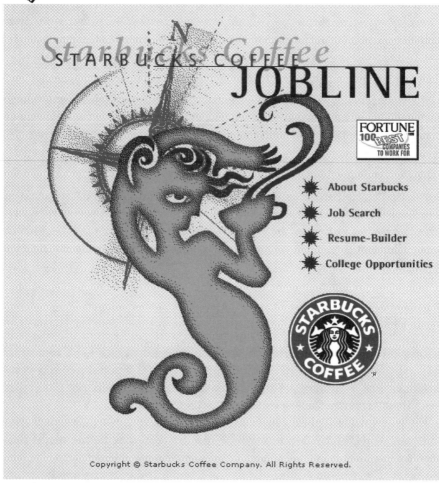

FIGURE 12.1   *Many companies provide information via their home pages.*

staffs. One person will respond to media inquiries, write news releases, produce a newsletter, design flyers, set up community relations activities, and do whatever else needs to be done. But in all jobs, they write.

Public relations is a respectable profession. Some people describe practitioners as hacks or flacks; they believe that practitioners tout the company's best interests and not society's at large. They view public relations as a way to cover up the bad things that organizations do and see public relations practitioners as the people who sidestep the truth. They criticize public relations people as trying to control the news and the slant on information.

When Diana, Princess of Wales, died, numerous organizations and individuals capitalized on her death to gain publicity. *The Wall Street Journal* even carried a story with examples of some of the news releases sent via wire services to the media. They ranged from FTD adding operators to be on call for flower orders to psychologists and photographers commenting on tabloids and paparazzi. Many observers question the ethics and good taste of tying certain public relations efforts to an individual's death.

Some criticism of a few individuals may be justified, just as in any profession. But most people today recognize that public relations practitioners adhere to a code of ethics, usually the code of the Public Relations Society of America (PRSA). Many professionals use the PRSA as a source of advice and continuing education. Information on how to join the organization and its student society can be found on its Web site at http://www.prsa.org. Practitioners who do not act ethically or who do not tell the truth hurt themselves and their organizations. They need the consistent trust and confidence of their publics if they are to survive. Once an organization loses the public's trust, it may take a major, costly public relations and advertising campaign to win it again. And the investment may not pay off.

Code of Professional Standards for the Practice of Public Relations

Public Relations Society of America

This Code was adopted by the PRSA Assembly in 1988. It replaces a Code of Ethics in force since 1950 and revised in 1954, 1959, 1963, 1977, and 1983. For information on the Code and enforcement procedures, please call the chair of the Board of Ethics through PRSA Headquarters.

Declaration of Principles

Members of the Public Relations Society of America base their professional principles on the fundamental value and dignity of the individual, holding that the free exercise of human rights, especially freedom of speech, freedom of assembly, and freedom of the press, is essential to the practice of public relations.

In serving the interests of clients and employers, we dedicate ourselves to the goals of better communication, understanding, and cooperation among diverse individuals, groups, and institutions of society, and of equal opportunity of employment in the public relations profession.

We pledge:

To conduct ourselves professionally, with truth, accuracy, fairness, and responsibility to the public;

To improve our individual competence and advance the knowledge and proficiency of the profession through continuing research and education;

And to adhere to the articles of the Code of Professional Standards for the Practice of Public Relations as adopted by the the governing Assembly of the Society.

Code of Professional Standards for the Practice of Public Relations

These articles have been adopted by the Public Relations Society of America to promote and maintain high standards of public service and ethical conduct among its members.

1. A member shall conduct his or her professional life in accord with the **public interest.**
2. A member shall exemplify high standards of **honesty and integrity** while carrying out dual obligations to a client or employer and to the democratic process.
3. A member shall **deal fairly** with the public, with past or present clients or employers, and with fellow practitioners, giving due respect to the ideal of free inquiry and to the opinions of others.
4. A member shall adhere to the highest standards of **accuracy and truth,** avoiding extravagant claims or unfair comparisons and giving credit for ideas and words borrowed from others.
5. A member shall not knowingly disseminate **false or misleading information** and shall act promptly to correct erroneous communications for which he or she is responsible.
6. A member shall not engage in any practice which has the purpose of **corrupting** the integrity of channels of communications or the processes of government.
7. A member shall be prepared to **identify publicly** the name of the client or employer on whose behalf any public communication is made.

8. A member shall not use any individual or organization professing to serve or represent an announced cause, or professing to be independent or unbiased, but actually serving another or **undisclosed interest.**

9. A member shall **not guarantee the achievement** of specified results beyond the member's direct control.

10. A member shall **not represent conflicting** or competing interests without the express consent of those concerned, given after a full disclosure of the facts.

11. A member shall not place himself or herself in a position where the member's **personal interest is or may be in conflict** with an obligation to an employer or client, or others, without full disclosure of such interests to all involved.

12. A member shall **not accept fees, commissions, gifts, or any other consideration** from anyone except clients or employers for whom services are performed without their express consent, given after full disclosure of the facts.

13. A member shall scrupulously safeguard the **confidences and privacy rights** of present, former, and prospective clients or employers.

14. A member shall not intentionally **damage the professional reputation** or practice of another practitioner.

15. If a member has evidence that another member has been guilty of unethical, illegal, or unfair practices, including those in violation of this Code, the member is obligated to present the information promptly to the proper authorities of the Society for action in accordance with the procedure set forth in Article XII of the By-laws.

(Reprinted with permission of Public Relations Society of America.)

The Role of Good Writing

Public relations practitioners must be good writers. They must be able to adopt different styles and tones when writing because they have many more audiences than the writer for a newspaper or specialized publication. In the morning they may write a general-interest news release and in the afternoon a speech in the language style of the company president. Or they may write an article for the employee newsletter and later consult with a production company on a video script for an upcoming stockholders meeting.

Much of public relations writing is grounded in journalistic writing. Many mass communications programs require public relations students to take media writing courses to learn the inverted pyramid and other formats. The courses also teach the fundamentals of grammar, punctuation, and style, and they stress the need for clear, concise, accurate writing that interests and attracts targeted audiences.

The need for accuracy in all aspects of public relations work is critical. Consider the public relations nightmare for CNN, the Atlanta-based cable news network, when it set up an 800 number so viewers could call in their questions and comments about programming. The number is 1–800-TALKCNN. But when CNN advertised the number, it mistakenly published it as 1–800-CNNTALK. The latter number dialed into a sex service. Or the correction Warner Bros., the film giant, had to make in its promotion of "In the Garden of Good and Evil." Publicity materials and even the film's final credits referred to author John Berendt's nonfiction work as a "novel." A novel is fiction. The misnomer required the film company to send out a correction that the movie was based on Berendt's book.

Informational versus Persuasive Writing

Public relations practitioners generally divide writing into two categories: informational and persuasive. The company's objective will determine the tone of the writing.

Informational writing is just what it says: It presents materials in a straightforward, factual manner—just as in journalistic writing. A brochure can be informational, simply listing an organization's history, services, address, and telephone number. A brochure may give specifics about an upcoming program.

A brochure can also be persuasive. Persuasive writing clearly pitches a particular point of view. Some public relations tools are deliberately persuasive. A direct mail letter to university alumni will try to persuade them to donate to endowed professorships. A public service announcement on radio will encourage listeners to donate canned goods to the local food bank.

Persuasive writing follows the tenets of good writing: accuracy, clarity, and conciseness. A brochure can be persuasive and still be informational, using facts and graphics to portray positively the company's position.

Most public relations writing adheres to journalism standards of fairness and impartiality. Experienced public relations practitioners know that arguments explained factually will have more impact than those that are biased and long-winded.

Considering Audiences, or Publics

Just as in any other mass communication field, public relations practitioners must consider their audiences, or what they call "publics." The publics are the people who will be reading news releases or viewing video news releases. They may be employees, customers, other businesses, town residents, lawmakers, reporters, or officials in local, state, or federal government agencies. Public relations practitioners must identify and know which publics are important to their organization.

Imagine you are the public information director for a university system that is planning a capital campaign to raise funds for new buildings. The university administration has set a goal of $120 million. In planning a public relations campaign, you would have to consider the university's publics: alumni, faculty members, staff members, students, students' parents, potential students, donors, legislature (if the university is public or state supported), the general public, and the media. From that list, you might identify five key or important publics.

Practitioners use research such as informal surveys or focus groups to learn about their publics. Specifically, practitioners need to know how their publics get information. Then they can decide which media, or communications tools, are most effective in reaching them. And they can decide the tone and style of the message.

For example, in Chapter 3 we had the example of the Amana Savings and Loan, which plans to open a fitness center in the old YMCA building next to corporate headquarters. The bank's corporate communications department is to make the announcement. The public relations manager decides to notify employees through the company newsletter and the media through a news release. The day the newsletter is delivered, the public relations manager will hand-carry a news release to the local newspaper.

For the newsletter, the important public is employees. Tone and structure are designed to aim information that is directly relevant to them:

```
Amana employees soon will be able to exercise daily at a
new fitness center the company will build next door to the
bank's headquarters on Sycamore Street.
```

> The bank will renovate the old YMCA building to provide
> a convenient way for employees to remain physically fit,
> says employee manager Kay Barnes. Employees will have to
> get a fitness privilege card but will not be charged to use
> the center.
>
> The estimated cost of the project is $1 million.

Whereas the newsletter article emphasizes employee benefits, the release to the local newspaper must take a broader angle and discuss the impact on the community.

> Amana Savings and Loan will renovate the old YMCA building
> on Sycamore Street into a fitness center for employees. The
> work is expected to be completed within six months.
>
> The project, estimated at $1 million, will rehabilitate
> prime downtown space that has been unused for a year. The
> YMCA moved into a larger building last summer.
>
> The center next door to company headquarters will
> provide a convenient way for employees to remain physically
> fit, says employee manager Kay Barnes. Employees will have
> to get a fitness privilege card but will not be charged to
> use the center.

The Media as a Public

An important public for any public relations practitioner is the media. The media learn about an organization through standard communications tools found in media kits, such as news releases. But they also use annual reports, Web sites, investor publications, executive speeches, brochures, and other means to find out information about companies. In turn, practitioners must know the media. They must know the media's audiences, formats, and content. They must convince the media to use information. Media are essential audiences because through newspapers, magazines, radio and television, specialty publications, and others, the practitioner reaches many publics. Two primary tools for public relations practitioners are media lists and media kits.

The Role of Media Lists

Media lists are necessary equipment for public relations. Developing a media list can be time-consuming. A media list should include the name of the reporter, editor, or producer; title; address; telephone number; fascimile number; and other useful information, such as videotape requirements, kinds of stories considered, deadlines, and Web site and e-mail addresses. Information should be updated every three months.

Obviously, media lists provide the addresses for mailing news releases. But many practitioners use their media lists to keep track of their media contacts. Reporters and editors are notorious for moving every few years to different jobs in different locations. Practitioners can also note on the media list when they have called to pitch a story idea or even personal tidbits, such as the names of reporters' children or favorite hobbies. Such knowledge serves as an icebreaker or a friendly way to wrap up a conversation.

Apart from media lists, most practitioners keep media logs. They note when a reporter called, the media outlet represented, the story or summary of questions, and who responded. The log can be a quantitative way to assess public relations efforts.

The Contents of Media Kits

Many organizations, whether major companies or nonprofit groups, produce materials for media kits. Among the standard pieces are fact sheets, backgrounders, news releases, and reprints of articles about the organization. Each may be subdivided further. These pieces may also be available at the organization's Web site. Even if the content of the Web site and the media kit are not identical, they need to be coordinated in appearance and tone. For example, the company logo and any slogan would appear in both places. All printed materials should show the address of the Web site; likewise, the Web site should offer printed material.

Once the basic pieces are developed, a practitioner can build a media kit depending on audience need. A reporter new to the financial services beat would get a package with backgrounders, fact sheets, the most recent annual report, the latest news release on company earnings, and any other information the public relations manager believes to be educational. When the bank announces a new retail service, fact sheets on the other services would be included in media kits distributed at a news conference.

The pieces together are called collateral pieces, that is, they have a similar look. The look or image of these pieces represents that of the company.

Refer to the news release example in Figure 12.2 and the report cover in Figure 12.3 on pages 318–319. The American Heart Association uses its identifiable single heart logo on all pieces. The slogan, "Fighting Heart Disease and Stroke," appears below the organization's name. The collateral pieces have unity, visual harmony, and an identifiable look.

With increased technology, organizations no longer rely solely on the U.S. mail to deliver media kits or information included in media kits. Companies use fascimiles or even post news on Web sites to reach the media. Some public and private companies, agencies, associations, municipalities, and other institutions hire companies to transmit news to the media.

For example, PR Newswire sends more than 150,000 full-text news releases each year to more than 2,000 newspapers, magazines, TV stations, and radio stations throughout the United States and to even more around the world. Medialink distributes printed press releases and kits by mail or broadcast fascimiles. But it also uses video, audio, and the Internet to make news for its clients available to television newsrooms and financial institutions. It uses video news releases and B-roll packages, satellite media tours, electronic press kits, interactive news conferences, and audio news releases. Video and audio clips are posted on the Web with links to clients' Web sites, and even live Web casts can be viewed as they are happening, then posted to Web sites for later viewing.

Printed Communications Tools

As discussed earlier, public relations practitioners have many ways to reach their important audiences. Some are used more often than others. The more commonly used ones, and those that require skilled writers, are discussed here.

FIGURE 12.2

National Center
Office of Communications
7272 Greenville Avenue
Dallas, Texas 75231-4596

**American Heart
Association.**
*Fighting Heart Disease
and Stroke*

FOR RELEASE:
4 p.m. ET, Thursday
January 8, 1998

CONTACT:
Brian Henry: (214-706-1135) or
Carole Bullock: (214-706-1279)
(for journal copies only, please
telephone: (214-706-1173)

NR 98-4834 (Stroke/Frey)

American Heart Association journal report:

Hispanics face higher risk for bleeding strokes than whites, Native Americans

DALLAS, Jan. 9 -- People who are Hispanic are more likely than whites and Native Americans to develop hemorrhagic strokes, caused by rupture of a brain artery, rather than ischemic strokes, caused by blockage of a brain artery, according to a new study appearing in *Stroke: Journal of the American Heart Association.*

Hemorrhage (bleeding) in the brain was more prevalent in Hispanics. Bleeding strokes occurred in 48 percent of Hispanics compared to 37 percent of whites and 27 percent of Native Americans.

The study is one of the largest to examine differences in stroke among minority populations. It included 1,290 whites, 242 Hispanics, 83 Native Americans, and 101 other patients hospitalized for stroke at the Barrow Neurological Institute in Phoenix, Arizona.

The authors observed that although Hispanics in the general population are less prone to high blood pressure than whites or Native Americans, Hispanics with stroke appear to have the greatest proportion of high blood pressure of any of the three groups. In this study, the rate of high blood pressure in stroke was reinforced. All groups had a high incidence of high blood pressure. It was found in 72 percent of Hispanics with stroke, compared to 71 percent of Native Americans and 66 percent of whites. Possible reasons for the high proportion of high blood pressure in Hispanics with stroke include less compliance with blood pressure treatment (especially in Hispanic Males) and special susceptibility of brain arteries to damage from high blood pressure in Hispanics.

Hispanics also had the second highest proportion of heavy alcohol intake and the second highest proportion of diabetes (behind Native Americans in these categories), both of which are known risk factors for stroke.

Whites ranked highest for heart disease and cigarette smoking and had the highest prevalence of cardioembolic strokes -- caused by blood clots that form within the heart and travel to the brain.

-more-

FIGURE 12.3

News Releases

News releases, such as those that follow, provide timely information to media. They may announce a promotion or staff change; a service or product; new information, such as the effects of legislation or the results of a survey; an upcoming event; or community service, such as a new scholarship program. Some news releases, especially those concerning events, are presented in the form of media advisories.

News Release

FOR RELEASE: CONTACT:
4 p.m. ET, Thursday   Brian Henry: (214) 706-1135 or
January 8, 1998   Carole Bullock: (214) 706-1279
                                For journal copies only, please
                                Telephone: (214) 706-1173

NR 98-4834 Stroke/Frey
American Heart Association journal report:
  Hispanics face higher risk for bleeding strokes than whites, Native Americans
  DALLAS, Jan. 9 — People who are Hispanic are more likely than whites and Native Americans to develop hemorrhage strokes, caused by rupture of a brain artery, rather than ischemic strokes, caused by blockage of a brain artery, according to a new study appearing in *Stroke: Journal of the American Heart Association.*
  Hemorrhage (bleeding) in the brain was more prevalent in Hispanics. Bleeding strokes occurred in 48 percent of Hispanics compared to 37 percent of whites and 27 percent of Native Americans.
  The study is the largest to examine differences in stroke among minority populations. It included 1,290 whites, 242 Hispanics, 83 Native Americans, and 101 other patients hospitalized for stroke at the Barrow Neurological Institute in Phoenix, Arizona.
  The authors observed that although Hispanics in the general population are less prone to high blood pressure than whites or Native Americans, Hispanics

with stroke appear to have the greatest proportion of high blood pressure of any of the three groups. In this study, the rate of high blood pressure in stroke was reinforced. All groups had a high incidence of high blood pressure. It was found in 72 percent of Hispanics with stroke, compared to 71 percent of Native Americans and 66 percent of whites. Possible reasons for the high proportion of high blood pressure in Hispanics with stroke include less compliance with blood pressure treatment (especially Hispanic males) and special susceptibility of brain arteries to damage from high blood pressure in Hispanics.

Hispanics also had the second highest proportion of heavy alcohol intake and the second highest proportion of diabetes (behind Native Americans in these categories), both of which are known risk factors for stroke.

Whites ranked highest for heart disease and cigarette smoking and had the highest prevalence of cardioembolic strokes—caused by blood clots that form within the heart and travel to the brain. Native Americans were most likely to be diabetic and develop lacunar strokes—caused by blockage of the smaller arteries of the brain.

The study's lead author, James L. Frey, M.D., chief, neurovascular section, division of neurology at the Barrow Neurological Institute, cautions that "because our data come from a population of patients hospitalized at a single institution, broad generalizations may be hazardous without confirmation from larger community-based studies. Nonetheless, our data are consistent with other data about the differences in the prevalence of stroke risk factors and stroke types among these populations. Interestingly, the different populations appear to respond to risk factors similarly, which means that efforts to prevent stroke in Hispanics and Native Americans should emphasize control of risk factors in the same way as is suggested for whites."

Co-researchers include Heidi K. Jahnke, R.N., R.S.N., and Eric Bulfinch, Ed.D.

Stroke: Journal of the American Heart Association is one of five journals published by the Dallas-based AHA.

(Reprinted with permission of the American Heart Association.)

The American Heart Association often writes about health topics, and the language must be clear and defined to help readers through technical topics. Some releases may contain interesting information but be difficult to navigate. The less research and rewriting a news organization must do, the more likely the release will be used. Consider the following news release:

today's news

Rawlings Sport Drink Signs Baseball Superstar Ken Caminiti

Del Mar, Calif., Jan. 14 / PR Newswire/—Beverage Source World-wide, Inc. (BSW), a wholly owned subsidary of Masadi Resources, Inc.. (MRI), announced today that pursuant to the company's marketing strategy, it has signed an athlete endorsement agreement with Ken Caminiti of the San Diego Padres.

As a shareholder and equity partner in BSW, Caminiti's 1998 agreement includes advertising, marketing and promoting the company's Rawlings Sport Drink line through print advertisements, point of sale merchandise, promotions and personal appearances.

Caminiti is a three-time Gold Glove winner and a three-time All-Star game player. In 1996, he was the fourth player ever to be unanimously selected as National League Most Valuable Player. Caminiti is just the third baseball player on record to hit .300 (.326) with at least 40 home runs and 130 RBIs.

BSW products include Rawlings Sport, a New Age sports beverage; Rawlings for Kids, the first vitamin and mineral fortified sports beverage for children; and Rawlings Sport Water, a premium spring water.

BSW is involved in licensing, co-branding and marketing of sports drinks, premium water, and other beverages. MRI is a diversified holding company with emphasis in the beverage industry.

Rawlings Sporting Goods Company is the exclusive Official Baseball Supplier to the Major and Minor Leagues and the exclusive supplier of the Official Basketball and Football for NCAA Championships. For more than 20 years, Rawlings has been the single provider of baseballs used in every All-Star and World Series game.

(*Source:* Beverage Source Worldwide, Inc. Reprinted with permission of PR Newswire.)

The release follows the business format, but news media may be more interested in the news about Caminiti first rather than the company and its subsidiaries. News releases must contain some of the news values discussed in Chapter 3: prominence, timeliness, proximity, impact, and magnitude. They may also include conflict, oddity, or emotional impact. The lead should summarize the relevant information. The rest of the release should be organized in the inverted pyramid style of writing discussed in Chapter 4 and follow Associated Press style, which most news outlets use.

The practitioner's goal in sending a news release is to get publicity. But the practitioner must remember that news releases are uncontrolled; the final story is up to the reporter's and editor's discretion. Reporters may use the release as a basis for an expanded story, or they may use the news release as is and even give the writer a byline. Reporters, editors, and producers need news releases that are complete, accurate, newsworthy, and appropriate for their audiences. Few will reject news releases in a ready-to-use format.

News releases should contain the public relations contact name, organization, organization address, organization phone number, fascimile number, e-mail address, and PR contact's home phone number. The information goes in the upper left-hand corner. If the organization's address is readily visible on letterhead, it can be omitted. Under this information go the date and the headline, setting up the contents of the news release.

Often PR practitioners will include a contact name and telephone number within the text of the news release, usually at the end, to ensure that further information is available to interested publics if the news release is run verbatim.

Fact Sheets

Fact sheets are generally one page long—or front and back of one sheet—and are designed to be read quickly. Information about the organization, a service, a product, or a special activity is highlighted in short segments.

An easy way to develop a fact sheet is to follow the news elements discussed in Chapter 3: who, what, when, where, how, and why. A statewide children's forum is planning its annual fund-raiser. The fact sheet would be organized:

Who: The Children's Forum

What: Annual fund-raiser—a black-tie dinner and dance

When: June 14

Where:	Downtowner Hotel
How:	Ticket prices $75 per individual for the dance and $150 for dinner and dance through the institute offices at 444-1234
Why:	To raise money for administrative and program costs.

Fact sheets should also contain the contact name, organization, and phone numbers for reporters and others who want additional information. When fact sheets are produced or updated, put the date at the bottom of the fact sheet to indicate how current the information is.

Facts sheets are also uncontrolled. Media can use the information any way they wish.

Backgrounders

Backgrounders are not news releases and do not carry news that has immediacy. A backgrounder supplements a news release and gives additional information a reporter may need about a company or its services. Information in a backgrounder does not have to be attributed as it would in a news release. The source is considered to be the company. The information is organized by section, such as introduction, history, specific services, demographics, and other information. The sections note specific information quickly.

Like a news release, a backgrounder must be well written and organized clearly and logically. Information must be accurate and should be updated periodically. Like news releases and fact sheets, a backgrounder is uncontrolled. The practitioner knows that anything in the backgrounder could appear in print or be heard on the airwaves and thus assimilated by the organization's publics.

Brochures

In writing and designing brochures, public relations practitioners are limited only by their talent, creativity, and budget. With the widespread use of desktop publishing, many more organizations can produce high-quality, good-looking brochures for little cost. They can also publish brochure content on the World Wide Web. The more work that is done in house, the more money saved.

Questions to determine in writing a brochure are these:

• Is the brochure persuasive or informative? If the brochure's primary role is to persuade, it will be written with emotional language, comparisons, and familiar concepts. If informative, material will be to the point and language straightforward.

• Who is the audience? Whether the audience is specialized or general will determine the level of language used.

• Will the brochure be read and thrown away or saved? Deciding how it will be used will affect the cost and design.

• Will the brochure be a stand-alone piece, such as those in a display rack at a state's welcome station, or a collateral piece in a media kit or with a related Web site? A stand-alone brochure must be complete because it cannot rely on information in other pieces or online links.

• What is the appropriate format? If the brochure is a self-mailer, it will have to have an address space. Information has to be arranged logically, and decisions have to be made on artwork, such as photographs, and on graphic elements and white space, the size, the number of folds or pages, and how the brochure will open.

Brochure copy should be short. Publics are looking for a quick read. Each panel should stand alone, and copy shouldn't jump from one panel to the next.

Brochures, whether printed or online, are appealing to public relations practitioners because they are controlled messages. The practitioner has the final say-so on copy and design. No one can change the content or wording; the only uncontrolled aspect is placement, for example, whether brochures are left at a doctor's office to be displayed or are given to volunteers to distribute. The concerns are visibility of the brochure rack and whether all brochures are handed out.

Newsletters

Some public relations practitioners debate the effectiveness of newsletters. They contend that they can be time-consuming and costly to produce and that few people read them. But newsletters are a primary method used by organizations to communicate with publics, particularly employees and donors.

Newsletters can also be produced efficiently and rather cheaply with desktop publishing systems. They can be quick-printed or even photocopied and folded in the office. Many are transmitted online via Web sites or e-mail.

Information for newsletters comes from other newsletters, employees, managers, news events, industry happenings, or seasonal topics. People within the organization or company may be correspondents, submitting ideas or actual copy from their departments. The newsletter editor writes stories based on the ideas or edits the correspondents' stories. The style can be news or feature, and more stories can have a beginning, middle, and end—not just written in inverted pyramid format. And all copy is controlled: The public relations practitioner ultimately determines the content and tone.

Newsletter editors must guard to keep publications interesting and lively. Many newsletters are deadly dull, containing column after column of information. To attract readers, newsletters must be enlightening, informative, and entertaining. Good design can capture readers, but good writing will hold them.

Speeches

Many people dread the thought of getting up in front of a crowd and giving a speech. The public relations practitioner who has to write a speech may be relieved that he or she doesn't have to deliver it, but the task of writing a speech for someone else can be daunting. Speeches are controlled, because they are delivered, but speakers must remember that they may be easy marks afterward for people who may have unflattering questions.

Speeches are needed for a variety of reasons: to educate, to state a position or advocate a certain belief, to praise someone's achievement, to entertain, to highlight a special occasion, or to establish rapport. Each one requires a special format and writing style. The speech reprinted on pages 326–329 was written in a style appropriate for the speech's audience, the National Press Club, and for its speaker. Eugene Roberts is former managing editor of *The New York Times*. His remarks follow the guidelines for effective speech writing.

Nothing Succeeds Like Substance

My first newspaper job was the *Goldsboro News-Argus,* which is, for the ill-informed, the leading newspaper in Wayne County, North Carolina. It then had a circulation of 9,000. I wrote its farm column, "Rambling in Rural Wayne." Farmers summoned me to the scene whenever there was a significant farming event.

I wrote, for example about the first farmer of the season to transplant tobacco plants from the seed bed to the field, and about the season's first cotton blossom. I clucked over farmers' wives who made the county's best strawberry preserves and pickled watermelon rind; and they, in turn, clucked over me. I wrote of volatile tobacco prices, of hailstorms and drought. I once wrote about a sweet potato that looked like Gen. Charles de Gaulle.

Because I was linked closely to events that were important to farm families, I—and what I wrote—became memorable to readers in a way that I never was, before or since.

I was reminded vividly of this more than a decade after I left the *News-Argus* and the "Rambling in Rural Wayne" column. It was in 1968 during the Tet offensive, when I was a war correspondent for *The New York Times* in Vietnam.

I heard vague reports of trouble in Hue. I made my way there by truck and helicopter and found that the Marines were surrounded and held only two blocks of the city. The Viet Cong and the North Vietnamese forces held on to the rest. Each day after the Marines were reinforced by fresh units, they retook two or three blocks of the city, only to lose most of it again during the night to enemy troops.

It took about 10 days for the Marines to get 10 blocks or so from their headquarters compound. When they did, they found several American advisors who had been hiding under a house since the night the enemy overran the city. They had little water, even less food, and were hanging on by their nerve ends when the Marines broke through.

The Marines took the survivors to the headquarters compound and, to give them a sense of security, put them in the safest place they could find—a bunker dug deep into the center of the compound. I heard about the survivors and went to interview them.

"My name is Gene Roberts," I said. "I'm with *The New York Times.* I've come to get your story."

Out of the darkness came a voice, and it said: "Hey, did you ever write the 'Rambling in Rural Wayne' column for the *Goldsboro News-Argus?*"

I learned valuable lessons from the *News-Argus* and my tobacco farmer readers. I learned never to underestimate readers. They can laugh with you at the Charles de Gaulle sweet potato stories, but they expect depth when stories arise that are important to them. I learned that if tobacco prices were going up or down there was no limit to their demand for detail. And when the government banned, as it once did, a very productive variety of tobacco seed, no amount of coverage was too great. I could have written the journalistic equivalent of *War and Peace* and the farmers would have read it.

I wish some of today's publishing executives had been out in the tobacco rows with me. They would have learned that formula and slickness cannot substitute for substantive news coverage.

It's interesting to note that when my old boss, John S. Knight, received the National Press Club's Fourth Estate Award 17 years ago, he reflected on the importance of giving readers plenitude of solid news coverage. He reminisced, for example, about how he won the newspaper war in Akron, Ohio, and with the *Beacon Journal* laid the cornerstone of what would become first Knight Newspapers and then Knight-Ridder, Inc. His strategy was simple: print more news than the opposition. "Too many publishers have forgotten that injunction today," Jack Knight told the club in 1976.

He was right then. And 17 years later, far more publishers have forgotten that it was the most substantive newspaper that became dominant in one competitive town after another: in New York, for example, and Philadelphia, Boston, Washington, Chicago, Dallas and Miami.

Today, as competition diminishes and disappears, many newspapers seem to be in a race to see which can be the most shortsighted and superficial. We are relying too much—far too much—on weather maps, charts, graphs, briefs, and color.

If we had looked upon these devices as nothing more, or less, than desirable improvements, then our papers would have been all the richer for the additions. But in far too many newspapers, we introduced these devices while slashing newsroom budgets and newsholes. The result, all too often, has been that instead of becoming *additions* to news coverage, the devices have become *substitutes* for news coverage. And this, in a word, is folly.

We, of course, introduced many devices in order to reach out to marginal readers and non-readers. This was good. But when we started cutting back on substance, we put serious, devoted readers at risk by becoming less essential to them. And this was, and is, a very bad tradeoff. I think, quite simply, that we are imperiling newspapers in the name of saving them.

Not only is this trend weakening our hold on to the most loyal readers, it is causing long-term confusion and instability on our staffs, which further threaten our readership. Evidence of this abounds.

Recently, I talked to a newspaper consultant who estimated that he had given advice to more than 100 newsrooms in the past two years. The consultant found a common problem at almost every paper. The mid-level tier of editors seemed traumatized.

The problem? Lack of resources. The mid-level editors didn't think it was possible to perform at an acceptable standard given the resources at their disposal.

You could go to my editors' meeting in the past three or four years and encounter widespread angst. And not meetings of mid-level editors. Top editors.

Reporters are also reeling. Let me tell you just one story. Eighteen months ago, Susumu Shimoyama came here from Japan to study investigative reporting. His plan was to seek out some of the country's best investigative reporters and do a paper on how they practiced their craft. But except at a bare handful of papers, he found it difficult to find reporters who were spending time on projects. Some investigative reporters had been reassigned. Some were leaving journalism. All gave the same reason. Their newspapers had lost interest in in-depth reporting.

"I interviewed quite a number of investigative reporters in this country for this project," Susumu later wrote. "There was one common word with which some of them described themselves in spite of themselves. That was 'dinosaur.'"

Susumu abandoned his original plan. Instead, he did a paper titled, "The Demise of Investigative Journalism in American Newspapers."

Hopefully, the gap between what Susumu expected to find and what he actually found led him to overstate the problem. I hope and believe that. But I wouldn't bet the farm on it.

But whether or not investigative reporting is threatened with extinction, it is, without question, seriously battered. So are many other forms of substantive reporting, including steady persistent coverage of news beats and subject areas.

Much of the newsroom cutting was done in the name of recession-related downsizing, although some companies say that the downsizing is permanent. But the recession is only part of the problem. The real problem is that we're further along in concentration of newspaper ownership and incorporation.

We're now in the second and third generation of professional corporate managers who are judged and compensated on the profits they generate during their tenure, not on what they do to guarantee the survival of newspapers. It should be noted that even in the worst of the recession, average operating profits, as a percentage of revenue, were in the 14 percent to 15 percent range for publicly held newspapers. Many basic American industries never reach that level of profit even in the best of times. And some newspaper companies reached those levels in recessionary times by mortgaging the future, by stripping away the glue that binds our most loyal readers to our papers.

Just how bleak is the situation? Scary to be sure, but not hopeless if corporations become aware that there is no security in superficiality and here and there, thankfully, are newspapers—a distinct minority—that understand this and are riding out the recession without shortchanging their readers. And there are executives on still other newspapers who are beginning to worry about what they are doing to the future of their papers by focusing on short-term, rather than long-term damage.

Let us hope there is enough understanding to produce a strong counter-movement for substance and continuity. Let us hope that more executives learn what some of us were taught in the streets and fields where the readers are—that you might get a large audience by being a quick, superficial read, but not an intense, dedicated audience.

And journalistic history is, of course, littered with the corpses of large-circulation newspapers that failed to make long-term and lasting reader relationships and, thus, were viewed as dispensable by their readers and consequently, by their advertisers.

Eugene L. Roberts Jr., former managing editor of *The New York Times,* was executive editor of the *Philadelphia Inquirer.* He teaches at the University of Maryland College of Journalism. He gave this speech at the National Press Club after receiving its Fourth Estate Award. (Reprinted by permission of the author.)

Primary Considerations

Writing a speech is like other mass communications writing. The writer must have a subject and a purpose or reason for giving the speech and must know the audience. Knowing what the audience already knows about the subject and whether it is likely to favor, oppose, or be undecided about the subject will determine the approach and how best to illustrate it.

A writer must create a speech that fits the speaker's way of talking and delivery. The style, however, must fit the audience's level of understanding and interest. The writer must use speech patterns that are suitable for the audience. For most audiences, the best bet is to use simple, precise language as is discussed in Chapter 5. Simple language will also help the speaker.

After you have completed the speech, read it aloud. Make sure the writing flows, the structure is appropriate, and the audience is addressed. Determine whether visuals are needed. Visuals should supplement what the speaker is saying and not detract from it. The speaker should be comfortable using visuals and should talk to the audience, not the screen. If possible, someone other than the speaker should be responsible for operating the audiovisual equipment.

As a public relations practitioner, remember that the speech will come back to you for changes and rewriting, perhaps several times. That's okay. One public relations practitioner, recalling a speech written for the company president, said she agonized over style and finally submitted a draft. A few days later it came back, completely revised and retyped. "When I read through the 10 pages, I saw one complete sentence that was my own," she said. "But the note from the president said, 'Great work!'"

Public Relations and Advertising

As the public relations director for your town's historical society, you want to let many publics know about plans for the society's annual Christmas tour of homes. To send a controlled message to many audiences, you decide to place an ad in the local newspaper. You would write the copy, and you might also solicit a local company to underwrite the cost and give it credit within the ad copy.

Advertising gives organizations the opportunity to produce a controlled message in both copy and placement. Once the message is determined, the ad is written. The organization buys space in a specific magazine or section of the newspaper or air time at a certain hour. The ad is printed or broadcast just as the organization produced it.

Most advertising is produced in advertising or marketing departments within large companies. Public relations practitioners are rarely involved in advertising except when their company produces image advertisements. A nonprofit organization, however, may have just one person who does all public relations and advertising work. Advertising is discussed further in Chapter 13.

Communications Planning

To implement a public relations campaign, practitioners need a plan. Plans are written during the second public relations stage, discussed earlier in the chapter. Plans are critical because they guide practitioners about their publics, communications tools, and timing. Once research is completed, practitioners can set out to match the types of communications tools with audiences.

Making the Match

In matching specific communications tools to publics, consider the example of the university capital campaign. As the public relations director, you would consider which media or tools would reach your targeted groups. You might decide to produce a general information brochure that would go to all publics or a Web site. But for individual publics, you might start a list like this:

• *Alumni.* Direct mail letters; news releases or news features to alumni publications; public service announcements to major radio and television stations in states where large numbers of alumni live; speeches and presentations to alumni club meetings; news releases and fact sheets to statewide media.

• *Faculty members.* News releases, feature releases, e-mail, and fact sheets to campus publications; direct mail; speeches and audiovisual presentations.

• *Students.* PSAs to popular radio stations; news releases, feature releases, and fact sheets to student publications; speeches and audiovisual presentations; advertisements in campus media.

If you continued the list, you probably would find that some communications tools serve the same publics. Different publics read newspapers and direct mail letters, watch television, and attend civic meetings. Each public has its own interests and language. The focus of the public relations message will vary depending on the audience.

For example, the direct mail letters to faculty members and alumni would carry the same message of the need for donations and would make a pitch for a contribution. But the faculty letter would explain how new buildings would add classrooms, laboratories, and offices—all to the benefit of teaching. The alumni letter would discuss how new buildings would benefit the university's reputation and thereby maintain the strength of degrees.

Writing a Plan for a Specific Occasion

Writing a plan requires thinking and often experience. Practitioners often begin by brainstorming or listing random ideas for communicating with publics. Then they start refining, based on time constraints, cost of producing materials, and company style. The final plan includes a statement of the issue or problem, campaign objectives, strategies for reaching objectives, and specific actions. Specific actions are assigned deadlines and an individual responsible for carrying out each action.

Think about the earlier example of the bank that is changing its checking service. Your role as the public relations person is to support the paid advertising done by the marketing department. Research says you need to target newcomers to town, existing customers who may switch type of account, and potential customers who may find the account more attractive than what their bank offers. You decide in the planning stage to develop a brochure that can be mailed to newcomers and to customers in their bank statements. For those who bank by computer, an online brochure may be needed. You also want to distribute news releases to area media to attract other nonbank customers.

Your plan would consider the time frame. The service will be introduced in three months. Brochure production takes time, so that is first on the to-do list. The news release will be done later. Your written plan looks like this:

Communications Plan for No-Frills Checking Service

Issue: First City Bank will introduce a new checking service in three months. It will offer customers free checking if they keep a minimum of $100 in a savings account. The first 200 checks will be free.

Objective: To attract customers to the service by positioning it as a less expensive way to maintain a checking account, particularly for people who don't need lots of attached services, such as credit cards.

Strategy: Use communications tools that will reach newcomers, existing customers, and nonbank customers.

Actions:

Date	Action	Responsibility
May 1	Develop outline and content for the brochure	PR manager
May 5	Hire a writer, designer, and Web master	PR manager
May 23	First draft of brochure copy	Freelance writer
May 24	Design for brochure complete	Freelance designer
May 28	Copy/design sent for approvals	PR manager
June 5	Final brochure complete	PR manager
June 7	Brochure copy to printer and Web master	PR staff
June 13	Brochure sent to account service to be stuffed in next check statement cycle	PR staff
June 15	Secure newcomers' names from chamber of commerce	PR staff
June 30	Mail brochure to newcomers, publish Web site	PR staff
July 1	Consider focus of local/statewide news release	PR manager
July 10	Complete draft of local/statewide news release	PR manager
July 20	Approvals returned on local/statewide news release	PR manager
July 25	Mail release to local and statewide media, publish copies of release on Web site	PR staff
Aug. 1	Checking service begins	

Crisis Planning

No organization expects or wants a crisis, but plans must be made in the event a crisis occurs. The crisis could be as large as an oil spill or as small as an error in a newsletter. If any event negatively affects audiences, an organization has a crisis.

A crisis plan can help an organization make lemonade out of lemons, says Joyce Fitzpatrick, senior vice president for Ruder-Finn, a major public relations firms in the United States. A crisis plan helps a company be prepared. Plans should be easily accessible and reviewed periodically.

Fitzpatrick notes when conducting crisis communication seminars that in a crisis plan, organizations should identify a specific spokesperson. If possible, the spokesperson should be someone who has been in a crisis before—and that person may not be the chief executive officer. Organizations should also establish a sequence of who will be informed first. Affected employees should hear about the crisis before they read about it in the media.

When the crisis occurs, Fitzpatrick advises the companies to respond within the first 24 hours. If the crisis is long-running, companies should set up a specific site and time each day for news conferences. The spokesperson should appear, even if there is no new development, and be ready to say when the company has new developments or information to share.

Wrap-up

This chapter is an introduction to the public relations field, its role, practitioners' responsibilities, and some communications tools. Students majoring in public relations will take specific courses on theory, case studies, public relations campaigns, public relations writing, and possibly video production. In each course, they will learn more about the field and its opportunities. At the core of each course will be the ability to write.

Public relations practitioners must be able to communicate quickly, accurately, and completely to be effective. They also must know their audiences. Public relations practitioners who can combine those two talents will be successful.

EXERCISES

1. You are the public relations officer for the Campus Literacy Program. You want to recruit more volunteers to serve as readers to children in the community.
   a. Identify the audience(s) you are trying to reach as potential volunteers.
   b. Knowing your audience interests and media usage, identify three communications tools you would use to reach each audience.

    c. What information would your audience(s) need to make a decision whether to volunteer? Make a list.

    d. How could you evaluate the success of your communications effort?

2. You are the public relations director for Bicycle World Equipment Co. You are to write a news release for the local newspaper based on the following information:

> Bicycle World is planning to sponsor bicycle safety clinics in the public schools that are located in Wayne County, the company headquarters. The clinics will be on two consecutive Saturdays from 10 a.m. to noon. Each of the county's six elementary schools will have the clinics. People who want to attend must call 555-3456 to register. The clinic is open to children 6-12 years of age. Each child must have a helmet.

> Bicycle World staff members will check each child's bicycle for safe operation and indicate on a check-off list any equipment that needs repair. Children will be advised of good bicycle safety, such as wearing helmets, riding in bike lanes, and using proper hand signals. Then each will be allowed to enter an obstacle course, which will test their riding proficiency. For example, as they ride down a "road," a dog may run out from between two cars. Children's reactions and reaction times will be monitored. After the road test, they will be briefed on what they did well and what they need to improve. At the end of the course, they will receive a certificate of accomplishment.

> "We believe bicycle safety is crucial for children," said company President Dennis Lester. "With just a little guidance, children can learn habits and rules that could save their lives. Those of us in the bicycle business want to ensure that children who use our products do so

competently and safely. We want them to enjoy bicycling
as a sport they can continue into adulthood."

The clinics are free.

Bicycle World is a three-year-old company that produces bike frames, components, bike helmets, clothing,
and road guides to bicycle routes. Company President
Dennis Lester is a master rider and formed the company
to provide quality equipment to bicycle enthusiasts.

3. From the above information, write a one-page fact sheet based on the bicycle clinics sponsored by Bicycle World Equipment Co. You would be the contact, 555–2345. The company's address is 67 W. Lane Blvd., Your town, Your zip code.

4. Bicycle World President Dennis Lester has been asked to speak to the local Girl Scout council about bike safety. The audience is girls 10–12 years of age. Develop an introduction that would attract them to the speech. Then write an outline of the information you would include when the actual speech is written.

5. Choose a nonprofit organization in your community. Contact the director about preparing a media kit for the organization. The kit could provide information about the organization itself or a special event. The kit would include a fact sheet; a backgrounder; a news release on a timely, relevant topic; and a news feature about the organization or one of its services. Use existing materials on the organization as part of your research plus interviews with the director, staff members, and any users of the organization's services.

REFERENCES

"Death of a Princess, Birth of a Thousand Press Releases," *Wall Street Journal*, September 10, 1997.

Thomas Bivins, *Handbook for Public Relations Writing*, 2nd ed. Chicago: NTC Business Books, 1993.

Scott M. Cutlip, Allen H. Center and Glen H. Broom, *Effective Public Relations*, 7th ed. Englewood Cliffs, NJ: Prentice-Hall, 1994.

J. E. Grunig and Todd Hunt, *Managing Public Relations*. Fort Worth, TX: Harcourt Brace Jovanovich College Publishers, 1984.

Medialink Web site. Available at: http://www.medialink.com.

Doug Newsom and Bob Carrell, *Public Relations Writing: Form and Style,* 3rd ed. Belmont, CA: Wadsworth Publishing, 1991.

PR Newswire Web site. Available at: http://www.prnewswire.com.

Public Relations Society of America Web site. Available at: http://www.prsa.org.

"Warner Bros. Issues Correction," CNN Custom:News [Online], November 24, 1997. Available at: http://www.cnn.com.

Dennis L. Wilcox and Lawrence W. Nolte, *Public Relations Writing and Media Techniques,* 2nd ed. New York: HarperCollins College Publishers, 1995.

13

Advertising

Advertising is probably the first form of media writing that children notice. Kids respond to ads, often before they can talk. Toddlers excitedly point at Ronald McDonald and "read" the golden arches as a sign for food even before they know their ABCs. By combining color, sound, movement, symbols, and language, advertising creates some of the most powerful messages in our world today.

Like all media presentations, good advertising depends on good writing. "Good advertising writers are writers first. They are personal writers—people who bring their own feelings and reactions to the product," observes Professor John Sweeney, former creative director for a major American advertising agency. "Good advertising slogans are some of the most effective communication available today. They have a concise, pithy, sensory quality that other writers would do well to study and adopt."

Clear, direct communication is and always has been required of ad writers, who are usually referred to as copywriters. Although many people think of ad writers as zany creative types—which they may be—copywriters primarily are just that: writers. Advertising copywriters learn to hook their audiences with the first sound or word of an ad. And, as Sweeney says, other writers can benefit from studying their techniques.

This chapter will explain

- Advertising goals in the information age,
- What is in an ad,
- The process of writing for advertising,

- Guidelines for effective ad writing, and
- What all writers can learn from advertising.

By reaching these goals, the ad writer fulfills the goal of marketing, which is to sell the product or service.

Advertising in the Information Age

Volney Palmer is generally credited with being the first advertising "agent." In 1841 he began selling newspaper advertising space for a profit. Advertisers prepared their ads; Palmer and other agents placed the ads for them. Such advertising agents became concerned with copy and artwork for the ads several years later. In 1869 F. W. Ayer started N. W. Ayer & Son, an advertising agency that provided writing, art, and media placement to its clients.

Advertising agencies have changed throughout the years, but the seeds of the modern agency were planted with N. W. Ayer & Son and other early agencies that still exist today. Advertisers also have myriad ways to reach consumers, not just newspapers or billboards. One company may advertise in newspapers, on radio and television, and on the Internet. The overwhelming number of new media and the changing media habits of audiences allow advertisers to funnel product information directly to specific and special audiences.

The goals of ad writers, regardless of medium, have remained constant over the years:

- To communicate availability of products to audiences,
- To communicate product benefits to audiences,
- To provide accessible information about products, and
- To communicate main ideas about products in a few words.

Other goals include image building, when a company wants consumers to view it as a good corporate citizen; response to a disaster, such as a utility company telling customers how soon power will be restored after massive hurricane damage; or public service messages, such as alerting audiences to the dangers of unprotected sex or the benefits of low-fat diets.

Like other media, advertising is a field that is changing daily. But almost all print advertisements are made by combining the same four elements:

1. A headline,
2. An illustration, which may be graphic (pictures) or dramatic,
3. Advertising text—from a few words to a few pages—describing the product, and
4. A signature or logo, usually at the close of the ad.

But simply putting these elements together will not create an advertisement. Advertisements that work must carefully select and intertwine these four elements.

Is Advertising Propaganda?

Some people think of advertising as propaganda—as distorted information designed to lead, or mislead, its audience. Propaganda is manipulative, and so is advertising, some people say.

Unlike most other forms of published writing, advertising is one-sided by its very nature; no one wants to spend his or her advertising budget extolling the benefits of the other guy's product. But the absence of other products from ads does not have to mean that an ad is unfairly biased if the information presented is accurate in and of itself.

"An advertisement is a known one-sided form, like a resumé," explains Professor John Sweeney. "It is not a sinister hiding of information; rather, it is a presentation of your best information."

Advertising writing has work to do; it substitutes for personal, face-to-face contact in the sales process. Like professional salespeople, advertisers deal with factual information and must never forget that they have a public responsibility. Once an advertiser loses public confidence in the accuracy of its claims, that confidence may not be recovered.

Presenting your best to the public, Sweeney explains, is a core value of advertising culture. A one-sided presentation need not be an unfair presentation, and understanding that aspect is part of being an effective professional, Sweeney says. He encourages advertisers to set ethical limits for themselves, adding, "We don't want billboards in the Grand Canyon."

Advertising that is less than ethical is not advertising; it is propaganda or huckstering or manipulation. Professional advertising writing is an accepted form of argument—a fair argument—and it abides by an ethical code. The Advertising Principles of American Business provide basic guidelines for advertisers that include truth, substantiation, taste, and decency. The voluntary code, shown here, demonstrates an overall concern with fairness and with public trust that most advertisers take seriously. More information on the American Advertising Federation can be found on its Web site, available at http://www.aaf.org.

The Advertising Principles of American Business*

Truth
Advertising shall tell the truth, and shall reveal significant facts, the omission of which would mislead the public.

Substantiation
Advertising claims shall be substantiated by evidence in possession of the advertiser and advertising agency, prior to making such claims.

Comparisons
Advertising shall refrain from making false, misleading, or unsubstantiated statements or claims about a competitor or his products or services.

Bait Advertising
Advertising shall not offer products or services for sale unless such offer constitutes a bona fide effort to sell the advertised products or services and is not a device to switch consumers to other goods or services, usually higher priced.

Guarantees and Warranties
Advertising of guarantees and warranties shall be explicit, with sufficient information to apprise consumers of their principal terms and limitations or, when space or time restrictions preclude such disclosures, the advertisement should clearly reveal where the full text of the guarantee or warranty can be examined before purchase.

Price Claims
Advertising shall avoid price claims which are false or misleading, or savings claims which do not offer provable savings.

Testimonials
Advertising containing testimonials shall be limited to those of competent witnesses who are reflecting a real and honest opinion or experience.

Taste and Decency
Advertising shall be free of statements, illustrations or implications which are offensive to good taste or public decency.

*Adopted by the American Advertising Federation Board of Directors, March 2, 1984, San Antonio, TX. (Reprinted with permission.)

Advertisers are subject to many government rules and regulations. The Capital Council of Better Business Bureaus advises that all advertisers stay abreast of regulations through subscription services such as Do's and Don'ts in Advertising or the National Advertising Case Reports. Such subscription services are quite expensive and typically are used by large agencies or companies. The industry has self-regulators, such as the National Advertising Review Council (NARC).

Under the Federal Trade Commission, the Division of Advertising Practices protects consumers from deceptive and unsubstantiated advertising. Its Web site notes that law enforcement activities focus on

- Tobacco and alcohol advertising, including monitoring for unfair practices or deceptive claims, and reporting to Congress on cigarette and smokeless tobacco labeling, advertising, and promotion.

- Advertising claims for food and over-the-counter drugs, particularly those relating to nutritional or health benefits of foods and safety and effectiveness of drugs or medical devices.

- Performance and energy-savings claims made for energy-related household and automotive products.

- Environmental performance claims made for consumer products, including claims that products are environmentally safe, ozone-friendly, or biodegradable.

- Infomercials, long-form (30-minute) broadcast advertising, to ensure that both the format and content of programs are nondeceptive.

- General advertising at the national and regional levels, particularly advertising making objective claims that are difficult for consumers to evaluate.

Advertising and Today's Audiences

The environment for advertising has changed tremendously in the past decade. New media and new products compete for audience attention, so that advertisers may no longer assume that mere publicity will lead to success or consumers using services and buying products. Today's advertisers must proceed with conscious, sophisticated attention to audiences and audience attitudes. Only through selecting likely audiences and streamlining ads for those groups can advertisers reach information-age consumers.

Ad production is seldom the work of the writer. In most cases, the copywriter is part of a team. For an advertising agency, the team could include market researchers, who determine audience interest and product competition; an account executive, who oversees the account and serves as the liaison with the client; the art director, who designs ads and other collateral pieces for the client; the creative director, who oversees the concept and production; and the media buyer, who places ads. All members of the team must know the others' roles. The copywriter often works mostly closely with the art designer on aspects such as typeface, length of copy, size of the ad, and graphic elements.

Newspapers still design ads for advertisers who do not have agencies or cannot afford to pay agencies to do the work. The newspaper staff would include an ad sales representative, art designer, and copywriter.

Advertising Strategy

Before a writer sits down to write an ad, a marketing strategy is already in place, based on decisions by the team and the client or business. Generally, the strategy is a written document and part of a plan that lists advertising goals, such as gaining more sales or improving corporate image; target audience; positioning, or how consumers perceive the service or product vis-a-vis competitors; benefits; creative approach, such as tone of the advertising message; and appropriate media to reach audiences.

The plan will enable the copywriter to know what structure will have the greatest appeal to the target audience. The creative approach is affected by the goal—selling a product, providing general information about a company, positioning a product as superior among its competitors, or boosting a corporate image. Target audiences will determine tone of language and whether the ad must be serious or can have humor. Even corporate image will affect how a copywriter pitches an ad.

One of the copywriter's first responsibilities to support the advertising strategy will be to come up with a theme. Philip Ward Burton notes in *Advertising Copywriting* that the theme "is the central idea—the imaginative spark plug—that will give your advertisements continuity, recall value, and thus, extra selling power. Your theme is the lifeline of your campaign...."

Targeting Audiences

The process of identifying and communicating with specific audiences is often called *targeting*. Maybelline may target girls aged 13–15 as a likely audience for messages about a new tinted lip gloss. With the target group in mind, Maybelline's ad writers design messages that will appeal to young teens and place these ads in publications and time slots of which teens are likely consumers. Maybelline, for example, might place an ad for its new lip gloss in *Seventeen* magazine and between scenes on the show *Beverly Hills 90210*.

Targeting is a necessity in an era of budget consciousness. Advertisers no longer can afford to waste funds by advertising to broad audiences that may contain only a few potential customers. To get maximum benefit from advertising dollars, advertisers select target audiences for specific products. Beer, tires, and trucks are advertised in sports sections and broadcasts; toys and sweet cereals are advertised with Saturday morning cartoons; and pain relievers, laxatives, and investments are sold with financial news.

Professional market research is used by major corporations to identify the best possible markets for particular ads. Cluster marketing attempts to impose some order on the new media-and-audience mix, dividing Americans into subgroups and predicting specific media behaviors, products, and services that each group is likely to use. Michael Weiss describes in his book, *The Clustering of America,* the nation's forty neighborhood types. One cluster commonly used by advertisers is the "Blue Blood Estates" group. It reads *The New York Times* and watches David Letterman; smart advertisers will place ads for upscale products here. Educated viewers know that such products already are advertised in appropriate places; David Letterman's sponsors include many luxury cars such as Infiniti and Lexus, whereas ads for furs and jewelry abound in the *Times.*

A common system is VALS, established in 1978 as one of the first major consumer segmentation systems based on lifestyle characteristics, according to its Web site. Companies throughout the United States use VALS for assistance in audience targeting, product development, product positioning, advertising, promotion, focus groups, media planning, and corporate image. In targeting, for example, VALS helps identify what audiences to target, what the audience buys, why it does what it does, where concentrations of the targeted audience live, and the best methods of reaching the targeted audience.

Tom Burrell, chairman of Burrell Advertising in Chicago, recognizes the need for all communicators to address specific audiences. He was one of the country's first advertising executives to focus his clients' advertisements on the needs, attitudes, interests, and even behaviors of a single ethnic group, African Americans.

"The future is destined to be more complex, more complicated, more diverse, and more segmented for media," Burrell predicts. He believes that the whole idea of mass marketing is dying and that agencies more and more will respond to the needs of specific consumer groups such as women, ethnic populations, seniors, urban dwellers, and rural residents.

Placement of Advertisements

Today's advertisers cannot afford to waste ad dollars on placing messages that will not reach their audiences; therefore Huggies, maker of disposable diapers and training pants, does not advertise in large newspapers or in general-interest magazines. Rather, the company advertises in magazines for parents; more specifically, it chooses magazines that appeal to consumers who value its product and can afford it. Huggies' ads for its Pull-Ups disposable training pants would appear in *Parents* magazine to reach conscientious parents of both genders working both in and outside the home.

For years, standard forms of advertising were limited to a few familiar media. Advertisers had access to audiences through television, radio, newspapers, magazines, billboards, and direct mail. Audiences for these forms were large and homogeneous: "middle America" for television, billboards, and general-circulation newspapers and magazines; "teen America" for radio and teen magazines; and "older Americans" for direct mail and specialty magazines.

Today, advertisers have more options as a result of audience fragmentation and new media development. They use fascimile, voice mail, and online services in addition to the traditional mix. Each may indicate other ways to reach the company. For example, Princess Cruises and Princess Tours advertises its Alaska tour in *Travel and Leisure* magazine. The ad includes a toll-free number and a tear-out, postage-paid card that can be sent for a free Alaska planning kit. The Ritz-Carlton hotel gives a toll-free number and its Web site address, www.ritzcarlton.com. Businesses are also flashing Web addresses in television commercials, such as a cookie ad with www.chipsahoy.com as part of the visuals. See Figure 13.1 on page 346 for an example of how a company incorporates its Web address into print ads.

FIGURE 13.1 *In This Ad the Internet Address Is Included under the Logo and Mailing Address.*

PERFORMANCE Bike Shop®

Holiday Sale

December 3rd – 24th

The bikes kids want are at *PERFORMANCE*®

'98 **DIAMONDBACK.** VIPER

SALE $169
Chrome version: $179

'98 **DIAMONDBACK.** JOKER

SALE $189
Chrome version: $199

DIAMONDBACK.

All bikes on sale!

Make the holidays hassle-free with our FREE professional assembly by trained mechanics

FREE storage until the holidays

Layaway and financing available

110% low price guarantee

2 Years FREE maintenance on every bike purchase

A huge sleigh full of items on sale: clothing, trainers, helmets, lights and bike components!

PERFORMANCE
Official Supplier of Technical Cycling Wear

PERFORMANCE Bike Shop®

Carrboro 404 E. Main Street 919-933-1491

Internet Address http://www.performancebike.com

Quantities, sizes, and color of items are limited to stock on hand—no rainchecks. These special prices are only available at the Performance Bike Shop locations indicated above, these prices will not be available through mail order, outlet stores, or other area Performance Bike Shop locations.

A number of businesses are developing links between print advertising and advertising on the Internet, according to a study by Assistant Professor Carol J. Pardun of the University of North Carolina at Chapel Hill School of Journalism and Mass Communication and Larry Lamb, assistant director at Kansas State University's School of Journalism and Mass Communication. They analyzed 1,249 ads that appeared in twenty magazines during June 1997. Two of five included Web addresses, and print ads for cars had Web addresses 98 percent of the time. Ads in *Business Week* magazine were most likely to include a Web address, whereas *Woman's Day* had the least number of ads with Web addresses. Half the ads that carried Web addresses made them part of the copy; others listed the address separately. See the ad in Figure 13.1 as an example.

Targeting and the Writer

When copywriters begin to write, they must consider the target audience and the medium or media that will be used. That information is in the strategy. As noted earlier, the audience's likes, dislikes, even educational level will determine the approach and tone of the ad. Where it will be placed and that medium's style and approach must also be assessed. Royal Caribbean, which offers luxury cruises, targets its advertising to different age groups. Scenes of activity appeal to younger vacationers, whereas serenity and sunsets attract older voyagers. The simple language is also directed to audience appeal. All ads end with the Royal Caribbean logo and the slogan "Like No Vacation on Earth."

Let's consider a copywriter who is directed to write an advertisement slogan to sell a new compact disc recording by pop artist Barry White. Research shows that young black women, who are frequent buyers of CDs and music videos, like romantic music and prefer a select group of magazines and newspapers that cater to their interests. Ads would appear in *Essence, People,* and *Spin* magazines, as well as on the Black Entertainment Network, which shows African American music videos.

Advertising for the new Barry White CD must appeal to young romantics. To reach that specific group, the copywriter could describe White's voice in the words of *People* magazine: ". . . smooth as satin sheets and soothing as a hot-oil backrub." The art director would arrange for photography to illustrate the words. The final ad would combine both to create the sense of

White's smooth and soothing voice. Garnering the small "young romantic" audience could increase sales of White's new CD by 5 to 10 percent, which would mean millions of dollars for the company. Remember: fame is not the goal of advertising; *sale* of the product is.

Copywriters have great pressure to keep advertising lean, direct, and on target so that no advertising words and minutes are wasted on an unlikely customer. This pressure affects the advertising writer at every point. The ad message must be structured as carefully as the placement. If an ad is directed to a specific audience, it needs to appear in the correct medium and to convey concepts immediately that are meaningful to the target group.

Here is effective ad writing pitched to its specific audience:

"I never worried too much about nutrition.

"Then, my doctor told me I was HIV positive.

"Now, I do everything I can to maintain my energy, strength, and quality of life."

The advertisement pictures a handsome, athletic man. The product is Advera, a nutrition supplement. The three written lines from the ad demonstrate how specific today's advertisements can be. For the most part, ads today strive not for mass communication but for complete communication with a particular group. The copywriter and art director work as a team, combining language and graphics in a powerful way to produce effective advertisements.

Advertising Writing: The Process

In reaching their audiences, ad writers go through the same process that other writers use: information gathering, thinking, listing, drafting, rewriting, sharing, and polishing. Just as in other media writing, deadline pressure may allow less time for each stage. Following is an explanation of how each stage works in advertising.

Stage 1: Information Gathering

Ad writers write nothing until they have information. But, as noted earlier in the chapter, most of that data is provided by market researchers and outlined in the strategy. Say the product is TrimWalk, an in-home exerciser. The strategy is to appeal to men and women 55 years of age and older who want a high quality of life and are concerned about looking healthy and vigorous and controlling weight. The positioning of TrimWalk notes that there is strong competition by other fitness products. The writer who has been assigned to the account knows that any comparison requires thorough research so that claims will be accurate and authentic.

Although the writer has research data, he may want to see how TrimWalk works. He uses it and describes his feelings: rejuvenated, relaxed, pleasantly tired, easy to use. That personal experience forms part of his information gathering.

Stage 2: Thinking

The thinking stage requires the writer to think about the purpose of the ad. He must examine who is in the audience. What qualities of the product, in this case TrimWalk, will appeal to older adults? The writer must ponder all the information in the advertising strategy and his own perceptions. He decides that the ad could emphasize health, vigor, and youthfulness. Once the thinking decision is made, he knows the purpose and can begin to make lists.

Stage 3: Listing

In this stage, the copywriter makes a simple list of the important selling points—that is, facts that will entice the audience of older adults to consider TrimWalk. The list of selling points might look like this:

1. TrimWalk is in your home, convenient for workouts at any time or in any weather.
2. TrimWalk is private; no one watches you exercise.
3. TrimWalk can be positioned so that you can watch television or listen to music while working out.
4. TrimWalk is safety inspected to guard against injury.
5. Regular use of TrimWalk leads to weight loss.
6. Regular use of TrimWalk leads to improved circulation.
7. Regular use of TrimWalk leads to improved skin and muscle tone.
8. Regular use of TrimWalk can possibly lead to better health and, in turn, a longer life.

Once the list is complete, the writer must look at which selling points are the most compelling for the audience. He cannot include all of them. So, although the copywriter knows his goal is to sell an exercise machine, he choses the appeal of better health and longer life. It will also satisfy points 5, 6, and 7 about specific health improvements.

Other lists prepare the copywriter for the task of writing: statistics on sales and satisfaction among older adults who use exercise equipment, most popular activities for older adults, income levels of older adults, demographics of designated media's audiences. Such lists help match the selling points with the audience. Although many facts surround any product, good ads will focus on only a few. With information, lists, and goals defined, the copywriter is ready to draft an ad.

Stage 4: Drafting the Ad

It is important to recall that this stage is called drafting rather than writing. Drafting is the stage of writing in which thoughts on a subject are recorded. Remember the ad elements listed earlier in the chapter: headline, graphic, ad copy, logo, slogan. The headline grabs the consumers' attention. Traditionally ad headlines served to name the targeted audience or the product. But writers have been become more sophisticated, using double meanings ("Love a fair"), addressing specific consumers directly ("Mothers need time out"), or telling how or why consumers will benefit from the ad's information ("How to reduce life's stresses in 20 minutes a day"). The headline might be dictated by a photograph or graphic element.

Good headlines grab attention while at the same time communicating some important information. Headlines jump-start the ad and lead the consumer into the body copy. They are not a summary of the ad, but like a lead, the opening salvo in an ad sets the tone and establishes the format for the rest of the message. Headlines are not limited in length. Long headlines are okay. Writers just need to ensure that such headlines are not confusing; copywriters do not want readers to stop and say "huh?"

Some guidelines for writing successful ad headlines are as follows:

- Address the public directly and personally, as if in conversation.
- Refer to a specific problem or goal. The examples just given deal with the problems of health and appearance.
- Offer a benefit. Notable benefits such as weight loss and improved circulation would be lost later in the copy, so they are communicated in the headline.

- Offer something new.
- Feature believable information. Rash claims will be ignored.
- Finally, good headlines are simple, simple, simple.

In the TrimWalk ad, the copywriter might use a question headline, which can make consumers pay attention and become involved. "Want to look and feel fit? Try taking a walk—in your living room." The writer would then move into body copy that describes how TrimWalk enhances skin and muscle tone, how it helps even the most fit seniors feel even better, and how convenient and even safe it is to exercise regularly at home. The closing paragraph would summarize that research shows that active people are healthier and tend to live longer.

Once the body copy is done, the writer usually wraps up with the product or service slogan and logos. The slogan may be written, or the copywriter may have to create one. Slogans can be attention-getting, product-enhancing, problem-solving, enduring. Truly clever or catchy slogans become markers for consumers: When they hear the phrases, they immediately think of the product—even if the product is not named. Most people can finish the slogan, "You deserve a break today," with the word "McDonalds," or associate "Be all that you can be" with the U.S. Army. "Eat mor' chicken" coupled with billboard-painting cows became a popular slogan for Chick Fil A. Logos also have recognition: the rainbow of NBC; the golden arches of McDonalds; the swoosh of Nike; or the lined globe of AT&T.

A draft of an ad is written quickly and reflects key points in the lists made in Stage 3. Never write a draft as if it were final. The loose words and organization of the draft will be fine-tuned—and perhaps entirely rewritten—several times before the final copy is produced. It helps to remember that what you draft is a work in progress; when you and the people you work with realize that drafts are raw rather than finished products, the words will flow more easily.

Stage 5: Rewriting

Even the cleverest ad writers must edit their own work before they pass it on. As we noted in Chapter 6, the first step in rewriting is to let the draft copy of the ad rest. It may rest on a desk or in a drawer; what's important is that the writer parts from it for at least ten or fifteen minutes. Ideally, a draft is put away overnight or for several hours. But when time is limited, leave the copy in a safe place and take a walk. Try to clear your head; perhaps you can get a snack or chat with a friend. Then return to the copy and check it over, answering the following checklist of questions:

- Does the ad, from the opening sentence, work to achieve its goal?
- Does the ad appeal to its intended audience? Will audience members see the benefits of your product after reading only the first few words of the ad?
- Is the language simple, varied, and conversational?
- Is the grammar correct? Are spellings standard?
- Are sentences and paragraphs short so that readers will have easy access to information?
- Have you stayed within space limitations?

Once you have edited your original work, eliminating any problems you detect, you have a revised draft and are ready for the next stage of writing.

Stage 6: Sharing

In an agency, copywriters share their work with the art director, creative director, account executive, and client. All will make comments and suggest changes. A freelancer who is a copywriter may also be the account executive, designer, and media buyer. In that case, he or she may want to share the ad copy with an outside reader, perhaps a member of the intended audience. The reader would tell the writer if the ad is appealing and if it would be noticed and read, and why or why not; make suggestions to improve the ad; and report any inaccuracies or errors. Whether a copywriter has the benefit of in-house people or an outside reviewer, sharing can provide helpful information to polish the advertising piece.

Stage 7: Polishing

If sharing resulted in a major rewrite of the ad, a copywriter may need to repeat stages 5 and 6, rewriting and sharing. But if only minor revisions are needed, the writer can present a final draft to the account executive or the client.

Polishing is a fine-tuning process, in which extra words are eliminated and white space is added by keeping words, sentences, and paragraphs as short as possible. All spellings, especially proper names, and all facts, especially statistics, are checked and rechecked. A computerized spell-check process is applied, and after one last read-through, the final draft is printed. This draft is usually typed and double-spaced and incorporated into the design.

In some settings, the copywriter also is responsible for desktop publishing and producing a finished advertisement, camera-ready for printing. Writers who face these responsibilities may want to take a course in graphic design or desktop publishing. Writers charged with complete ad design must also remember that writing is the first and most important step in producing ads that reach audiences.

Tips for Ad Copy That Sells

Advertising Professor Jim Plumb, who has thirty years of experience in all aspects of advertising, gives the following broad tips to copywriters:

1. *Touch on selling points.* Focus on concrete reasons for purchase. An abstract reason to buy a Subaru wagon is safety, but a concrete selling point is that buying a Subaru keeps the driver from shoveling snow or paying a tow truck.

2. *Sell the benefits.* Find and list the benefits of your product that are important to your audience. Build your ad writing around these benefits. List them in the ad if you can, but be sure to mention them in some way. Don't forget to look for intangible benefits. Sometimes the most powerful benefits are intangibles, such as the mood that a perfume creates or a feeling of belonging that comes from a health club. Again, the viewer or reader should experience the product.

3. *Identify the single greatest benefit of your product and feature it in the headline.* Research should identify the quality of your product that is most meaningful to your intended audience. Then create a headline or slogan that will convey this benefit to your audience. With "Mmmmm, good!" Campbell's is selling the benefit of good taste. With "Just Do It," Nike sells discipline, an intangible benefit, as its star quality. A slogan in ads for *The Washington Post* reads, "If you don't get it, you don't get it." That is, if you don't take the *Post* regularly, you'll be left out socially. By communicating benefits in a few words, ad writing has the power to modify attitudes and behaviors. The same technique, among others used by copywriters, can work in all forms of writing.

Other experts in the field remind copywriters of more specifics. In their book, *The New How to Advertise,* advertising executives Kenneth Roman and Jane Maas list elements of good advertising strategy. They note that a good ad will show solutions to a problem; effective ads will aim for target audiences; and every good ad projects the tone, manner, and personality of the product. Other experts also recommend that ad copy note details; use well-chosen language; have strong, clear words; have one unifying idea or theme; contain a beginning, a middle, and an end; and for the most part, use correct grammar.

But some contend if such rules are followed, the result will be well-produced but boring ads. Other techniques are needed for fun or zany, truly creative advertisements. George Felton in his book, *Advertising Concepts,* discusses reversal as an approach to writing ads. He notes

All great ads employ reversal: Something significant has been put in, left out, inverted, photographed oddly, colored wrong, talked about differently, or in some way had violence done to its ordinariness. Otherwise, if our preconceptions have been fulfilled instead of violated, we'll be looking at clichés.

He gives as an example the classic Volkswagen ad that took the maxim "Think big" and reversed it to "Think small." The print advertisement used exceptional white space and put a small Volkswagen near the upper lefthand corner. "The ad reversed our expectations twice: once as user of clichés and once as viewers of ads," Felton notes.

If copywriters want to use reversal, among the questions they should ask are: Who doesn't use the product? Where don't you find it? When isn't it used? What's an unusual use for it? When is the one time it won't come in handy? The answers would be clues to an ad. Reversal would also allow a copywriter to capitalize on negatives or liabilities. One arena to watch will be the positioning of ads in the United States for the 2000 Summer Olympics in Australia. The distance and cost to travel there will have to be overcome with other aspects of the games and the country.

All Writers Can Learn from Advertising

Many advertising students argue that there is no connection between news writing and advertising writing. Likewise, news writing students argue that their work has nothing to do with advertising technique. But Associate Professors Katherine McAdams and John Sweeney studied prize-winning ads and news stories and found that the two have much in common.

"Award-winning news competes for the reader's attention, as does ad copy; both kinds of writing require techniques that catch and reward readers with concise, informative, pleasurable reading," McAdams and Sweeney concluded. They list five factors that they found in both groups of award-winning writing:

1. *Audience.* Both news writing and ad writing aim messages at specific audiences and demonstrate a clear knowledge of audience interests and concerns.

2. *Distillation.* News articles and advertisements both must distill large amounts of information into very limited space, resulting in careful, early placement of key information.

3. *Freshness.* Excellent news writing is involving and rewarding for the reader. The same is true of advertising. The means to success in both fields lies in presenting information with interest and liveliness.

4. *Substance.* Both kinds of writing depend on substantive writing that presents facts. Information—especially new or surprising information—is top priority in both advertising and news.

5. *Easy access.* Unless facts are presented with the reader's ease in mind, the information may not be read. That's why both news writing and advertising writing emphasize short words, short paragraphs, and simple sentences. Both may have one-sentence paragraphs.

Advertising copy may have some quirky differences, however. Necessary transitions may require starting sentences with "because" or "which." Because rhythm is key, just as in newswriting, sentences will vary in length. Ad copy may contain more sentence fragments. A sentence in a news article might use semicolons between independent clauses when ad copy would use periods. Because of its persuasive nature, ad copy language can be bolder, more suggestive, even "cuter" than that found in a news article. And that aspect sells many students on striving to become copywriters—or to have some advertising job in the information age. In producing good writing for any medium, today's writers must be concerned with reaching audiences.

Because of competition among products and brands, ad writers were first to identify and target audiences. Today, as all media become conscious of competition, we can learn from their techniques how to satisfy the public hunger for new and relevant information.

EXERCISES

1. Imagine that you have been asked to create an ad that describes the benefits of dining in your campus cafeteria. The ad will appear in your campus newspaper. The audience is undergraduate students.

   a. Begin by doing product research: Visit the cafeteria for a meal, and take note of important information and impressions. List the facts and impressions you gathered in your research visit. Be prepared to discuss the items on your list.

   b. Supplement your product research with audience research. List at least five questions about cafeteria dining that you could use in brief interviews with students. Discuss your questions with your professor and classmates, then use your best questions in interviews with six or more students.

   c. Consider what you learned from your efforts in product and audience research. Divide a blank sheet of paper in half. On one side, list the major benefits that you could write about for your advertising copy. On the other side, list prominent characteristics of your audience. Turn the page over and write at least three possible headlines for your ad. Each headline should feature at least one cafeteria benefit and appeal to at least one audience characteristic.

2. Invite an advertising professional from your campus or community to visit your class. Ask this person to talk briefly about advertising in today's competitive media environment. You may also want to ask your speaker to look over any headlines or advertising copy the class has written and to select some examples of good writing.

3. Imagine that you have been asked to write a headline and three paragraphs of advertising copy about the car that you drive most often. Your audience is your fellow students; the ad will appear in a student publication. Begin by taking a research drive and listing the benefits of your automobile; then develop the copy.

4. Find a poorly written advertisement in a newspaper or magazine. Clip the ad, then get out a fresh piece of paper. Rewrite the ad, improving the writing and targeting. Do any research that is needed.

5. Find a copy of an advertisement that you think uses reversal to make its point. Explain how the ad deviates from what would be the expected presentation. Take a product you use regularly and come up with a creative approach that uses reversal.

6. Choose a company and visit its Web site. How much of the site is information and how much is advertising? Does the site allow browsers to order products? Compare the company's Web site with the site for a nonprofit organization such as Save the Children at www.savethe children.org.

REFERENCES

American Advertising Federation Web site, Available at: http://www.aaf.com

Philip Ward Burton, *Advertising Copywriting,* 6th ed. Lincolnwood, IL: NTC Business Books, 1990.

Federal Trade Commission Web site, Available at: http://www.ftc.gov.

George Felton, *Advertising Concepts and Copy.* Englewood Cliffs, NJ: Prentice Hall, 1994.

Katherine McAdams and John Sweeney, "Copy Writing and Newswriting Need Similar Skills." *Journalism Educator,* Winter 1987.

David Ogilvy, *Ogilvy on Advertising.* New York: Crown Publishers, 1983.

Carol Pardun and Larry Lamb, "The Presence of the Corporate Web Site in Traditional Print Advertising." Paper presented to the International, Interdisciplinary Research Conference of the Public Relations Society of America, Baltimore, MD, June 1998.

James Plumb, "Writing Advertising Copy." Lecture. College Park, MD, University of Maryland College of Journalism, 1990.

Kenneth Roman and Jane Maas, *The New How to Advertise.* New York: St. Martin's Press, 1992.

John Sweeney, "Principles of Advertising." Lecture series. Chapel Hill, NC, University of North Carolina at Chapel Hill, 1986.

John Sweeney, Personal interview. Chapel Hill, NC, University of North Carolina, 1995.

Michael J. Weiss, *The Clustering of America.* New York: Harper & Row, 1988.

APPENDIX A

Libel and Privacy

Writers can unknowingly or carelessly damage an individual's reputation. Even if a slip is unintentional, if the libel is in print or is aired, the writer can be sued successfully. So can the newspaper, the television station, the church administration, or the nonprofit group.

Libel can occur in any writing: a news article, a news release, a public service announcement, annual reports, corporate financial statements, a television talk show, or a church bulletin. If a news release is mailed but not published, the writer could still be sued for libel because dissemination of the falsity occurred. While oral defamation is known as slander, a radio or television station that broadcasts slander or libelous statements can be sued under the state's libel laws.

Most libel results when people write about topics they do not really understand. Inexperienced reporters, student writers, and occasional writers are most at risk. Good data collection and good writing techniques can prevent many libel problems, however. Mass communication professors advise their students to be absolutely accurate and scrupulously fair in what they write.

The legal system will protect writers who do a good job of investigating and who use many sources. And the protection often will extend even if they write something that turns out to be false and defamatory.

A huge body of law exists on libel. Thousands of libel cases have been filed. Although most writers do not need to be lawyers, they do need to know the basics of libel law. A writer may be the only member of a nonprofit organization's communication staff; he or she needs to know what might cause trouble. Libel laws differ from state to state. For example, the statute of limitations, or time within which a person can file a libel suit, varies; it is usually from one to two years. Writers should be familiar with the libel laws in their states or in the states in which the material will be published.

358

Elements of Libel

In being aware of libel, writers do not have to be afraid to write negative information. If they know the essential elements of libel, they won't be chilled into self-censorship.

An individual—or the person written about—has to prove six essential elements to win a libel case:

- *Defamation.* The individual has to show that the information was defamatory or bad.
- *Identification.* The story clearly identified the individual by name, in a recognizable photo, or through specific description.
- *Publication.* The memo was circulated, the story printed, the news release received, the report aired, or the message was read by just one person other than the writer or person written about.
- *Falsity.* The information published was not true. Sometimes the burden of proof falls on the media, which attempt to prove the information was true.
- *Harm or injury.* The individual has to show harm to his or her reputation or emotional well-being. Proof of monetary loss can increase the amount of money the media have to pay if they lose.
- *Fault.* The individual has to prove that the newspaper, radio station, or other party was at fault in presenting the libel.

To win a case, most plaintiffs have to prove all six elements. On the sixth item, court decisions have set different criteria for private citizens and public figures.

In most cases ordinary folks have to prove a standard of fault called *negligence* to win a libel suit. They must show that the writer failed to follow professional standards or acted unreasonably in carrying out his or her research and in writing.

Celebrities or people in power or politics have to go further in establishing fault. They must prove that the writer knew that the information was false or showed reckless disregard as to whether the information was true or false. That is called *actual malice.* That element came about through the 1964 *New York Times* v. *Sullivan* case, in which the United States Supreme Court ruled that a public official cannot recover damages for a defamatory falsehood relating to his or her official conduct unless he or she proves that the statement was made with actual malice.

Let's say you are writing a story about your town's mayor. During interviews, an unreliable source tells you that the mayor leaves town twice a year to meet his childhood sweetheart—not his wife—at a mountain cabin. If you were to write that bit of information without further investigation, you would be setting yourself up for a libel suit. Your action would be reckless disregard for whether the information was true.

People are defamed, perhaps falsely, every day. Just think about the hundreds of police reports naming people who have been arrested. They can prove many of the elements above, such as publication, identification, and defamation. But would they win a libel suit? Rarely.

A Writer's Defenses in a Libel Suit

Within the legal system are defenses writers can use to protect themselves against a libel suit even if the person they wrote about can prove the elements listed earlier. The major defenses are these:

• *Truth.* The writer can prove the information was true through reliable witnesses and documentary evidence.

• *Fair reporting or reporter's privilege.* Writers are protected when they report fairly and accurately material from official government proceedings or documents. That is one reason that news media rely so heavily on government meetings and sessions. A witness can falsely accuse someone in court of committing murder, and you as a reporter can print the accusation. You are protected if the charges were made during a court session. Your reporting must be accurate, fair and balanced, attributed to the government meeting or record, and not motivated by malice.

• *Wire service defense.* Some states have adopted what is known as the wire service defense. Newspapers and other media organizations are protected if they get a story from the wire services, such as the Associated Press, and reprint it. It would be impossible for writers to verify every fact that appeared in a wire service story. Wire service clients have to trust that the information sent to them is true.

• *Opinion defense.* The opinion defense protects two kinds of statements. Writers are protected if they are critiquing a performance or service as long as they give a general assessment that is incapable of being proved true or false.

For example, a restaurant critic could write that the restaurant food is not good. He could not say that the chef stole the high-quality meats for his family, leaving lesser meats for the restaurant dishes—unless that were true, of course.

The opinion defense also protects what is known as hyperbole: wild exaggeration that no one would believe to be true. For example, in the 1980s, the federal courts said *Hustler* magazine had a First Amendment right to publish an outrageous insult directed at television evangelist Jerry Falwell. Falwell had sued the magazine after it published a cartoon parody of Campari liqueur's "first time" advertising campaign. The cartoon depicted the Rev. Falwell as having his "first time"—his first sexual encounter—while drunk with his mother in an outhouse. The courts said no one would believe such an outrageous allegation, so the evangelist's reputation had not been damaged. A reporter may state that the university's chancellor was dressed in 1960s-style clothes and got up on stage to dance at a Dead Heads concert. If the story were printed, reasonable people would not believe it was true. If the chancellor sued, the courts would likely rule that no one would believe such an outrageous story, so the chancellor's reputation had not been damaged.

As a footnote, writers should know that they cannot libel the government—state, local, or federal. Writers can say that the federal government or some part of it is an overgrown, bumbling bureaucratic mess without fear of being sued. But they cannot use the same words to describe the head of a particular agency without getting into trouble.

How to Avoid Libel Suits

Writers do not want to be sued for libel even if they win. Libel suits are costly, time-consuming, and emotionally draining. They can go on for years. People do win libel cases against media. For example, CapCities Communications lost a $11.5 million libel suit when one of its New York television stations incorrectly identified a restaurant owner as having ties with organized crime. In 1994, an attorney won a $24 million judgment against *The Philadelphia Inquirer,* which had reported he quashed a homicide investigation when he was an assistant district attorney because it involved the son of a police officer.

Ninety percent of libel cases filed never make it to court. Some are dropped, and some end up in out-of-court settlements, which cost media actual payouts and attorneys' fees. Libel suits are to be avoided.

Some recommendations:

- Don't write lies and publish them.
- Use credible, reliable, multiple sources.
- Recognize the importance of fairness.
- Be accurate.

Also, be polite if someone complains about inaccuracy. One study showed that most people who sued decided to do so after they were treated rudely when they pointed out the mistake.

Right of Privacy

Writers must also be careful not to violate individuals' right to privacy. The doctrine of the right to privacy has evolved to protect individuals and to give them the right to be let alone, particularly from unwarranted publicity. Decisions from lower courts up to the United States Supreme Court have involved individuals' right to privacy.

Privacy law varies considerably from state to state, and writers should know what constitutes invasion of privacy in their states or in the state where articles will be published or stories aired. Generally, however, there are three ways writers sometimes invade individuals' privacy while gathering and writing information.

First, a journalist might go on private property without permission to get a story. He then could be sued for intruding on the property owner's privacy. In such cases, he is sued for his means of gathering information, not for the content of what he wrote. The writer could be sued successfully even if no story resulted.

Second, a writer might disclose private and embarrassing but true facts about an individual, who could claim the facts should not have been published. But winning that suit could be difficult for the person who sues, because courts are hesitant to punish the news media for publishing the truth. Also, if individuals become part of a newsworthy event, they forfeit their right to privacy. The courts have upheld the forfeiture even if the individual became part of the news event involuntarily. For example, a private citizen may become a hostage in a bank robbery and therefore is part of the news event.

Third, *The Associated Press Stylebook and Libel Manual* notes that the news media "may be liable for invasion of privacy if the facts of a story are changed deliberately or recklessly, or 'fictionalized.'" These privacy cases closely resemble libel cases, and just as with libel considerations, writers must be careful to be accurate and thorough.

In some states privacy law is so protective of the media that privacy is more of an ethical problem than a legal one. In dealing with the ethics of privacy, many media outlets have categories of individuals and treat them differently. Politicians and public officials are held to a higher standard of behavior in what journalists will or will not pursue. A classic case was Democratic presidential candidate Gary Hart, who challenged the media to find out if he was committing adultery. Journalists pursued Hart, photographed and witnessed him in intimate situations with Donna Rice, a woman who was not his wife. Hart eventually resigned from the presidential race.

Media also hold to a high standard public figures who trade on their public image or who are briefly prominent in the news. Other people, the common folk if you will, garner more privacy from the media. Journalists rarely go through their garbage.

REFERENCES

Harold Nelson and Dwight L. Teeter Jr., *Law of Mass Communications: Freedom and Control of Print and Broadcast Media.* Westbury, NY: The Foundation Press, 1986.

Cathy Packer, Personal interview, School of Journalism and Mass Communication at the University of North Carolina at Chapel Hill, Chapel Hill, NC, December 1997.

Norm Goldstein (Ed.), *The Associated Press Stylebook and Libel Manual.* New York: The Associated Press, 1997.

APPENDIX B

The Abused Words List

Writers must pay attention to words that sound alike but are spelled differently and have different meanings. The words can be confusing and can be used incorrectly.

When writers fail to select the correct word, often readers know it, and the writers' credibility suffers. Writers also teach readers incorrect usage when their writing is not specific and accurate.

Many good writers have come up with lists that caution other writers about the tricky words. Becoming familiar with such a list is extremely important in the age of computers, which may overlook incorrect usage in spell-check programs.

Professor Thom Lieb of Towson State University has developed what he calls "the abused words list." Writers need to review the list periodically so that red flags of warning are raised when a word from the list is used. Writers can refer to the list to ensure they use words correctly. Here is Lieb's list, with a few additions from the authors:*

abdicate, abrogate: Abdicate means give up formally (an office, throne, authority) or to surrender or repudiate (a right, responsibility). Abrogate means cancel or repeal by authority, annul.

accept, except: Accept means receive. Except means exclude.

adapt, adopt: Adapt means make fit or suitable by changing or adjusting. Adopt means take up and use, vote to accept, select.

adopted, passed, enacted: Resolutions are adopted or approved; bills are passed. Laws are enacted when they go into effect.

adverse, averse: Adverse is poor or bad; averse is opposed to.

*Adapted from Thomas Lieb, *Editing for Clear Communication.* Copyright © 1996 Times Mirror Higher Education Group, Inc., Dubuque, IA. All Rights Reserved. Reprinted by permission.

advice, advise: Advice is an opinion given. Advise means to give advice.

affect, effect: To affect is to have an effect on; effect is the noun. But effect as a verb means "bring about."

after, following: After means next in time; following means next in order.

aggravate, irritate: Aggravate means make worse; irritate means to incite or provoke.

agnostic, atheist: An agnostic believes it is impossible to know whether there is a God. Atheists believe there is no God.

aid, aide: Aides (assistants) give aid (help) to their bosses. Aid can also be a verb, but aide can only be a noun.

alleged, intended: Alleged means so declared before proof; intended means meant, planned, or proposed.

all ready, already: All ready means prepared: The team was all ready for the game. Already means beforehand: The opponents were already there.

allusion, delusion, illusion: Allusion is a hint, indirect reference: He made an allusion to her vanity. Note that to allude to something is not to name the thing specifically. Delusion is a false belief, especially a psychotic one. Illusion is unreal perception, misconception, unreal image perception: He had an illusion he could fly across the sea. And there is also, of course, elude, meaning avoid.

alot: It's a lot, and it's best saved for real estate stories.

alright: It's not; it's all right.

altar, alter: Altar is a table-like platform used in a church service; alter, a verb meaning change.

alternative, alternate: Alternative involves a choice; alternate, a verb or adjective that means in turns.

alumna, alumni, alumnus: An alumnus can be of either sex, but is typically male. An alumna is female; plural is alumnae pronounced with a long e sound. Plural of both sexes or males is alumni.

amateur, novice: Amateur is a nonprofessional; novice is a beginner.

among, between: Among refers to more than two things. Between refers to two.

amount, number: Amount is the quantity of things: The amount of testimony was small. Number refers to individual or separate units in a group: The number of times she testified was too small to make a difference.

anxious, eager: You can only be anxious about something; you cannot be anxious to do that thing. Anxious implies fear and anxiety. If you are stimulated and excited at the prospect of doing something, then you are *eager* to do it.

avenge, revenge: Avenge for another, revenge for self.

assume, presume: Assume means take to be fact without a basis for belief; to presume is to regard as true because there is reason to do so and no contrary evidence. Presume also means take upon oneself without permission or authority.

bad, badly: Bad is an adjective, used when you want to describe the subject: He felt bad about the report of campaign irregularities. Badly describes some quality of the verb rather than the subject. She took her defeat badly.

bale, bail: A farmer's hay is baled; water is bailed out of a boat; a prisoner is released on bail. (Bond is cash or property given as a security for an appearance or performance.)

basis: Unnecessary in "weekly basis," "timely basis," and so forth.

bi-, semi-: Bi means two; semi means half. Bimonthly—every two months. Semimonthly—twice a month. However: Biannual means the same as semiannual—twice a year. Biennial means every two years.

bills, legislation: Legislation is laws enacted by legislative body. A president can send proposed legislation or bills.

bloc, block: Bloc is a group or coalition; block has many meanings, but none is the same as bloc.

blond, blonde: The first is an adjective for all sexes and a noun for male; the second is a noun for females.

breach, breech: The first is a failure to observe terms (e.g., of a contract). Breech is the rump, the lower or back part of a thing (breech birth) or part of a gun.

burglary, robbery, theft: Burglary involves breaking into a building to commit theft or another felony. Robbery is taking something from another person through the use of violence or intimidation. Theft is the general term for taking another's property without consent. Larceny is the legal term.

canvas, canvass: First is a cloth; second means to solicit.

capital, capitol: Capital: City that is official seat of government; wealth. Capitol: Capital "C," the building in which Congress meets in Washington, D.C. Lowercase "c," the building in which a state legislature meets.

carat, caret, karat: Carat expresses the weight of precious stones. Caret is a proofreader's mark. Karat is the proportion of pure gold used in an alloy.

careen: Leaning sideways or tossing about like a boat under sail—*not* skidding or veering. For that, try CAREER.

censor, censure: A censor is a person who can censor a publication, cutting out anything offensive, obscene, etc. To censure is to condemn as wrong or to strongly disapprove.

center around: Something can be centered at, centered in, or centered on, but not around.

chafe, chaff: Chafe means to irritate. Chaff means to ridicule good-naturedly; it also means husks or rubbish.

cite, site, sight: Cite means refer or quote. Site is a location. Sight is a view.

collision: Violent contact between moving bodies. A car cannot collide with a telephone pole or other unmoving object.

combine: Must involve putting together at least two things: "Maid o' Silk" combined the spirit of old America in modern dress.

compared to, compared with: When you put one thing in the same class or category without examining it closely, use compared to: The inflation rate can be compared to a hot-air balloon with an endless supply of fuel. When you put things side by side to examine similarities and differences, use compared with: The inflation rate is 8 percent, compared with last year's figure of 10 percent.

compliment, complement: They can be noun or verb. Compliment is praise; complement adds to something to make it complete.

compose, comprise: To compose is to make up; to comprise is to include. Fifty states compose the United States. The United States comprises fifty states.

conclude: Arguments conclude. Speeches close or end.

confidant, confident: Confidant is a close, trusted friend in whom one can confide. Confident is sure of oneself.

connote, denote: Connote means suggest or imply something beyond explicit meaning. Denote means be explicit about the meaning.

conscious, aware: We are conscious of what we feel and aware of what we know.

contact: As a verb, it means the physical touching of things: His toe contacted the football.

continual, continuous: Continual means repeated or intermittent; continuous means unbroken.

cord, chord: Cord is a string or small rope, or anatomical structure such as spinal or vocal cord. Or it may be a ribbed fabric or a unit of wood. Chord is a string of a musical instrument or a combination of tones.

council, counsel, consul: Council is an assembly, usually a legislative body. Counsel is advice, a lawyer. Consul is a person appointed by his government to serve his country's interests abroad.

couple of: Like "a pair," needs the "of." Never "a couple tomatoes."

damage, damages: First means loss or harm. Second is only a legal term meaning money paid or ordered to be paid as compensation for loss or injury.

data: Is plural, as are media, strata, phenomena, criteria, and alumni. When the group or quantity is regarded as a unit, it takes a singular verb: The data is invalid. If the word refers to individual items, use plural verb: The data were collected by a team of twenty.

deign: Means to condescend, not to dare or care.

dilemma: An argument necessitating a choice between two equally unfavorable or disagreeable alternatives.

discreet, discrete: First means prudent, circumspect; second is detached or separate.

disinterested, uninterested: Disinterested is impartial; uninterested means lack interest.

disorganize, unorganized: The first is a verb, meaning disrupt the organization of. The second is an adjective, meaning lacking order, system, or unity.

due to: Not a synonym for "because of." It should modify a noun: It was an omission due to oversight. BUT: The name was omitted because of oversight.

egregious: (pronounced i gre jes): Outstanding for undesirable qualities; remarkably bad.

either: Not synonymous with both. Incorrect: The teams lined up at either end of the field. Correct: The teams lined up at both ends.

enrage, outrage: Enrage is a verb meaning put in a rage. Outrage is a noun, meaning an act of extreme violence or viciousness.

emigrate, immigrate: The first means leave a country; the second, enter.

enormity: Applies preferably to abnormal wickedness, but it is often misused to mean enormous.

ensure, insure: First is guarantee: A good writer takes every possible measure to ensure accuracy. Insure is used in references to insurance. And let us not forget assure: make a person sure of something, or convince.

envelop, envelope: To envelop is to wrap up, obscure, hide. An envelope is the paper product that envelops your letters and bills.

epitaph, epithet: The first is an inscription on a tombstone. The second is a descriptive adjective applied to someone.

farther, further: Farther refers to physical distance, further to degree, time, or quantity.

faze, phase: Faze is embarrass or disturb; phase is an aspect or stage.

feel: Generally, best saved for touching and feeling things. Don't use as a synonym for thinking or believing. It is acceptable when you mean to be convinced emotionally rather than intellectually: "The parents of the kidnapped girl feel certain she is safe."

fewer, less: The general rule is that if you can't count it, use less: fewer students, but less interest.

fiance, fiancee: The man has one "e," the woman, two.

flair, flare: Flair is a conspicuous talent; flare means blaze with sudden, bright light or to burst out in anger. Also a noun meaning flame.

flaunt, flout: To flaunt is to show off; to flout is to mock, scoff, or show disdain for.

flounder, founder: Horses flounder—struggle or thrash about—in the mud. Ships founder or sink.

fortunate, fortuitous: The first means coming by good luck, the second means happening by chance.

fulsome: Fulsome praise is insincere, not copious. It means offensively excessive.

gantlet, gauntlet: A gantlet is a section of railroad tracks over a narrow passage where two lines of track overlap (two lines using only three rails). A gauntlet is a former military punishment in which an offender had to run between two rows of men with clubs. It is also a long glove.

get: Often used instead of a more precise verb. Get around—evade. Get behind—endorse. AND get does not substitute for become: I become cold rather than get cold.

gibe, jibe: The first is to jeer, taunt, or flout. The second is to shift sails, alter a course, or be in harmony.

gorilla, guerrilla: The first is an ape, the second a soldier or raider.

grant, subsidy: A grant is money given to public companies; subsidy is help to a private enterprise.

hanged, hung: Hang, hung, hung refers to objects; hanged refers to people.

hike: What a Boy Scout takes. Not synonymous for increase.

historic, historical: Historic means famous in history. Historical pertains to history, such as historical sites and historical novels.

holdup, holed up: A man with a gun can commit a holdup by forcibly stopping another person and robbing him or her. If the gunman hides out at the place of the holdup, he is holed up.

hopefully: Full of hope. "The hungry child sat hopefully on the steps of the candy shop."

impact: Means a collision or a violent striking together. Does not mean influence or effect: When the car hit the guardrail, the impact caused the front end to jackknife.

impassable, impassible: The first means that a passage is impossible. The second describes lack of sensitivity to pain or suffering.

imply, infer: The speaker implies; the listener infers.

in, into (also: on, onto): If you're in the lake and feel like jumping, you jump in the lake. If you're in a boat on the lake and you feel like jumping overboard, you jump into the lake.

ironically: The contrary of what is expressed, for example, calling a stupid plan clever. Irony is a form of sarcasm.

last, latest, past: Last few days, in the past, his latest book.

launch: Send into space, not begin, as in "New Sewer System Launched."

liable: Not a good substitute for likely, unless the event designated is injurious or undesirable. It is likely to be sunny and clear; it is liable to rain.

lie, lay: To lie is to recline; to lay, to place. Confusion results mainly from past and past perfect tenses: lie, lay, lay (or lain); lay, laid, laid.

like, as: Like joins nouns and pronouns: "He blocks like a pro." Use as with verbs: "Winston tastes good as a cigarette should."

likewise: Avoid using as a transition. WRONG: He went home. Likewise, his sister went. CORRECT: He went home. So did his sister.

loath, loathe: The first means unwilling; the second means hate.

mad: Means insane, not angry.

majority, plurality: First is more than half of an amount. Second is more than the next highest number.

masterly, masterful: The first means skillful; the second means domineering.

mean, median, average, mode: Mean and average are generally interchangeable: the sum of the units divided by the number of units. Median is the number in the middle (such as the middle score or income); half lie above, half below. Mode is the most commonly occurring number.

meanwhile: Should be used only when a close relationship exists in subject matter and intervening time is actually meant.

measles: A child has measles, not the measles; same too with mumps. Treat both as singular.

meld: A card game term, it does not mean blend or combine.

meticulous: Being overcareful, finical, or fussy about trivial details.

moral, morale: Moral refers to ethics; morale to mood or spirits. The moral life is the good life. His morale was lifted by the phone call.

nauseated, nauseous: If you are nauseated, you feel or become sick. Something nauseous is sickening or disgusting.

negotiate: You negotiate a loan or treaty; you climb a hill.

noisy, noisome: Noisy is making or accompanied by noise. Noisome is injurious to health, noxious, harmful, or foul smelling.

off of: Off suffices: Get off my back.

only: Almost invariably misplaced, altering the meaning of the sentence. Try it in front of each word in this sentence to see how it alters meaning: I hit him in the eye yesterday.

oral, verbal: The use of the mouth is essential to oral communications; verbal means simply "using words."

ordinance, ordnance: An ordinance is a direction or command of an authoritative nature. Ordnance is a cannon or artillery.

pedal, peddle: The first is what you do on a bike or what you put your feet on. The second means sell.

penultimate: The next to the last. The penultimate month of the year is November. The antepenultimate month is October.

percentage, percentage point: They are not the same. When unemployment falls from 10 percent to 8 percent, it is a drop of 2 percentage points—but 20 percent!

persuade, convince: Persuade means induce someone to believe or do something, plead with, or urge. Convince means bring someone to belief or conviction beyond doubt, satisfy by proof. Grace has tried to persuade her to change her story. Finally, she was convinced that Grace was right.

podium, lectern: First is a footstool or platform; second is what speakers thump.

pointed out: You can point out only what is a fact. Make sure you are accepting a statement as a fact if you have someone "pointing it out."

populous, populated, populace: First means crowded or thickly populated; populated means inhabited; populace means common people of a community.

pore, pour: Pore, as a verb, means read or study carefully. Pour is what you do with a liquid.

portentous: Ominous, portending evil.

precipitate, precipitous: Precipitate means cause to happen before anticipated. Precipitous is steep like a precipice.

presently: Means soon, not now. Not synonymous with currently.

pretense, pretext: Pretense is a false show, a more overt act used to conceal personal feelings: "Her compliments were all pretense." Pretext is something put forward to conceal a truth: "They said he was dismissed for tardiness, but that was just a pretext for incompetence."

principal, principle: The first is the head of a school; also means "main." The second is a rule, truth, etc.

prior to, in advance of: Use "before" instead.

prison, jail: Prison is a maximum-security facility for persons convicted of felonies. Jail is a facility normally used to confine persons awaiting trial or sentencing on misdemeanors or felonies, persons serving sentences for misdemeanors, and persons confined for civil matters, such as failure to pay alimony.

prophecy, prophesy: Prophecy is a noun, meaning a forecast. Prophesy is a verb, meaning foretell, predict, forecast.

prone: If a man is lying prone on the beach, no one can step on his stomach. Prone means lying face down. Supine means lying face up.

prostate, prostrate: Prostate is of or relating to the male body. Prostrate is lying with the face downward in a show of great humility or abject submission.

quell, quench: Uprisings, disorders, riots, and the like are quelled. A fire is quenched.

quintessential: Quintessence is the pure, concentrated essence of anything.

rack, wrack: To rack is to trouble, torment or afflict, or to oppress by unfair demands. Also, you rack your brains, and something exasperating is nerve-racking. Wrack is properly used as a noun meaning ruin or destruction.

raise, rear, raze: Raise animals, rear children. To raze is to destroy.

ravage, ravish: To ravage is to destroy or ruin: The tornadoes ravaged the town. To ravish is to fill with joy, carry away forcibly, or rape: The army ravished the Trojan women.

record: You do not set a new record or an all-time record; neither is it a record first. It is simply a record.

refute: Means disprove—almost always implies editorial. Generally, rebut or dispute is better.

regime, regimen, regiment: A regime is a political ruling system. A regimen is a system of diet, etc., for improving health. A regiment is a military unit consisting of two or more battalions.

reign, rein: Reign is royal power, authority, or rule. Rein is a strap of leather used to control a horse.

reluctant, reticent: First is unwilling to act; the second is to speak.

role, roll: Role is a part assumed by an actor or a function assumed by someone. Roll is a noun and verb meaning more than a dozen different things—but not what role does.

sensual, sensuous: Sensual refers to the gratification of the grosser bodily senses of appetite (sex, food); sensuous suggests a strong appeal of that which is pleasing to the senses. A sensuous person is susceptible to the pleasures of sensation. She was given to sensual excesses. The music playing was sensuous.

set, sit: To set is to place: Set the book here. Sit is what you do when you take a seat.

sewage, sewerage: Sewage is human waste, sometimes called sanitary waste. Sewerage is the system to carry away sewage.

since, because: Since is best used when it denotes a period of time, either continuous or broken. Because gives a reason or cause.

suit, suite: You can have a suit of clothes, cards, or a lawsuit. There are suites of music, rooms, and furniture.

tall, high: A building, tree, or man is tall; a plane, bird, or cloud is high.

temperature, weather: The temperature can move higher or lower, but only the weather can become warmer or cooler.

than, then: Than is a conjunction of comparison. Then is an adverb denoting time.

that, which: That restricts or defines; which is nonrestrictive, adding extra but not necessarily essential information.

their, there, they're: Their is the possessive form of the pronoun "they." There is an adverb denoting place or, when used to begin a sentence, it is called an expletive or a false subject: There are only 20 shopping days left until Christmas. They're is the contraction of they and are.

til, till: Use until.

troop, troupe: The first is a group of persons or animals. The second is an ensemble of actors, dancers, singers, etc.

try and: The correct usage is "try to."

via: By way of, not by means of: via I-79, not via bus.

wasted words: These words add nothing: kind of, little, pretty, rather, really, some, sort of. The most wasted: VERY.

would, could, should: Saying a child COULD remain in an institution until age 18 is different from saying he WOULD remain there—or SHOULD. Be careful with these.

APPENDIX C

Spelling in the Computer Age

Writers, BEWARE: Spelling skills are essential in the computer age. This warning sounds exaggerated when computers can check spellings of hundreds of words in minutes. But take heed. The following paragraph passed a spell-check program in less than one second without a hitch:

```
They're know miss steaks in this newsletter cause we used
special soft wear witch checks yore spelling. It is mower
or lass a weigh to verify. How ever it can knot correct
arrows in punctuation ore usage, an it will not fined words
witch are miss used butt spelled rite. Four example, a
paragraph could have mini flaws but wood bee past by the
spell checker. And it wont catch the sentence fragment
witch you. Their fore, the massage is that proofreading is
know eliminated but is berry much reek wired.
```

Although the example is exaggerated, it serves to remind that a spell-checker only "checks." It looks to see that all typed words correspond exactly to real words listed in the computer's dictionary. Here's how it works: Spell-checkers look at each word, then check to see whether they have a match in the dictionaries stored in computer memory. A spell-checker highlights only the words that have no match in the computer's dictionary, stopping the checking process at those words so that they may be manually checked by the writer or editor.

What Spell-Checkers Will (and Won't) Do

Memory-based checking systems are a great invention, virtually eliminating senseless typographical errors such as "scuh" and "typograpical," as well as common spelling problems such as seperate for separate and mispell for misspell. Unfortunately, however, it is not a perfect invention.

Here's the problem: If the computer merely finds a word in its dictionary, it "checks" that word, assuring the writer that the spelling is correct. Say, for example, the computer encounters this sentence: "Robin was going too the fare." The sentence checks. The words "too" and "fare" exist in the dictionary, so they pass muster. And if Robin happens to be spelled correctly "Robyn," that error will go unchecked because "robin" would be found in the computer's dictionary and sail through. Or perhaps the typo is an actual word, such as count instead of court. The error would slip by as correct, and the writer would have created an immediate audience-stopper and confusion.

Remember that a spell-checker indicates only the words that have no match. So spell-checkers aid writers in only some spelling instances, not all of them. Some of the most challenging spelling tasks, which are listed in the following section, still are the writer's responsibility.

A Do-It-Yourself List

By now it should be clear that spell-checkers will not do everything. The writer has the hands-on, do-it-yourself responsibility of checking the following problems that spell-checkers do not correct.

HOMONYMS. Writers must distinguish among homonyms or words that sound alike but have different meanings and are spelled differently. Any writer's credibility would drop if his readers saw these sentences:

> *Mrs. Margolis consulted two professional piers before suspending the student.*
> Readers will see Mrs. Margolis conferring in a lakeside setting.
> *Barnes said he didn't want to altar his plans.*
> Will Barnes offer his plan during religious services?
> *All navel movements will be approved by the commanding officer.*
> Whose belly buttons?
> *Investigators found millions of land mines sewn into the earth.*
> Did someone use a needle and thread?

Such homonyms as pier and peer, alter and altar, and sewn and sown escape highlighting by the spell-checker, which recognizes each as dictionary words. Writers may leave simple errors in their writing because of overconfidence in the ability of spell-checkers. Some words writers should watch include the following:

To, two, too	Aid, aide
Their, they're, there	It's, its
No, know	Whose, who's
Not, knot	

More subtle—but no less damaging—are the errors made when writers confuse other commonly occurring homonyms, such as those listed here. Good writers distinguish between or among homonyms.

affect (verb)
effect (noun, meaning result, verb meaning bring about)

a lot (colloquial expression substituted for "many" or "much")
allot (to distribute)

allude (refer to)
elude (escape)

altar (in a church)
alter (change)

altogether (adverb meaning entirely)
all together (adjective meaning in a group)

canvas (cloth)
canvass (poll)

capitol (building)
capital (city)

compliment (flattering statement)
complement (fills up or completes)

counsel (advise, legal adviser)
council (assembly)
consul (diplomatic officer)

dual (two)
duel (combat between two people)

flair (style; panache)
flare (torch)

guerrilla (person who engages in warfare)
gorilla (ape)

immigrate (come to a new country)
emigrate (leave one's country)

legislature (body)
legislator (individual officials)

miner (in a mine)
minor (under age)

naval (of the navy)
navel (belly button)

pore (small opening; to examine closely)
pour (to cause to flow)

pier (water walkway)
peer (social equal)

principal (head, first)
principle (lesson, belief)

role (in a play)
roll (list)

stationery (paper)
stationary (permanent)

vein (blood vessel)
vain (conceited)
vane (wind detector)

Note: There is no such word as "alot." A lot is two distinct words.

SIMILAR WORDS WITH DIFFERENT USES. No spell-checker knows the difference between conscience and conscious, affect and effect, flout and flaunt, loose and lose, lead and led, read and red, or border or boarder, populace and populous. Some grammar-check programs will highlight such problematic words, but these programs require the writer to make the correct choice. Keeping a good stylebook or grammar guide on your desk is the best way to make distinctions among similar words. Again, the writer or editor must catch the error, even though a spell-checker lives within the computer.

IRREGULAR VERBS. Computer programs leave verb choice to the writer, so irregular verbs, used incorrectly, may appear to be spelling errors. The sentence "We sat the boat in the water" should be "We set the boat in the water," but it would most certainly pass spell-checking. Frequently confused pairs of irregular verbs include the following:

lie (recline)
lay (place)

rise (elevate)
raise (nurture, as crops or plants)
rear (nurture throughout childhood; applies to humans only)

sit (be seated)
set (put or place)

COMPOUND WORDS. Some compound words, such as speedboat and bookkeeper, will pass spell-checkers as two words, even though they are correctly spelled as single words. The reason? The spell-checker recognizes the separate words—speed, boat, book, and keeper—as valid entries, leaving the writer appearing not to know the correct spelling.

PROPER NAMES. As we noted earlier, proper names—unlike most units of language—may be spelled any way an individual desires. The infinite variety of name spellings makes it standard for all names to be checked and double-checked, regardless of what spell-checking approves. Many names, such as Robin and Lily, are also common nouns listed in computer dictionaries. Often the correct spelling for the proper name is different from that offered by a spell-checker. For example, Robin may be "Robyn," and Lily may spell her name "Lillie." Double-check names in any document.

New-Age Spelling Problems

Overall, spell-checking systems help. They solve problems with words that contain "ie" and with words that have idiosyncratic endings, such as -ence, -ance, -ere, -are, -tion, -sion, and so on. But new technologies still leave writers struggling to select from possible spellings and check words not found in the computer dictionary.

Writers should always edit before and after spell-checking because it actually creates some new, computer-age spelling hazards. Keep in mind these problems:

1. Spell-checkers approve any words found in the dictionary. Errors such as using "too" for "to" and "count" for "court" go undetected by checking systems.

2. Spell-checkers require intelligent choices. When checkers encounter an unfamiliar word, the word is highlighted for editing by the writer. Even if the spell-checker offers suggestions for proper spelling from the computer's memory, it asks the writer to do the thinking and to make the correct choice. So writers still must know how to spell.

3. Spell-checkers inspire confidence that may be unwarranted, allowing for careless or lazy editing. Confident that a document has been checked, writers may leave many unwitting and even embarrassing errors. (One professor recalled an instance in which the computer approved "dick" in a sentence that called for the word "disk.") Such errors may be detected when careful, nonmachine editing is combined with the computer spell-checking process.

Both spell-checking and manual, word-by-word editing still are "berry much reek wired," as our earlier example stated. No machine can replace the complex decision making that an editor provides. In the information age, good writers and editors are even more essential to ensure accurate writing.

APPENDIX D

Key to Grammar Quizzes

After years of working with these exercises, the authors recognize that no single answer exists for any exercise item. Each answer we provide is what we consider to be the BEST or PREFERRED answer, rather than the only answer.

Grammar Diagnostic Quiz (pages 202–204):

1. (4.) Clauses on either side of a semicolon must be independent.
2. (3.) It is the LIST that HAS BEEN TRIMMED.
3. (3.) Commas may not separate independent clauses.
4. (2.) Commas follow all elements in a complete date.
5. (1.) The modifying phrase, in its present location, modifies INSE-CURITY rather than FRESHMEN.
6. (2.) Use LIE when no action is taken.
7. (1.) Modifying the council with hopefully leaves them filled with hope.
8. (2.) Semicolons are used to separate punctuated items in a list.
9. (3.) Use neither and nor as a matched pair.
10. (2.) Use the pronoun IT to agree with the noun COMPANY, a singular thing.
11. (2.) Phrases that rename subjects are nonessential. Comma after COM-MISSION.
12. (3.) LIVES is the verb that agrees with the subject ONE.
13. (2.) Commas follow both elements of a city and state combination that occurs in midsentence.
14. (1.) The past tense, USED, is correct usage in this idiom.
15. (2.) Including WILL PLAY in this phrase makes for faulty parallelism.
16. Sentence fragment.

17. Comma error. Semicolon or period needed.
18. The coordinate conjunction AND is used where a subordinate conjunction, such as BECAUSE or THAT, is needed.
19. Modifier problem. His muscles are not being a weight lifter.
20. Agreement: ITS SKIN.

1. Correct. Your princiPAL is your PAL. PrincipLES are LESSONS.
2. Sheriff, with one r. SHE and RIFF called the sheriff.
3. Marshal, in all cases except for the proper noun, the name.
4. Correct. There is A RAT in sepARATe.
5. Correct. StationERy is sold by stationERs.
6. Correct. To REpeatedly commend.
7. Correct. Note also bookkeeper and withholding.
8. Seize. Spell carefully in all cases of I-E. Computer checkers help.

Slammer for Commas, Semicolons, and Colons (pages 208–209):

1. 4		7. 4 and 10
2. 7		8. 1
3. 9 and 10		9. 7
4. 2		10. 10
5. 2, 5, and 6		11. 6 and 7
6. 8		12. 2 and 12

Slammer for Subject–Verb Agreement (pages 212–213):

1. includes	13. believes
2. appear	14. is
3. gives	15. decides
4. results	16. typifies
5. have	17. are
6. do	18. are
7. is	19. is
8. are	20. is
9. exhibits	21. teach
10. are	22. is
11. constitute	23. consider

12. was	24. disagree

Slammer for Pronouns (pages 215–216):

1. his or her	9. their
2. its	10. is
3. himself	11. its
4. its	12. it
5. its	13. are
6. is	14. himself or herself
7. was	15. his or her
8. was	

Slammer for Who/Whom and That/Which (pages 217–218):

1. whom
2. who
3. whom
4. who
5. whose

1. gun, which sale,	5. gun, which compartment,
2. that	6. who
3. car, which plates,	7. gun, which
4. Texans, who drawl,	8. that

Modifier Slammer (pages 219–220):

1. The waiter served ice cream, which started melting immediately, in glass bowls.
2. Correct.
3. On the way to our hotel, we saw a herd of sheep.
4. Correct.
5. The house where Mrs. Rooks taught ballet is one of the oldest in Rockville.
6. Correct.
7. Without yelling, I could not convince the child to stop running into the street.

8. The critic said that after the first act of the play, Brooke's performance improves.
9. While we were watching the ball game, Sue's horse ran away.
10. Correct.
11. The bank approves loans of any size to reliable individuals.
12. After I was wheeled into the operating room, the nurse placed a mask over my face.
13. Correct.
14. Aunt Helen asked us to call on her before we left.

INDEX